C000044951

GCSE Biology Vocabulary Workbook

By Lewis Morris

www.insiderswords.com/gcse-bio

ISBN-13:978-1694086167

We hope you find this vocabulary workbook helpful with your studies. If you do, please consider
leaving a brief review at this link:

http://www.amazon.com/review/create-review?&asin=169408616X

Table of Contents

What is "Insider Language"?

Recent research has confirmed what we have known for decades: The strongest students and leaders in industry have a mastered an Insider Language in their subject and field. This Insider language is made up of the technical terms and vocabulary necessary to communicate effectively in classes or the workplace. For those who master it, learning is easier, faster, and much more enjoyable.

Most students who are surveyed report that the greatest challenge to any course of study is learning the vocabulary. When we examine typical college courses, we discover that there is, on average, 250 Insider Terms a student must learn over the course of a semester. Further, most exams rely heavily on this set of words for assessment purposes. The structure of multiple choice exams lends itself perfectly to the testing of this Insider Language. Students who can differentiate between Insider Language terms can handle challenging exam questions with ease and confidence.

From recent research on learning and vocabulary we have learned:

- Your knowledge of any subject is contained in the content-specific words you know. The more of these terms that you know, the easier it is to understand and recall important information; the easier it will be to communicate your ideas to peers, professors, supervisors, and co-workers. The stronger your content-area vocabulary is, the higher your scores will be on your exams and written assignments.

- Students who develop a strong Insider Language perform better on tests, learn faster, retain more information, and express greater satisfaction in learning.

- Familiarizing yourself with subject-area vocabulary before formal study (pre-learning) is the most effective way to learn this language and reap the most benefit.

- The vocabulary on standardized exams come directly from the stated objectives of the test-makers. This means that the vocabulary found on standardized exams is predictable. Our books focus on this vocabulary.

- Most multiple-choice exams are glorified vocabulary quizzes. Think about the format of a multiple-choice question. The question stem is a definition of a term and the choices (known as distractors) are 4 or 5 similar words. Your task is to differentiate between the meanings of those terms and choose the correct word.

- It takes a person several exposures to a new word to be able to use it with confidence in conversation or in writing. You need to process these words several different ways to make them part of your long-term memory.

The goals of this book are:
- To give you an "Insider Language" for your subject.
- Pre-teach the most important words before you set out on a traditional course of review or study.
- Teach you the most important words in your subject area.
- Teach you strategies for learning subject-area words on your own.
- Boost your confidence in your ability to master this language and support you in your study.
- Reduce the stress of studying and provide you with fun activities that work.

How it works:

The secret to mastering Insider Language is through repetition and exposure. We have eleven steps for you to follow:

1. Read the word and definition in the glossary out loud. "See it, Say it"
2. Identify the part of speech the word belongs to such as noun, verb, adverb, or adjective. This will help you group the word and identify similar words.
3. Place the word in context by using it in a sentence. Write this sentence down and read it aloud.
4. Use "Chunking" to group the words. Make a diagram or word cloud using these groups.
5. Make connections to the words by creating analogies.
6. Create mnemonics that help you recognize patterns and orders of words by substituting the words for more memorable items or actions.
7. Examine the morphology of the word, that is, identify the root, prefix, and suffix that make up the word. Identify similar and related words.
8. Complete word games and puzzles such as crosswords and word searches.
9. Complete matching questions that require you to differentiate between related words.
10. Complete Multiple-choice questions containing the words.
11. Create a visual metaphor or "memory cartoon" to make a mental picture of the word and related processes.

By completing this word study process, you will be exposed to the terminology in various ways that will activate your memory and create a lasting understanding of this language.

The strategies in this book are designed to make you an independent expert at learning insider language. These strategies include:

- Verbalizing the word by reading it and its definition aloud ("See It, Say It"). This allows you to make visual, auditory, and speech connections with its meaning.

- Identifying the type of word (Noun, verb, adverb, and adjective). Making this distinction helps you understand how to visualize the word. It helps you "chunk" the words into groups, and gives you clues on how to use the word.

- Place the word in context by using it in a sentence. Write this sentence down and read it aloud. This will give you an example of how the word is used.

- "Chunking". By breaking down the word list into groups of closely related words, you will learn them better and be able to remember them faster. Once you have group the terms, you can then make word clouds using a free online service. These word clouds provide visual cues to remembering the words and their meanings.

- Analogies. By creating analogies for essential words, you will be making connections that you can see on paper. These connections can trigger your memory and activate your ability to use the word in your writing as you begin to use them. Many of these analogies also use visual cues. In a sense, you can make a mental picture from the analogy.

- Mnemonics. A device such as a pattern of letters, ideas, or associations that assists in remembering something. A mnemonic is especially useful for remembering the order of a set of words or the order of a process.

- Morphology. The study of word roots, prefixes, and suffixes. By examining the structure of the words, you will gain insight into other words that are closely related, and learn how to best use the word.

- Visual metaphors. This is the most sophisticated and entertaining strategy for learning vocabulary. Create a "memory cartoon" using one or more of the vocabulary terms. This activity triggers the visual part of your memory and makes fast, permanent, imprints of the word on your memory. By combining the terms in your visual metaphor, you can "chunk" the entire set of vocabulary terms into several visual metaphors and benefit from the brain's tendency to group these terms.

The activities in this book are designed to imprint the words and their meanings in your memory in different ways. By completing each activity, you will gain the necessary exposures to the word to make it a permanent part of your vocabulary. Each activity uses a different part of your memory. The result is that you will be comfortable using these words and be able to tell the difference between closely related words. The activities include:

A. Crossword Puzzles and Word Searches- These are proven to increase test scores and improve comprehension. Students frequently report that they are fun and engaging, while requiring them to analyze the structure and meaning of the words.

B. Matching- This activity is effective because it forces you to differentiate between many closely related terms.

C. Multiple Choice- This classic question format lends itself to vocabulary study perfectly. Most exams are in this format because they are simple to make, easy to score, and are a reliable type of assessment. (Perfect for the Vocabulary Master!) One strategy to use with multiple choice questions that enhance their effectiveness is to cover the answer choices while you read the question. After reading the question, see if you can answer it before looking at the choices. Then look at the choices to see if you match one of them.

Conducting a thorough "word study" of your insider language will take time and effort, but the rewards will be well worth it. By following this guide and completing the exercises thoughtfully, you will become a stronger, more effective, and satisfied student. Best of luck on your mastery of this Insider Language!

Insider Language Strategies

"See It, Say It!" Reading your Insider Language set aloud

"IT IS BETTER TO FAIL IN ORIGINALITY THAN TO SUCCEED IN IMITATION."
–HERMAN MELVILLE

Reading aloud is the foundation for the development of an Insider Language. It is the single most important thing you can do for vocabulary acquisition. Done correctly, it engages the visual, auditory, and speech centers of the brain and hastens its storage in your long-term memory.

Reading aloud demonstrates the relationship between the printed word and its meaning.

You can read aloud on a higher level than you can initially understand, so reading aloud makes complex ideas more accessible and exposes you to vocabulary and patterns that are not part of your typical speech. Reading aloud helps you understand the complicated text better and makes more challenging text easier to grasp and understand. Reading aloud helps you to develop the "habits of mind" the strongest students use.

Reading aloud will make connections to concepts in the reading that requires you to relate the new vocabulary to things you already know. Go to the glossary at the end of this book and for each word complete the five steps outlined below:

1. Read the word and its definition aloud. Focus on the sound of the word and how it looks on the paper.
2. Read the word aloud again try to say three or four similar words; this will help you build connections to closely related words.
3. Read the word aloud a third time. Try to make a connection to something you have read or heard.
4. Visualize the concept described in the term. Paint a mental picture of the word in use.
5. Try to think of the opposite of the word. Discovering a close antonym will help you place this word in context.

Create a sentence using the word in its proper context

"OPPORTUNITIES DON'T HAPPEN. YOU CREATE THEM." –CHRIS GROSSER

Context means the circumstances that form the setting for an event, statement, or idea, and which it can be fully understood and assessed. Synonyms for context include conditions, factors, situation, background, and setting.

Place the word in context by using it in a sentence. Write this sentence down and read it aloud. By creating sentences, you are practicing using the word correctly. If you strive to make these sentences interesting and creative, they will become more memorable and effective in activating your long-term memory.

Identify the Parts of Speech
"SUCCESS IS NOT FINAL; FAILURE IS NOT FATAL: IT IS THE COURAGE TO CONTINUE THAT COUNTS." –WINSTON S. CHURCHILL

Read through each term in the glossary and make a note of what part of speech each term is. Studying and identifying parts of speech shows us how the words relate to each other. It also helps you create a visualization of each term. Below are brief descriptions of the parts of speech for you to use as a guide.

VERB: A word denoting action, occurrence, or existence. Examples: walk, hop, whisper, sweat, dribbles, feels, sleeps, drink, smile, are, is, was, has.

NOUN: A word that names a person, place, thing, idea, animal, quality, or action. Nouns are the subject of the sentence. Examples: dog, Tom, Florida, CD, pasta, hate, tiger.

ADJECTIVE: A word that modifies, qualifies, or describes nouns and pronouns. Generally, adjectives appear immediately before the words they modify. Examples: smart girl, gifted teacher, old car, red door.

ADVERB: A word that modifies verbs, adjectives and other adverbs. An "ly" ending almost always changes an adjective to an adverb. Examples: ran swiftly, worked slowly, and drifted aimlessly. Many adverbs do not end in "ly." However, all adverbs identify when, where, how, how far, how much, etc. Examples: run hot, lived hard, moved right, study smart.

Chunking

Chunking is when you take a set of words and break it down into groups based on a common relationship. Research has shown that our brains learn by chunking information. By grouping your terms, you will be able to recall large sets of these words easily. To help make your chunking go easily use an online word cloud generator to make a set of word clouds representing your chunks.

1. Study the glossary and decide how you want to chunk the set of words. You can group by part of speech, topic, letter of the alphabet, word length, etc. Try to find an easy way to group each term.
2. Once you have your different groups, visit www.wordclouds.com to create a custom word cloud for each group. Print each one of these clouds and post it in a prominent place to serve as constant visual aids for your learning.

Analogies

An analogy is a comparison in which an idea or a thing is compared to another thing that is quite different from it. Analogies aim at explaining an idea by comparing it to something that is familiar. Metaphors and similes are tools used to create analogies.

Analogies are useful for learning vocabulary because they require you to analyze a word (or words), and then transfer that analysis to another word. This transfer reinforces the understanding of all the words.

As you analyze the relationships between the analogies you are creating, you will begin to understand the complex relationships between the seemingly unrelated words.

_A_ is to _B_ as _C_ is to _D_

This can be written using colons in place of the terms "is to" and "as."

A:B::C:D

The two items on the left (items A & B) describe a relationship and are separated by a single colon. The two items on the right (items C & D) are shown on the right and are also separated by a colon. Together, both sides are then separated by two colons in the middle, as shown here: Tall: Short :: Skinny: Fat. The relationship used in this analogy is the antonym.

How to create an analogy

Start with the basic formula for an analogy:

_____ : _____ :: _____ : _____

Next, we will examine a simple synonym analogy:

automobile : car :: box : crate

The key to figuring out a set of word analogies is determining the relationship between the paired set of words.

Here is a list of the most common types of Analogies and examples

Synonym	Scream : Yell :: Push : Shove
Antonym	Rich : Poor :: Empty : Full
Cause is to Effect	Prosperity : Happiness :: Success : Joy
A Part is to its Whole	Toe : Foot :: Piece : Set
An Object to its Function	Car : Travel :: Read : Learn
A Item is to its Category	Tabby : House Cat :: Doberman : Dog
Word is a symptom of the other	Pain : Fracture :: Wheezing : Allergy
An object and it's description	Glass : Brittle :: Lead : Dense
The word is lacking the second word	Amputee : Limb :: Deaf : Hearing
The first word Hinders the second word	Shackles : Movement :: Stagger : Walk
The first word helps the action of the second	Knife : Bread :: Screwdriver : Screw
This word is made up of the second word	Sweater : Wool :: Jeans : Denim
A word and it's definition	Cede: Break Away :: Abolish : To get rid of

Using words from the glossary, make a set of analogies using each one. As a bonus, use more than one glossary term in a single analogy.

_____ : _____ :: _____ : _____

Name the relationship between the words in your analogy:_____

_____ : _____ :: _____ : _____

Name the relationship between the words in your analogy:_____

_____ : _____ :: _____ : _____

Name the relationship between the words in your analogy:_____

Mnemonics

"IT ISN'T THE MOUNTAINS AHEAD TO CLIMB THAT WEAR YOU OUT; IT'S THE PEBBLE IN YOUR SHOE."   –MUHAMMAD ALI

A mnemonic is a learning technique that helps you retain and remember information. Mnemonics are one of the best learning methods for remembering lists or processes in order. Mnemonics make the material more meaningful by adding associations and creating patterns. Interestingly, mnemonics may work better when they utilize absurd, startling, or shocking examples and references. Mnemonics help organize the information so that you can easily retrieve it later. By giving you associations and cues, mnemonics allow you to form a mental structure ordering a list or process to help you remember it better. This mental structure allows you to create a structure of association between items that may not appear to have any relationship. Mnemonics typically use references that are easy to visualize and thus easier to remember. Through visualization of vivid images and references, the information is much easier to imprint into long-term memory. The power of making mnemonics lies in converting dull, inert and uninspiring information into something vibrant and memorable.

How to make simple and effective mnemonics
Some of the best mnemonics help us remember simple rules or lists in order.

Step 1. Take a list of terms you are trying to remember in order. For example, we will use the scientific method:

observation, question, hypothesis, methods, results, and conclusion.

Next, we will replace each word on the list with a new word that starts with the same letter. These new words will together form a vivid sentence that is easy to remember:

Objectionable Queens Haunted Macho Rednecks Creatively.

As silly as the above sentence seems, it is easy to remember, and now we can call on this sentence to remind us of the order of the scientific method.

Visit http://www.mnemonicgenerator.com/ and try typing in a list of words. It is fun to see the mnemonics that it makes and shows how easy it is to make great mnemonics to help your studying.

Using vivid words in your mnemonics allows you to see the sentence you are making. Words that are gross, scary, or name interesting animals are helpful. Profanity is also useful because the shock value can trigger memory. The following are lists of vivid words to use in your mnemonics:

Gross words

Moist, Gurgle, Phlegm, Fetus, Curd, Smear, Squirt, Chunky, Orifice, Maggots, Viscous, Queasy, Bulbous, Pustule, Putrid, Fester, Secrete, Munch, Vomit, Ooze, Dripping, Roaches, Mucus, Stink, Stank, Stunk, Slurp, Pus, Lick, Salty, Tongue, Fart, Flatulence, Hemorrhoid.

Interesting Animals

Aardvark, Baboon, Chicken, Chinchilla, Duck, Dragonfly, Emu, Electric Eel, Frog, Flamingo, Gecko, Hedgehog, Hyena, Iguana, Jackal, Jaguar, Leopard, Lynx, Minnow, Manatee, Mongoose, Neanderthal, Newt, Octopus, Oyster, Pelican, Penguin, Platypus, Quail, Racoon, Rattlesnake, Rhinoceros, Scorpion, Seahorse, Toucan, Turkey, Vulture, Weasel, Woodpecker, Yak, Zebra.

Superhero Words

Diabolical, Activate, Boom, Clutch, Dastardly, Dynamic, Dynamite, Shazam, Kaboom, Zip, Zap, Zoom, Zany, Crushing, Smashing, Exploding, Ripping, Tearing.

Scary Words

Apparition, Bat, Chill, Demon, Eerie, Fangs, Genie, Hell, Lantern, Macabre, Nightmare, Owl, Ogre, Phantasm, Repulsive, Scarecrow, Tarantula, Undead, Vampire, Wraith, Zombie.

There are several types of mnemonics that can help your memory.

1. Images

Visual mnemonics are a type of mnemonic that works by associating an image with characters or objects whose name sounds like the item that must be memorized. This is one of the easiest ways to create effective mnemonics. An example would be to use the shape of numbers to help memorize a long list of them. Numbers can be memorized by their shapes, so that: 0 -looks like an egg; 1 -a pencil, or a candle; 2 -a snake; 3 -an ear; 4 -a sailboat; 5 -a key; 6 -a comet; 7 -a knee; 8 -a snowman; 9 -a comma.

Another type of visual mnemonic is the word-length mnemonic in which the number of letters in each word corresponds to a digit. This simple mnemonic gives pi to seven decimal places:

3.141582 becomes "How I wish I could calculate pi."

Of course, you could use this type of mnemonic to create a longer sentence showing the digits of an important number. Some people have used this type of mnemonic to memorize thousands of digits.

Using the hands is also an important tool for creating visual objects. Making the hands into specific shapes can help us remember the pattern of things or the order of a list of things.

2. Rhyming

Rhyming mnemonics are quick ways to make things memorable. A classic example is a mnemonic for the number of days in each month:
"30 days hath September, April, June, and November.
All the rest have 31
Except February, my dear son.
It has 28, and that is fine
But in Leap Year it has 29."

Another example of a rhyming mnemonic is a common spelling rule:
"I before e except after c
or when sounding like a
in neighbor and weigh."

Use **rhymer.com** to get large lists of rhyming words.

3. Homonym

A homonym is one of a group of words that share the same pronunciation but have different meanings, whether spelled the same or not.

Try saying what you're attempting to remember out loud or very quickly, and see if anything leaps out. If you know other languages, using similar-sounding words from those can be effective.

You could also browse this list of homonyms
at http://www.cooper.com/alan/homonym_list.html.

4. Onomatopoeia

An Onomatopeia is a word that phonetically imitates, resembles or suggests the source of the sound that it describes. Are there any noises made by the thing you're trying to memorize? Is it often associated with some other sound? Failing that, just make up a noise that seems to fit.

Achoo, ahem, baa, bam, bark, beep, beep beep, belch, bleat, boo, boo hoo, boom, burp, buzz, chirp, click clack, crash, croak, crunch, cuckoo, dash, drip, ding dong, eek, fizz, flit, flutter, gasp, grrr, ha ha, hee hee, hiccup, hiss, hissing, honk, icky, itchy, jiggly, jangle, knock knock, lush, la la la, mash, meow, moan, murmur, neigh, oink, ouch, plop, pow, quack, quick, rapping, rattle, ribbit, roar, rumble, rustle, scratch, sizzle, skittering, snap crackle pop, splash, splish splash, spurt, swish, swoosh, tap, tapping, tick tock, tinkle, tweet, ugh, vroom, wham, whinny, whip, whooping, woof.

5. Acronyms

An acronym is a word or name formed as an abbreviation from the initial components of a word, such as NATO, which stands for North Atlantic Treaty Organization. If you're trying to memorize something involving letters, this is often a good bet. A lot of famous mnemonics are acronyms, such as ROYGBIV which stands for the order of colors in the light spectrum (Red, Orange, Yellow, Green, Blue, Indigo, and Violet).

A great acronym generator to try is: www.all-acronyms.com.

A different spin on an acronym is a backronym. A **backronym** is a specially constructed phrase that is supposed to be the source of a word that is an acronym. A backronym is constructed by creating a new phrase to fit an already existing word, name, or acronym.

The word is a combination of *backward* and *acronym*, and has been defined as a "reverse acronym." For example, the United States Department of Justice assigns to their Amber Alert program the meaning "**A**merica's **M**issing: **B**roadcast **E**mergency **R**esponse." The process can go either way to make good mnemonics.

Visit: https://arthurdick.com/projects/backronym/ to try out a simple backronym generator.

6. Anagrams

An anagram is a direct word switch or word play, the result of rearranging the letters of a word or phrase to produce a new word or phrase, using all the original letters exactly once; for example, the word anagram can be rearranged into nag-a-ram.

Try re-arranging letters or components and see if anything memorable emerges. Visit http://www.nameacronym.net/ to use a simple anagram generator.

One particularly memorable form of anagram is the spoonerism, where you swap the initial syllables or letters of words to make new phrases. These are usually humorous, and this makes them easier to remember. Here are some examples:

"Is it kisstomary to cuss the bride?" (as opposed to "customary to kiss")
"The Lord is a shoving leopard." (instead of "a loving shepherd")
"A blushing crow." ("crushing blow")
"A well-boiled icicle" ("well-oiled bicycle")
"You were fighting a liar in the quadrangle." ("lighting a fire")
"Is the bean dizzy?" (as opposed to "is the dean busy?")

7. Stories

Make up quick stories or incidents involving the material you want to memorize. For larger chunks of information, the stories can get more elaborate. Structured stories are particularly good for remembering lists or other sequenced information. Have a look at https://en.wikipedia.org/wiki/Method_of_loci for a more advanced memory sequencing technique.

Visual Metaphors

"LIMITS, LIKE FEAR, IS OFTEN AN ILLUSION." –MICHAEL JORDAN

What is a Metaphor?

A metaphor is a figure of speech that refers to one thing by mentioning another thing. Metaphors provide clarity and identify hidden similarities between two seemingly unrelated ideas. A visual metaphor is an image that creates a link between different ideas.

Visual metaphors help us use our understanding of the world to learn new concepts, skills, and ideas. Visual metaphors help us relate new material to what we already know. Visual metaphors must be clear and simple enough to spark a connection and understanding. Visual metaphors should use familiar things to help you be less fearful of new, complex, or challenging topics. Metaphors trigger a sense of familiarity so that you are more accepting of the new idea. Metaphors work best when you associate a familiar, easy to understand idea with a challenging, obscure, or abstract concept.

How to make a visual metaphor

1. Brainstorm using the words of the concept. Use different fonts, colors, or shapes to represent parts of the concept.

2. Merge these images together

3. Show the process using arrows, accents, etc.

4. Think about the story line your metaphor projects.

Examples of visual metaphors:

A skeleton used to show a framework of something.

A cloud showing an outline.

A bodybuilder whose muscles represent supporting ideas and details.

A sandwich where the meat, tomato, and lettuce represent supporting ideas.

A recipe card to show a process.

Your metaphor should be accurate. It should be complex enough to convey meaning, but simple and clear enough to be easily understood.

Morphology
"SCIENCE IS THE CAPTAIN, AND PRACTICE THE SOLDIERS." LEONARDO DA VINCI

Morphology is the study of the origin, roots, suffixes, and prefixes of the words. Understanding the meaning of prefixes, suffixes, and roots make it easier to decode the meaning of new vocabulary. Having the ability to decode using morphology increases text comprehension when initially reading as well.

The capability of identifying meaningful parts of words (morphemes), including prefixes, suffixes, and roots can be helpful. Identifying morphemes improves decoding accuracy and fluency. Reading speed improves when you can decode larger chunks of text quickly. When you can recognize morphemes in words, you will be better able to make sense of new words in context. Below are charts containing the most common prefixes, suffixes, and root words. Use them to help you decode your vocabulary terms.

Prefixes

Prefix	Meaning	Example words and meanings	
a, ab, abs	away from	absent abdicate	not to be present, to give up an office or throne.
ad, a, ac, af, ag, an, ar, at, as	to, toward	Advance advantage	To move forward To have the upper hand
anti	against	Antidote antisocial antibiotic	To repair poisoning refers to someone who's not social
bi, bis	two	bicycle binary biweekly	two-wheeled cycle two number system every two weeks
circum, cir	around	circumnavigate circle	Travel around the world a figure that goes all around
com, con, co, col	with, together	Complete Complement	To finish To go along with
de	away from, down, the opposite of	depart detour	to go away from to go out of your way
dis, dif, di	apart	dislike dishonest distant	not to like not honest away
En-, em-	Cause to	Entrance	the way in.
epi	upon, on top of	epitaph epilogue epidemic	writing upon a tombstone speech at the end, on top of the rest
equ, equi	equal	equalize equitable	to make equal fair, equal
ex, e, ef	out, from	exit eject exhale	to go out to throw out to breathe out
Fore-	Before	Forewarned	To have prior warning

Prefix	Meaning	Example Words and Meanings	
in, il, ir, im, en	in, into	Infield	The inner playing field
		Imbibe	to take part in
in, il, ig, ir, im	not	inactive	not active
		ignorant	not knowing
		irreversible	not reversible
		irritate	to put into discomfort
inter	between, among	international	among nations
		interact	to mix with
mal, male	bad, ill, wrong	malpractice	bad practice
		malfunction	fail to function, bad function
Mid	Middle	Amidships	In the middle of a ship
mis	wrong, badly	misnomer	The wrong name
mono	one, alone, single	monocle	one lensed glasses
non	not, the reverse of	nonprofit	not making a profit
ob	in front, against, in front of, in the way of	Obsolete	No longer needed
omni	everywhere, all	omnipresent	always present, everywhere
		omnipotent	all powerful
Over	On top	Overdose	Take too much medication
Pre	Before	Preview	Happens before a show.
per	through	Permeable	to pass through,
		pervasive	all encompassing
poly	many	Polygamy	many spouses
		polygon	figure with many sides
post	after	postpone	to do after
		postmortem	after death
pre	before, earlier than	Predict	To know before
		Preview	To view before release
pro	forward, going ahead of, supporting	proceed	to go forward
		pro-war	supporting the war
		promote	to raise or move forward
re	again, back	retell	to tell again
		recall	to call back
		reverse	to go back
se	apart	secede	to withdraw, become apart
		seclude	to stay apart from others
Semi	Half	Semipermeable	Half-permeable

Prefix	Meaning	Example Words and Meanings	
Sub	under, less than	Submarine	under water
super	over, above, greater	superstar superimpose	a start greater than her stars to put over something else
trans	across	transcontinental transverse	across the continent to lie or go across
un, uni	one	unidirectional unanimous unilateral	having one direction sharing one view having one side
un	not	uninterested unhelpful unethical	not interested not helpful not ethical

Roots

Root	Meaning	Example words & meanings	
act, ag	to do, to act	Agent Activity	One who acts as a representative Action
Aqua	Water	Aquamarine	The color of water
Aud	To hear	Auditorium	A place to hear music
apert	open	Aperture	An opening
bas	low	Basement Basement	Something that is low, at the bottom A room that is low
Bio	Living thing	Biological	Living matter
cap, capt, cip, cept, ceive	to take, to hold, to seize	Captive Receive Capable Recipient	One who is held To take Able to take hold of things One who takes hold or receives
ced, cede, ceed, cess	to go, to give in	Precede Access Proceed	To go before Means of going to To go forward
Cogn	Know	Cognitive	Ability to think
cred, credit	to believe	Credible Incredible Credit	Believable Not believable Belief, trust
curr, curs, cours	to run	Current Precursory Recourse	Now in progress, running Running (going) before To run for aid
Cycle	Circle	Lifecycle	The circle of life
dic, dict	to say	Dictionary Indict	A book explaining words (sayings)

Root	Meaning	Examples and meanings	
duc, duct	to lead	Induce Conduct Aqueduct	To lead to action To lead or guide Pipe that leads water somewhere
equ	equal, even	Equality Equanimity	Equal in social, political rights Evenness of mind, tranquility
fac, fact, fic, fect, fy	to make, to do	Facile Fiction Factory Affect	Easy to do Something that is made up Place that makes things To make a change in
fer, ferr	to carry, bring	Defer Referral	To carry away Bring a source for help/information
Gen	Birth	Generate	To create something
graph	write	Monograph Graphite	A writing on a particular subject A form of carbon used for writing
Loc	Place	Location	A place
Mater	Mother	Maternity	Expecting birth
Mem	Recall	Memory	The recall experiences
mit, mis	to send	Admit Missile	To send in Something sent through the air
Nat	Born	Native	Born in a place
par	equal	Parity Disparate	Equality No equal, not alike
Ped	Foot	Podiatrist	Foot doctor
Photo	Light	Photograph	A picture
plic	to fold, to bend, to turn	Complicate Implicate	To fold (mix) together To fold in, to involve
pon, pos, posit, pose	to place	Component Transpose Compose Deposit	A part placed together with others A place across To put many parts into place To place for safekeeping
scrib, script	to write	Describe Transcript Subscription	To write about or tell about A written copy A written signature or document
sequ, secu	to follow	Sequence	In following order

Root	Meaning	Examples and Meanings	
Sign	Mark	Signal	to alert somebody
spec, spect, spic	to appear, to look, to see	Specimen Aspect	An example to look at One way to see something
sta, stat, sist,	to stand, or make stand	Constant	Standing with
stit, sisto	Stable, steady	Status Stable Desist	Social standing Steady (standing) To stand away from
Struct	To build	Construction	To build a thing
tact	to touch	Contact Tactile	To touch together To be able to be touched
ten, tent, tain	to hold	Tenable Retentive Maintain	Able to be held, holding Holding To keep or hold up
tend, tens, tent	to stretch	Extend Tension	To stretch or draw out Stretched
Therm	Temperature	Thermometer	Detects temperature
tract	to draw	Attract Contract	To draw together An agreement drawn up
ven, vent	to come	Convene Advent	To come together A coming
Vis	See	Invisible	Cannot be seen
ver, vert, vers	to turn	Avert Revert Reverse	To turn away To turn back To turn around

1. *Using the Across and Down clues, write the correct words in the numbered grid below.*

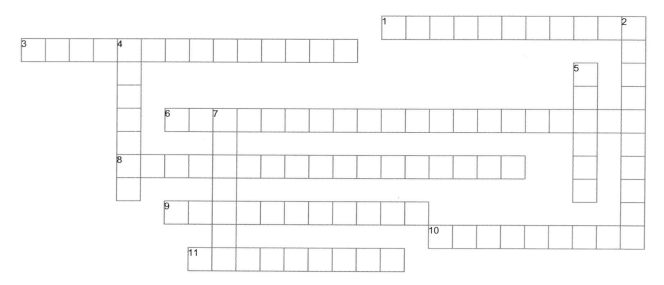

ACROSS

1. The practice of cultivating land, growing food, and raising stock.

3. The double helix is unwound and each strand acts as a template for the next strand. Bases are matched to synthesize the new partner strands.

6. The branch of biology concerned with the relations between organisms and their environment.

8. The independent evolution of similar traits, starting from a similar ancestral condition.

9. When two genes are close together on the same chromosome, they do not assort independently.

10. The interaction of genes that are not alleles, in particular the suppression of the effect of one such gene by another.

11. the tendency of a crossbred individual to show qualities superior to those of both parents.

DOWN

2. A process by which the contents of a cell vacuole are released to the exterior through fusion of the vacuole membrane with the cell membrane.

4. Describes a genetically distinct geographic variety, population or race within a species, which is adapted to specific environmental conditions.

5. A molecule with the same chemical formula as another molecule, but with a different chemical structure.

7. Refers to the number of elements to which it can connect.

A. Ecotype
D. Exocytosis
G. Linked Genes
J. Agriculture

B. Valence
E. Epistasis
H. Heterosis
K. Isomer

C. Environmental Biology
F. Parallel Evolution
I. DNA Replication

2. *Using the Across and Down clues, write the correct words in the numbered grid below.*

ACROSS

3. Sperm units with egg in the open, rather than inside the body of the parents

4. The collection of glands that produce hormones that regulate metabolism, growth and development, tissue function, sexual function, reproduction, sleep, and mood.

6. The study of insects.

9. A class of organic compounds containing an amino group and a carboxylic acid group

10. A biochemical assembly that contains both proteins and lipids, bound to the proteins, which allow fats to move through the water inside and outside cells.

DOWN

1. The application of concepts and methods of biology to solve real world problems.

2. A gene whose individual effect on a phenotype is too small to be observed, but which can act together with others to produce observable variation.

5. Any organism whose cells contain a nucleus and other organelles enclosed within membranes.

7. A heterocyclic compound of carbon, nitrogen, oxygen, and hydrogen. It forms ions and salts known as urates and acid urates, such as ammonium acid urate.

8. One of the four main nucleobases found in the nucleic acids DNA and RNA, the others being adenine, cytosine, and thymine.

9. One of the proteins into which actomyosin can be split; can exist in either a globular or a fibrous form.

A. Actin
B. Bioengineering
C. Polygene
D. Amino acid
E. Endocrine System
F. Uric acid
G. Entomology
H. Lipoprotein
I. External Fertilization
J. Eukaryote
K. Guanine

3. Using the Across and Down clues, write the correct words in the numbered grid below.

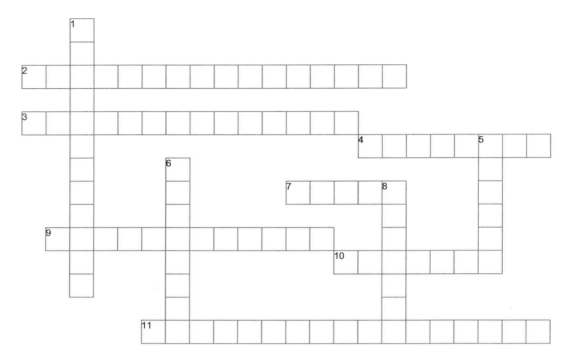

ACROSS

2. An interdisciplinary branch of biology and engineering.

3. A measure of the potential energy in water as well as the difference between the potential in a given water sample and pure water.

4. The smallest particle in a chemical element or compound that has the chemical properties of that element or compound.

7. The vascular tissue in plants that conducts water and dissolved nutrients upward from the root and also helps to form the woody element in the stem.

9. The branch of science that explores the chemical processes within and related to living organisms.

10. A system of physical units-based on the meter, kilogram, second, ampere, kelvin, candela, and mole, together with a set of prefixes.

11. A measure of the tendency of an atom to attract a bonding pair of electrons. The Pauling scale is the most commonly used.

DOWN

1. A process in which proteins or nucleic acids lose the quaternary structure, tertiary structure and secondary structure which is present in their native state.

5. The organ in the lower body of a woman or female mammal where offspring are conceived and in which they gestate before birth; the womb.

6. The stock of different genes in an interbreeding population.

8. The continuation of the spinal cord within the skull, forming the lowest part of the brainstem and containing control centers for the heart and lungs.

A. Denaturation
E. Uterus
I. Molecule
B. Synthetic Biology
F. Medulla
J. Biochemistry
C. SI units
G. Electronegativity
K. Xylem
D. Gene Pool
H. Water Potential

4. *Using the Across and Down clues, write the correct words in the numbered grid below.*

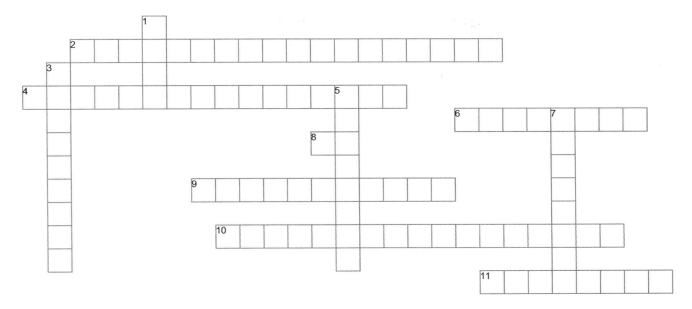

ACROSS

2. The study of genetic variation within populations, and involves the examination and modeling of changes in the frequencies of genes and alleles.

4. The genetic contribution of an individual to the next generation's gene pool relative to the average for the population.

6. A cell filled with basophil granules, found in numbers in connective tissue and releasing histamine and other substances during inflammatory and allergic reactions.

8. A numeric scale used to specify the acidity or basicity (alkalinity) of an aqueous solution. It is roughly the negative of the logarithm to base 10 of the concentration.

9. The deep sea (2000 meters or more) where there is no light.

10. Threatened by factors such as habitat loss, hunting, disease and climate change, and usually have declining populations or a very limited range.

11. The ecological state of a species being unique to a defined geographic location, such as an island, nation, country or other defined zone, or habitat type.

DOWN

1. An unstable subatomic particle. Among all known unstable subatomic particles, only the neutron (lasting around 15 minutes) and some atomic nuclei have a longer decay lifetime.

3. Any member of two classes of chemical compounds derived from carbonic acid or carbon dioxide.

5. The scientific and objective study of non-human animal behavior rather than human behavior and usually with a focus on behavior under natural conditions.

7. A compound of chlorine with another element or group, especially a salt of the anion or an organic compound with chlorine bonded to an alkyl group.

A. Carbonate
E. Endemism
I. Abyssal zone

B. Endangered Species
F. Darwinian Fitness
J. Ethology

C. Population Genetics
G. Mast Cell
K. pH

D. Chloride
H. Muon

5. *Using the Across and Down clues, write the correct words in the numbered grid below.*

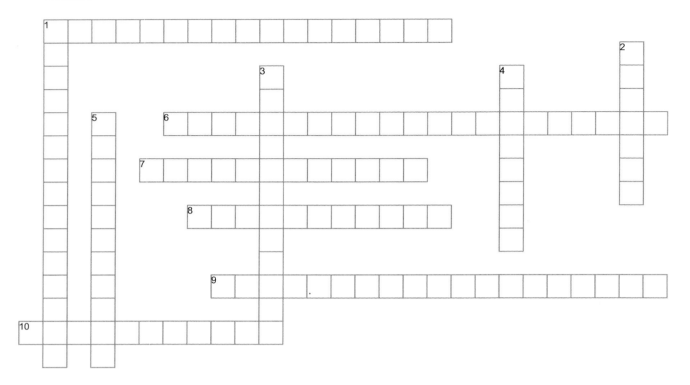

ACROSS

1. Threatened by factors such as habitat loss, hunting, disease and climate change, and usually have declining populations or a very limited range.

6. Sperm units with egg in the open, rather than inside the body of the parents

7. a plant hormone.

8. The yellow colored photosynthetic pigments.

9. The subfield of biology that studies the evolutionary processes that produced the diversity of life on Earth starting from a single origin of life.

10. The study of organic particles, such as bacteria, fungal spores, very small insects, pollen grains and viruses, which are passively transported by the air.

DOWN

1. Any of various molecules that are capable of accepting one or two electrons from one molecule and donating them to another in the process of electron transport.

2. The spontaneous net movement of solvent molecules through a semi-permeable membrane into a region of higher solute concentration.

3. The study of parasites, their hosts, and the relationship between them.

4. A heterocyclic compound of carbon, nitrogen, oxygen, and hydrogen. It forms ions and salts known as urates and acid urates, such as ammonium acid urate.

5. The act of transferring pollen grains from the male anther of a flower to the female stigma.

A. External Fertilization   B. Uric acid   C. Evolutionary Biology
D. Abscisic acid   E. Osmosis   F. Pollination
G. Electron Carrier   H. Xanthophyll   I. Parasitology
J. Endangered Species   K. Aerobiology

6. *Using the Across and Down clues, write the correct words in the numbered grid below.*

ACROSS

1. Rain containing acids that form in the atmosphere when industrial gas emissions (especially sulfur dioxide and nitrogen oxides) combine with water.

6. One of the four nucleobases in the nucleic acid of RNA that are represented by the letters A, G, C and U.

7. A biological agent that reproduces inside the cells of living hosts.

9. The application of concepts and methods of biology to solve real world problems.

10. The branch of science that explores the chemical processes within and related to living organisms.

11. The branch of biology concerned with the relations between organisms and their environment.

DOWN

2. Helps keep blood sugar level from getting too high (hyperglycemia) or too low (hypoglycemia).

3. Density is mass per volume.

4. Known as Fish Science, is the branch of biology devoted to the study of fish.

5. The study of the microscopic anatomy of cells and tissues of plants and animals.

8. Animals, like flatworms and jellyfish, that have no body cavity (coelom).

A. Acid precipitation
D. Virus
G. Mass Density
J. Bioengineering

B. Insulin
E. Biochemistry
H. Histology
K. Uracil

C. Acoelomate
F. Environmental Biology
I. Ichthyology

7. *Using the Across and Down clues, write the correct words in the numbered grid below.*

ACROSS

4. The highest range of electron energies in which electrons are normally present at absolute zero temperature.

6. The study of viruses-submicroscopic, parasitic particles of genetic material contained in a protein coat and virus-like agents.

7. Organisms that produce an egg composed of shell and membranes that creates a protected environment in which the embryo can develop out of water

9. The practice of cultivating land, growing food, and raising stock.

10. A microbially facilitated process of nitrate reduction that may ultimately produce molecular nitrogen.

11. A straightforward extension of Lewis structures. States that electrons in a covalent bond reside in a region that is the overlap of individual atomic orbitals.

DOWN

1. A very large molecule, such as protein, commonly created by polymerization of smaller subunits (monomers).

2. Refers to the provision of essential nutrients necessary to support human life and health.

3. A molecule that can be bonded to other identical molecules to form a polymer.

5. A small dense spherical structure in the nucleus of a cell during interphase.

8. A unit of concentration measuring the number of moles of a solute per liter of solution.

A. Agriculture
B. Amniotes
C. Virology
D. Nucleolus
E. Denitrification
F. Human Nutrition
G. Macromolecule
H. Molarity
I. Valence band
J. Monomer
K. Valence bond theory

8. *Using the Across and Down clues, write the correct words in the numbered grid below.*

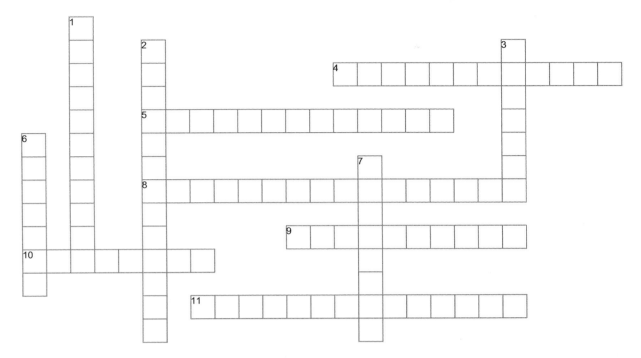

ACROSS

4. Plasma cells, also called plasma B cells, plasmocytes, plasmacytes, or effector B cells, are white blood cells that secrete large volumes of antibodies.

5. Virus that infects and multiplies within bacteria.

8. Variations of genomes between members of species, or between groups of species thriving in different parts of the world as a result of genetic mutation.

9. A process by which the contents of a cell vacuole are released to the exterior through fusion of the vacuole membrane with the cell membrane.

10. One of the three primary germ layers in the very early human embryo. The other two layers are the ectoderm (outside layer) and mesoderm (middle layer).

11. The process of reversing the charge across a cell membrane (usually a NEURON), so causing an ACTION POTENTIAL.

DOWN

1. A complex organic substance present in living cells, especially DNA or RNA, whose molecules consist of many nucleotides linked in a long chain.

2. An evolutionary theory that explains the origin of eukaryotic cells from prokaryotes.

3. Large biomolecules, or macromolecules, consisting of one or more long chains of amino acid residues.

6. Often defined as the largest group of organisms in which two individuals are capable of reproducing fertile offspring, typically using sexual reproduction.

7. A heterocyclic compound of carbon, nitrogen, oxygen, and hydrogen. It forms ions and salts known as urates and acid urates, such as ammonium acid urate.

A. Exocytosis
E. Bacteriophage
I. Nucleic Acid
B. Genetic Variation
F. Effector Cell
J. Species
C. Symbiogenesis
G. Protein
K. Depolarization
D. Endoderm
H. Uric acid

9. *Using the Across and Down clues, write the correct words in the numbered grid below.*

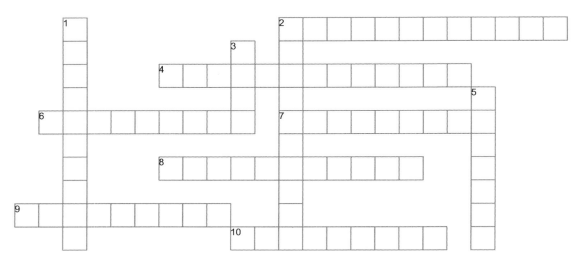

ACROSS

2. The lowest theoretically attainable temperature (at which the kinetic energy of atoms and molecules is minimal)

4. Also known as antibodies, They act as a critical part of the immune response by specifically recognizing and binding to particular antigens, and aiding in their destruction.

6. The preying of one animal on others.

7. A colorless cell which circulates in the blood and body fluids and is involved in counteracting foreign substances and disease; a white (blood) cell.

8. The branch of biology that deals with classification and nomenclature; taxonomy.

9. Any of the elongated contractile threads found in striated muscle cells.

10. A chemical substance produced and released into the environment by an animal, especially a mammal or an insect, affecting the behavior or physiology of others of its species.

DOWN

1. A process in which one substance permeates another; a fluid permeates or is dissolved by a liquid or solid.

2. Animals, like flatworms and jellyfish, that have no body cavity (coelom).

3. An unstable subatomic particle. Among all known unstable subatomic particles, only the neutron (lasting around 15 minutes) and some atomic nuclei have a longer decay lifetime.

5. The midsection of the small intestine of many higher vertebrates like mammals, birds, reptiles. It is present between the duodenum and the ileum.

A. Immunogloblin
E. Systematics
I. Absorption

B. Absolute zero
F. Pheromone
J. Muon

C. Acoelomate
G. Jejunum
K. Leukocyte

D. Myofibril
H. Predation

10. *Using the Across and Down clues, write the correct words in the numbered grid below.*

ACROSS

2. A chemical synapse formed by the contact between a motor neuron and a muscle fiber.

7. The energy that an atomic system must acquire before a process (such as an emission or reaction) can occur.

9. A heterocyclic compound of carbon, nitrogen, oxygen, and hydrogen. It forms ions and salts known as urates and acid urates, such as ammonium acid urate.

10. An interdisciplinary branch of biology and engineering.

11. Single-cell microscopic organisms which lack a true nucleus. They represent one of the three domains.

DOWN

1. The study of the physical properties of molecules, the chemical bonds between atoms as well as the molecular dynamics.

3. The science of drug action on biological systems.

4. A steroidal prohormone of the major insect molting hormone is secreted from the prothoracic glands.

5. When two genes are close together on the same chromosome, they do not assort independently.

6. The branch of biology that studies the effects of low temperatures on living things within Earth's cryosphere or in science.

8. A plant that grows harmlessly upon another plant and derives its moisture and nutrients from the air, rain, and sometimes from debris accumulating around it.

A. Molecular physics
D. Bacteria
G. Cryobiology
J. Pharmacology

B. Neuromuscular Junction
E. Activation energy
H. Epiphyte
K. Ecdysone

C. Synthetic Biology
F. Linked Genes
I. Uric acid

11. *Using the Across and Down clues, write the correct words in the numbered grid below.*

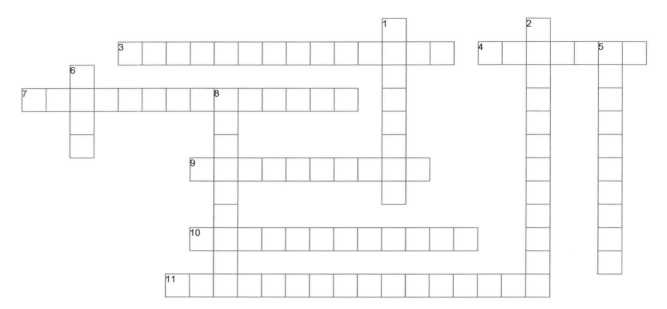

ACROSS

3. The application of concepts and methods of biology to solve real world problems.

4. A species of atoms having the same number of protons in their atomic nuclei (i.e. the same atomic number, Z).

7. The application of computer technology to the management of biological information.

9. A kind of swallowing cell, which means it functions by literally swallowing up other particles or smaller cells.

10. The study of parasites, their hosts, and the relationship between them.

11. An enzyme that catalyzes the formation of cyclic AMP from ATP.

DOWN

1. The study of viruses-submicroscopic, parasitic particles of genetic material contained in a protein coat and virus-like agents.

2. A steroid hormone from the androgen group and is found in humans and other vertebrates.

5. Organic molecules that serve as the monomers, or subunits, of nucleic acids like DNA (deoxyribonucleic acid) and RNA (ribonucleic acid).

6. The yellow internal part of a bird's egg, which is surrounded by the white, is rich in protein and fat, and nourishes the developing embryo.

8. The third phase of mitosis, the process that separates duplicated genetic material carried in the nucleus of a parent cell into two identical daughter cells.

A. Macrophage
E. Adenylate cyclase
I. Nucleotide

B. Yolk
F. Parasitology
J. Element

C. Bioengineering
G. Bioinformatics
K. Testosterone

D. Virology
H. Metaphase

12. *Using the Across and Down clues, write the correct words in the numbered grid below.*

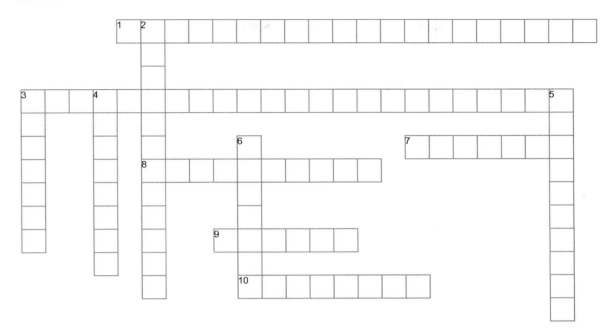

ACROSS

1. The branch of biology concerned with the relations between organisms and their environment.

3. The collective term for all possible frequencies of electromagnetic radiation.

7. Application of biological methods and systems found in nature to the study and design of engineering systems and modern technology.

8. A group of signaling proteins made and released by host cells in response to the presence of several pathogens, such as viruses, bacteria, parasites, and also tumor cells.

9. A unit of mass (also known as an atomic mass unit, amu), equal to the mass of a hydrogen atom (1.67 x 1024 g).

10. A subatomic particle with a negative elementary electric charge.

DOWN

2. The study of cells of the nervous system and the organization of these cells into functional circuits that process information and mediate behavior.

3. The scientific analysis and study of interactions among organisms and their environment. It is an interdisciplinary field that includes biology, geography and Earth science.

4. A compound of chlorine with another element or group, especially a salt of the anion or an organic compound with chlorine bonded to an alkyl group.

5. The total number of protons and neutrons (together known as nucleons) in an atomic nucleus

6. An enzyme that synthesizes short RNA sequences called primers.

A. Mass Number
D. Primase
G. Chloride
J. Electromagnetic Spectrum

B. Ecology
E. Neurobiology
H. Dalton
K. Environmental Biology

C. Electron
F. Interferon
I. Bionics

13. *Using the Across and Down clues, write the correct words in the numbered grid below.*

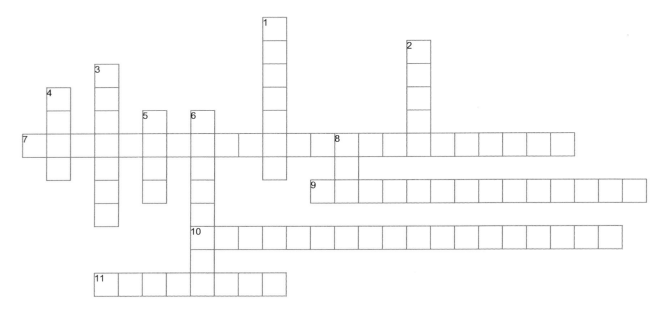

ACROSS

7. A technique used in molecular biology to amplify a single copy or a few copies of a piece of DNA across several orders of magnitude.

9. The double helix is unwound and each strand acts as a template for the next strand. Bases are matched to synthesize the new partner strands.

10. A type of microscope that uses a beam of electrons to create an image of the specimen. It is capable of much higher magnifications.

11. The study of viruses-submicroscopic, parasitic particles of genetic material contained in a protein coat and virus-like agents.

DOWN

1. Refers to the number of elements to which it can connect.

2. A liquid by-product of the body secreted by the kidneys through a process called urination (or micturition) and excreted through the urethra.

3. A large molecule, or macromolecule, composed of many repeated subunits.

4. An unstable subatomic particle. Among all known unstable subatomic particles, only the neutron (lasting around 15 minutes) and some atomic nuclei have a longer decay lifetime.

5. The structural and functional unit of all organisms; an autonomous self

6. A cell filled with basophil granules, found in numbers in connective tissue and releasing histamine and other substances during inflammatory and allergic reactions.

8. An atom or molecule with a net electric charge due to the loss or gain of one or more electrons.

A. Polymerase Chain Reaction
D. Electron Microscope
G. Urine
J. Virology

B. Polymer
E. Muon
H. DNA Replication
K. Mast Cell

C. Valence
F. Cell
I. Ion

14. *Using the Across and Down clues, write the correct words in the numbered grid below.*

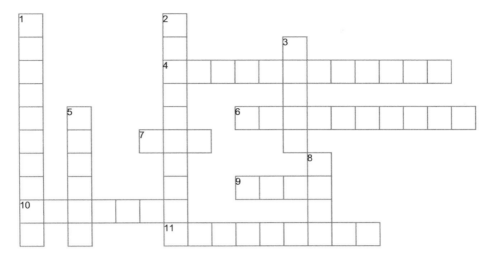

ACROSS

4. A lasting attraction between atoms that enables the formation of chemical compounds.

6. The theory that all living things are made up of cells.

7. An atom or molecule with a net electric charge due to the loss or gain of one or more electrons.

9. A dark green to yellowish brown fluid, produced by the liver of most vertebrates, that aids the digestion of lipids in the small intestine.

10. Often defined as the largest group of organisms in which two individuals are capable of reproducing fertile offspring, typically using sexual reproduction.

11. An animal that is dependent on or capable of the internal generation of heat; a warm

DOWN

1. A mammalian blastula in which some differentiation of cells has occurred.

2. Cytosine, Guanine, Adenine (which can be found in DNA and RNA), Thymine (found only in DNA), and Uracil (found only in RNA).

3. A lymphocyte of a type produced or processed by the thymus gland and actively participating in the immune response.

5. The vascular tissue in plants that conducts sugars and other metabolic products downward from the leaves.

8. A gene is a locus (or region) of DNA that encodes a functional RNA or protein product, and is the molecular unit of heredity.

A. Cell theory
B. Gene
C. Chemical bond
D. Species
E. Blastocyst
F. Nucleobase
G. Phloem
H. Endotherm
I. Ion
J. Bile
K. T Cell

15. *Using the Across and Down clues, write the correct words in the numbered grid below.*

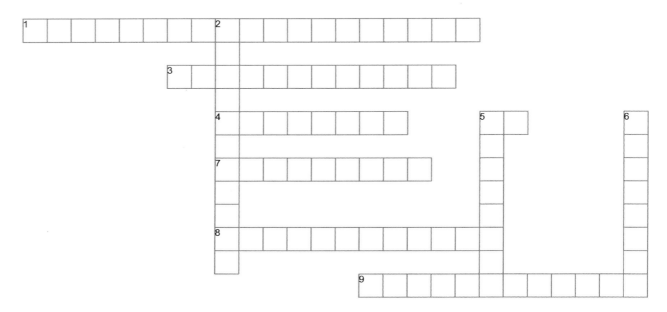

ACROSS

1. The subfield of biology that studies the evolutionary processes that produced the diversity of life on Earth starting from a single origin of life.

3. A field of scientific study that is based on the hypothesis that social behavior has resulted from evolution and attempts to explain and examine social behavior within that context.

4. A steroidal prohormone of the major insect molting hormone is secreted from the prothoracic glands.

5. A numeric scale used to specify the acidity or basicity (alkalinity) of an aqueous solution. It is roughly the negative of the logarithm to base 10 of the concentration.

7. Any member of two classes of chemical compounds derived from carbonic acid or carbon dioxide.

8. A group of animals that have no backbone, unlike animals such as reptiles, amphibians, fish, birds and mammals who all have a backbone.

9. The branch of science that explores the chemical processes within and related to living organisms.

DOWN

2. A complex organic substance present in living cells, especially DNA or RNA, whose molecules consist of many nucleotides linked in a long chain.

5. A gene whose individual effect on a phenotype is too small to be observed, but which can act together with others to produce observable variation.

6. The inactive X chromosome in a female somatic cell, rendered inactive in a process called lionization

A. Ecdysone
D. Evolutionary Biology
G. Polygene
J. Biochemistry

B. Nucleic Acid
E. Barr body
H. pH

C. Invertebrate
F. Carbonate
I. Sociobiology

16. *Using the Across and Down clues, write the correct words in the numbered grid below.*

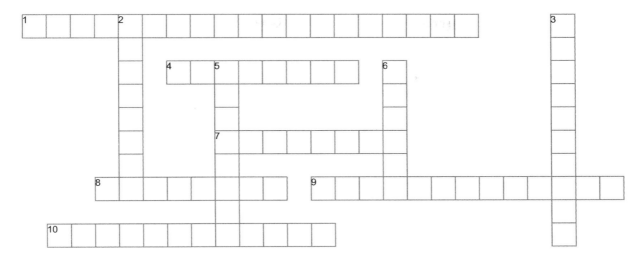

ACROSS

1. The scientific study of nature and of Earth's biodiversity with the aim of protecting species, their habitats, and ecosystems from excessive rates of extinction.

4. A cell filled with basophil granules, found in numbers in connective tissue and releasing histamine and other substances during inflammatory and allergic reactions.

7. The smallest particle in a chemical element or compound that has the chemical properties of that element or compound.

8. One of the three primary germ layers in the very early human embryo. The other two layers are the ectoderm (outside layer) and mesoderm (middle layer).

9. The first step of gene expression, in which a particular segment of DNA is copied into RNA (mRNA) by the enzyme RNA polymerase.

10. Catalysis in living systems. In biological processes, natural catalysts, such as protein enzymes, perform chemical transformations on organic compounds.

DOWN

2. A subatomic particle with a negative elementary electric charge.

3. The part of an enzyme or antibody where the chemical reaction occurs

5. An undifferentiated cell of a multicellular organism that is capable of giving rise to indefinitely more cells of the same type.

6. A motor protein in cells which converts the chemical energy contained in ATP into the mechanical energy of movement

A. Molecule
D. Mast Cell
G. Biocatalysts
J. Active site

B. Conservation Biology
E. Electron
H. Dynein

C. Transcription
F. Stem cell
I. Endoderm

17. *Using the Across and Down clues, write the correct words in the numbered grid below.*

ACROSS

3. A lymphocyte of a type produced or processed by the thymus gland and actively participating in the immune response.

6. Type of reproduction in which cells from two parents unite to form the first cell of a new organism.

7. Large biomolecules, or macromolecules, consisting of one or more long chains of amino acid residues.

8. The fibrous connective tissue that connects bones to other bones.

9. Component of the blood that functions in the immune system. Also known as a leukocyte.

10. The study, in the field of genetics, of cellular and physiological phenotypic trait variations that are caused by external or environmental factors that switch genes on and off.

DOWN

1. The set of observable characteristics of an individual resulting from the interaction of its genotype with the environment.

2. An organelle formed from a centriole, and a short cylindrical array of microtubules.

3. The decoding of genetic instructions for making proteins.

4. The inner layer of the stems of woody plants; composed of xylem.

5. The variety of life in the world or in a particular habitat or ecosystem.

A. Phenotype   B. Wood   C. White Blood Cell   D. Ligament
E. Basal body   F. Epigenetics   G. T Cell   H. Translation
I. Biodiversity   J. Protein   K. Sexual Reproduction

18. *Using the Across and Down clues, write the correct words in the numbered grid below.*

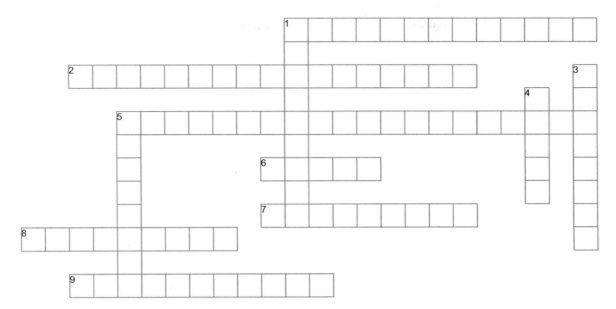

ACROSS

1. The reduced genetic diversity that results when a population is descended from a small number of colonizing ancestors.

2. When a nerve or muscle cell is at "rest", its membrane potential is called the resting membrane potential.

5. The term used to describe what happens to an ecological community over time.

6. A distinct juvenile form many animals undergo before metamorphosis into adults. Animals with indirect development such as insects, amphibians, or cnidarians.

7. A tissue produced inside the seeds of most of the flowering plants around the time of fertilization.

8. An animal that is dependent on or capable of the internal generation of heat; a warm

9. The practice of cultivating land, growing food, and raising stock.

DOWN

1. A hierarchical series of organisms each dependent on the next as a source of food.

3. The stock of different genes in an interbreeding population.

4. Very large ecological areas on the earth's surface, with fauna and flora (animals and plants) adapting to their environment.

5. An organ or cell that acts in response to a stimulus.

A. Endosperm
D. Ecological Succession
G. Membrane Potential
J. Founder Effect

B. Effector
E. Agriculture
H. Gene Pool
K. Larva

C. Endotherm
F. Food Chain
I. Biome

19. *Using the Across and Down clues, write the correct words in the numbered grid below.*

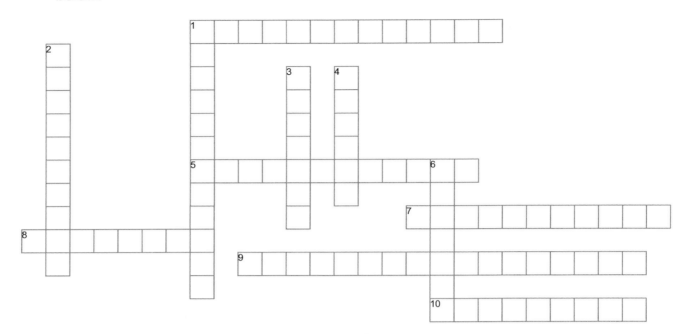

ACROSS

1. One cell dividing into two identical daughter cells.
5. The study of microscopic organisms, such as bacteria, viruses, archaea, fungi and protozoa.
7. The yellow colored photosynthetic pigments.
8. The fibrous connective tissue that connects bones to other bones.
9. Rain containing acids that form in the atmosphere when industrial gas emissions (especially sulfur dioxide and nitrogen oxides) combine with water.
10. An interaction of living things and non-living things in a physical environment.

DOWN

1. The branch of science that explores the chemical processes within and related to living organisms.
2. A process by which the contents of a cell vacuole are released to the exterior through fusion of the vacuole membrane with the cell membrane.
3. An organic compound with four rings arranged in a specific configuration. Examples include the dietary lipid cholesterol and the sex hormones.
4. A motor protein in cells which converts the chemical energy contained in ATP into the mechanical energy of movement
6. One of the four main nucleobases found in the nucleic acids DNA and RNA, the others being adenine, cytosine, and thymine.

A. Steroid
B. Dynein
C. Binary fission
D. Xanthophyll
E. Exocytosis
F. Ligament
G. Biochemistry
H. Ecosystem
I. Acid precipitation
J. Microbiology
K. Guanine

20. *Using the Across and Down clues, write the correct words in the numbered grid below.*

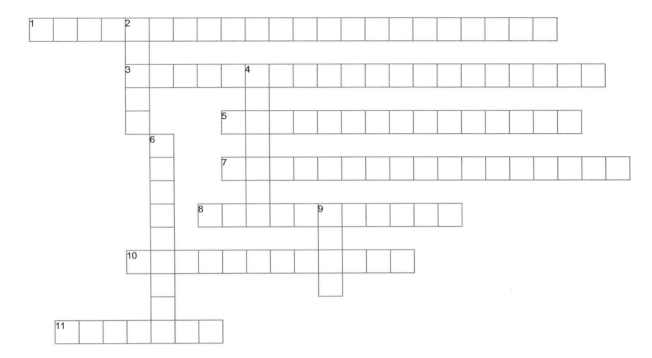

ACROSS

1. The site of oxidative phosphorylation in eukaryotes.
3. A network of membranous tubules within the cytoplasm of a eukaryotic cell, continuous with the nuclear membrane.
5. The local voltage change across the cell wall as a nerve impulse is transmitted.
7. When a nerve or muscle cell is at "rest", its membrane potential is called the resting membrane potential.
8. The highest range of electron energies in which electrons are normally present at absolute zero temperature.
10. The science of drug action on biological systems.
11. A large molecule, or macromolecule, composed of many repeated subunits.

DOWN

2. A lymphocyte of a type produced or processed by the thymus gland and actively participating in the immune response.
4. A lymphatic capillary that absorbs dietary fats in the villi of the small intestine.
6. A organism in which internal physiological sources of heat are of relatively small or quite negligible importance in controlling body temperature. "Cold blooded".
9. The structural and functional unit of all organisms; an autonomous self

A. Action potential
D. Cell
G. Endoplasmic Reticulum
J. Polymer

B. T Cell
E. Membrane Potential
H. Ectotherm
K. Electron Transport Chain

C. Valence band
F. Lacteal
I. Pharmacology

21. *Using the Across and Down clues, write the correct words in the numbered grid below.*

ACROSS

3. The total number of protons and neutrons (together known as nucleons) in an atomic nucleus

4. A label frequently used to describe various forms of cross-disciplinary and multitaxon research.

7. The study of genetic variation within populations, and involves the examination and modeling of changes in the frequencies of genes and alleles.

8. The inactive X chromosome in a female somatic cell, rendered inactive in a process called lionization

9. A type of cell division that reduces the number of chromosomes in the parent cell by half and produces four gamete cells.

10. An interdisciplinary science that applies the approaches and methods of physics to study biological systems.

11. A series of chemical reactions used by all aerobic organisms to generate energy through the oxidation of acetyl

DOWN

1. The double helix is unwound and each strand acts as a template for the next strand. Bases are matched to synthesize the new partner strands.

2. An organelle formed from a centriole, and a short cylindrical array of microtubules.

5. An unstable subatomic particle. Among all known unstable subatomic particles, only the neutron (lasting around 15 minutes) and some atomic nuclei have a longer decay lifetime.

6. A cell filled with basophil granules, found in numbers in connective tissue and releasing histamine and other substances during inflammatory and allergic reactions.

A. Biophysics
B. Basal body
C. Muon
D. Mass Number
E. Meiosis
F. Integrative Biology
G. Barr body
H. DNA Replication
I. Krebs Cycle
J. Population Genetics
K. Mast Cell

22. *Using the Across and Down clues, write the correct words in the numbered grid below.*

ACROSS

1. Density is mass per volume.
3. The four bases found in DNA are adenine, cytosine, guanine and thymine. These four bases are attached to the sugar
5. A process in nature in which organisms possessing certain genotypic characteristics that make them better adjusted to an environment tend to survive.
6. A gene whose individual effect on a phenotype is too small to be observed, but which can act together with others to produce observable variation.
8. The scientific analysis and study of interactions among organisms and their environment. It is an interdisciplinary field that includes biology, geography and Earth science.
9. Any organism whose cells contain a nucleus and other organelles enclosed within membranes.
11. Usually defined as a chemical reaction that involves the loss of a water molecule from the reacting molecule.

DOWN

2. A short branched extension of a nerve cell, along which impulses received from other cells at synapses are transmitted to the cell body
4. An inner layer of cells in the cortex of a root and of some stems, surrounding a vascular bundle.
7. Any part of a gene that will become a part of the final mature RNA produced by that gene after introns have been removed by RNA splicing.
10. One of the proteins into which actomyosin can be split; can exist in either a globular or a fibrous form.

A. Dehydration Reaction
D. Exon
G. Natural Selection
J. Ecology

B. Polygene
E. Deoxyribonucleic Acid
H. Actin
K. Endodermis

C. Mass Density
F. Dendrite
I. Eukaryote

23. *Using the Across and Down clues, write the correct words in the numbered grid below.*

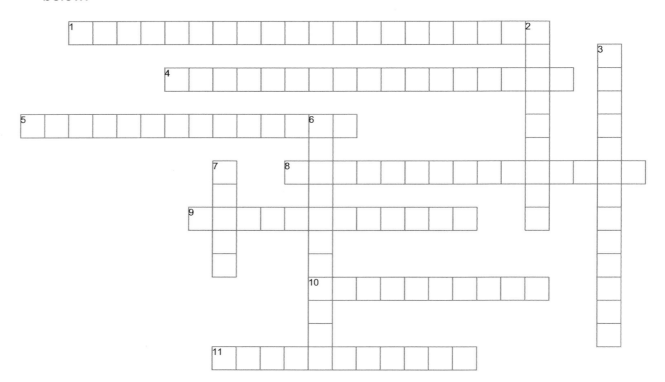

ACROSS

1. A network of membranous tubules within the cytoplasm of a eukaryotic cell, continuous with the nuclear membrane.

4. A measure of the tendency of an atom to attract a bonding pair of electrons. The Pauling scale is the most commonly used.

5. An epithelial tissue that secretes mucus and that lines many body cavities and tubular organs including the gut and respiratory passages.

8. Adaptation to a new climate (a new temperature or altitude or environment).

9. The branch of science that explores the chemical processes within and related to living organisms.

10. The part of an enzyme or antibody where the chemical reaction occurs

11. Density is mass per volume.

DOWN

2. The third phase of mitosis, the process that separates duplicated genetic material carried in the nucleus of a parent cell into two identical daughter cells.

3. The application of the principles of biology to the study of physiological, genetic, and developmental mechanisms of behavior in humans and other animals.

6. A complex organic substance present in living cells, especially DNA or RNA, whose molecules consist of many nucleotides linked in a long chain.

7. A liquid by-product of the body secreted by the kidneys through a process called urination (or micturition) and excreted through the urethra.

A. Psychobiology
D. Metaphase
G. Active site
J. Endoplasmic Reticulum

B. Mass Density
E. Acclimatization
H. Urine
K. Biochemistry

C. Electronegativity
F. Mucous Membrane
I. Nucleic Acid

24. *Using the Across and Down clues, write the correct words in the numbered grid below.*

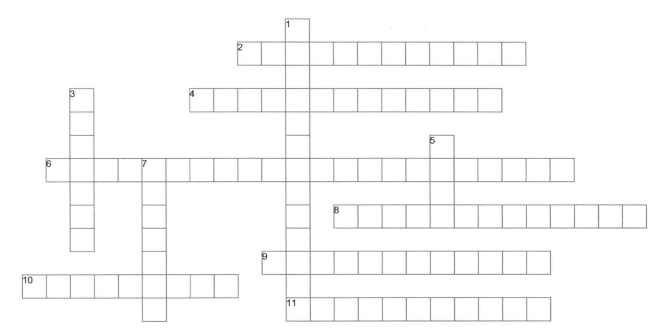

ACROSS

2. Catalysis in living systems. In biological processes, natural catalysts, such as protein enzymes, perform chemical transformations on organic compounds.

4. Also known as antibodies, They act as a critical part of the immune response by specifically recognizing and binding to particular antigens, and aiding in their destruction.

6. A form of asexual reproduction of a plant. Only one plant is involved and the offspring is the result of one parent. The new plant is genetically identical to the parent.

8. The scientific study of organisms in the ocean or other marine bodies of water.

9. The form of RNA in which genetic information transcribed from DNA as a sequence of bases is transferred to a ribosome.

10. Any member of two classes of chemical compounds derived from carbonic acid or carbon dioxide.

11. RNA consisting of folded molecules that transport amino acids from the cytoplasm of a cell to a ribosome.

DOWN

1. The reduced genetic diversity that results when a population is descended from a small number of colonizing ancestors.

3. Refers to the number of elements to which it can connect.

5. An unstable subatomic particle. Among all known unstable subatomic particles, only the neutron (lasting around 15 minutes) and some atomic nuclei have a longer decay lifetime.

7. One of the four nucleobases in the nucleic acid of DNA that are represented by the letters G–C–A–T.

A. Thymine
D. Valence
G. Muon
J. Marine Biology

B. Carbonate
E. Messenger RNA
H. Immunogloblin
K. Founder Effect

C. Transfer RNA
F. Biocatalysts
I. Vegetative reproduction

25. *Using the Across and Down clues, write the correct words in the numbered grid below.*

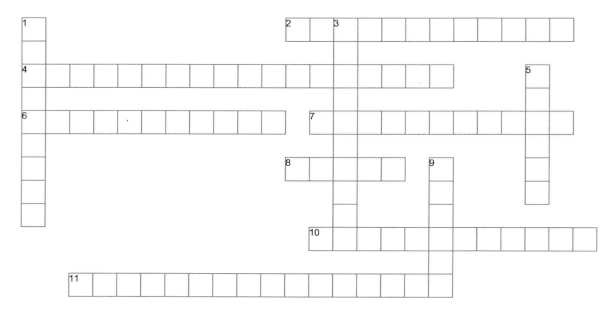

ACROSS

2. The science of drug action on biological systems.

4. A type of microscope that uses a beam of electrons to create an image of the specimen. It is capable of much higher magnifications.

6. A branch of zoology that concerns the study of birds.

7. The branch of biology that studies the effects of low temperatures on living things within Earth's cryosphere or in science.

8. A human embryo after eight weeks of development.

10. A group of animals that have no backbone, unlike animals such as reptiles, amphibians, fish, birds and mammals who all have a backbone.

11. A process in nature in which organisms possessing certain genotypic characteristics that make them better adjusted to an environment tend to survive.

DOWN

1. The set of observable characteristics of an individual resulting from the interaction of its genotype with the environment.

3. A process in which one substance permeates another; a fluid permeates or is dissolved by a liquid or solid.

5. A diploid cell resulting from the fusion of two haploid gametes; a fertilized ovum.

9. An elementary, half-integer spin particle that does not undergo strong interactions.

A. Zygote
E. Cryobiology
I. Electron Microscope

B. Invertebrate
F. Pharmacology
J. Ornithology

C. Lepton
G. Fetus
K. Absorption

D. Natural Selection
H. Phenotype

26. *Using the Across and Down clues, write the correct words in the numbered grid below.*

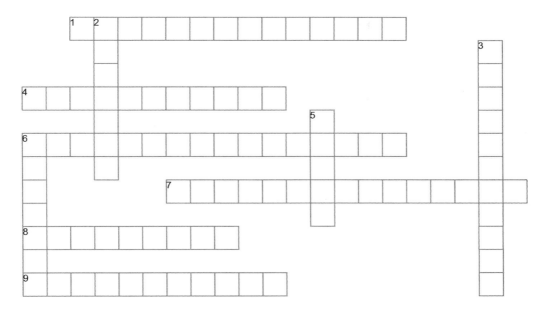

ACROSS

1. How your body recognizes and defends itself against bacteria, viruses, and substances that appear foreign and harmful.

4. The branch of biology that studies the effects of low temperatures on living things within Earth's cryosphere or in science.

6. A branch of science concerning biological activity at the molecular level.

7. Any of various molecules that are capable of accepting one or two electrons from one molecule and donating them to another in the process of electron transport.

8. A colorless cell which circulates in the blood and body fluids and is involved in counteracting foreign substances and disease; a white (blood) cell.

9. The study of plant nutrition and growth especially as a way to increase crop yield

DOWN

2. A molecule that can be bonded to other identical molecules to form a polymer.

3. The highest range of electron energies in which electrons are normally present at absolute zero temperature.

5. The red liquid that circulates in the arteries and veins of humans and other vertebrate animals, carrying oxygen to and carbon dioxide from the tissues of the body.

6. The continuation of the spinal cord within the skull, forming the lowest part of the brainstem and containing control centers for the heart and lungs.

A. Valence band
E. Medulla
I. Electron Carrier

B. Monomer
F. Blood
J. Immune Response

C. Cryobiology
G. Molecular biology

D. Leukocyte
H. Agrobiology

27. *Using the Across and Down clues, write the correct words in the numbered grid below.*

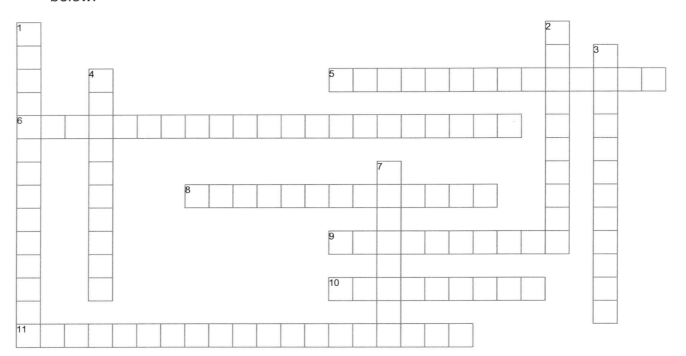

ACROSS

5. A measure of the potential energy in water as well as the difference between the potential in a given water sample and pure water.

6. A chemical synapse formed by the contact between a motor neuron and a muscle fiber.

8. Virus that infects and multiplies within bacteria.

9. Organic molecules that serve as the monomers, or subunits, of nucleic acids like DNA (deoxyribonucleic acid) and RNA (ribonucleic acid).

10. the tendency of a crossbred individual to show qualities superior to those of both parents.

11. The subfield of biology that studies the evolutionary processes that produced the diversity of life on Earth starting from a single origin of life.

DOWN

1. How your body recognizes and defends itself against bacteria, viruses, and substances that appear foreign and harmful.

2. In cell biology, an organelle that is the main place where cell microtubules get organized. They occur only in plant and animal cells.

3. The variety of life in the world or in a particular habitat or ecosystem.

4. A threadlike strand of DNA in the cell nucleus that carries the genes in a linear order.

7. The region of an embryo or seedling stem above the cotyledon.

A. Biodiversity
D. Nucleotide
G. Bacteriophage
J. Evolutionary Biology

B. Epicotyl
E. Immune Response
H. Heterosis
K. Chromosome

C. Centrosome
F. Water Potential
I. Neuromuscular Junction

28. *Using the Across and Down clues, write the correct words in the numbered grid below.*

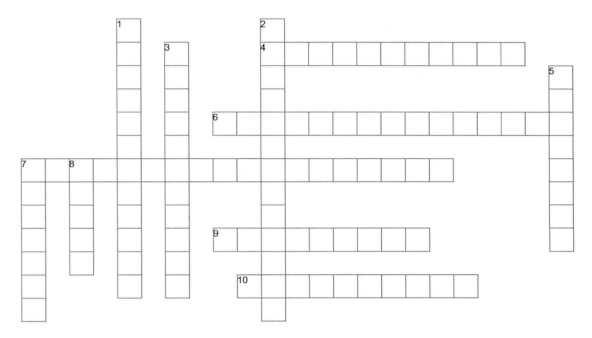

ACROSS

4. A group of cytokines (secreted proteins and signal molecules) that were first seen to be expressed by white blood cells (leukocytes)

6. A microbially facilitated process of nitrate reduction that may ultimately produce molecular nitrogen.

7. The pursuit of answers to medical questions. These investigations lead to discoveries, which in turn lead to the development of new preventions, therapies and cures.

9. A medical specialty that is concerned with the diagnosis of disease based on the laboratory analysis of bodily fluids such as blood and urine.

10. Animals, like flatworms and jellyfish, that have no body cavity (coelom).

DOWN

1. A group of animals that have no backbone, unlike animals such as reptiles, amphibians, fish, birds and mammals who all have a backbone.

2. The study of the transformation of energy in living organisms.

3. The ecological region at the lowest level of a body of water such as an ocean or a lake, including the sediment surface and some sub

5. The study of heredity

7. A form of terrestrial locomotion where an organism moves by means of its two rear limbs or legs.

8. a part of an organism that is typically self-contained and has a specific vital function, such as the heart or liver in humans.

A. Denitrification
B. Acoelomate
C. Invertebrate
D. Bioenergetics
E. Interleukin
F. Genetics
G. Biomedical research
H. Organ
I. Benthic zone
J. Pathology
K. Bipedal

29. Using the Across and Down clues, write the correct words in the numbered grid below.

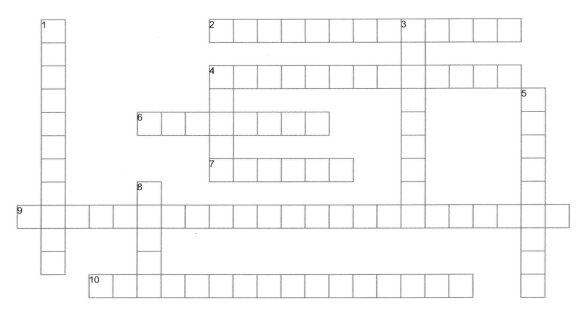

ACROSS

2. Virus that infects and multiplies within bacteria.

4. The study of the transformation of energy in living organisms.

6. The outermost layer of cells or tissue of an embryo in early development, or the parts derived from this, which include the epidermis, nerve tissue, and nephridia.

7. A motor protein in cells which converts the chemical energy contained in ATP into the mechanical energy of movement

9. A technique used in molecular biology to amplify a single copy or a few copies of a piece of DNA across several orders of magnitude.

10. An interdisciplinary branch of biology and engineering.

DOWN

1. The nucleotide triplets of DNA and RNA molecules that carry genetic information in living cells.

3. The set of observable characteristics of an individual resulting from the interaction of its genotype with the environment.

4. The red liquid that circulates in the arteries and veins of humans and other vertebrate animals, carrying oxygen to and carbon dioxide from the tissues of the body.

5. The female gametophyte of a seed plant, within which the embryo develops.

8. Hadronic subatomic particles composed of one quark and one antiquark, bound together by the strong interaction.

A. Synthetic Biology
D. Dynein
G. Embryo Sac
J. Genetic Code

B. Ectoderm
E. Polymerase Chain Reaction
H. Bioenergetics
K. Blood

C. Phenotype
F. Bacteriophage
I. Meson

30. *Using the Across and Down clues, write the correct words in the numbered grid below.*

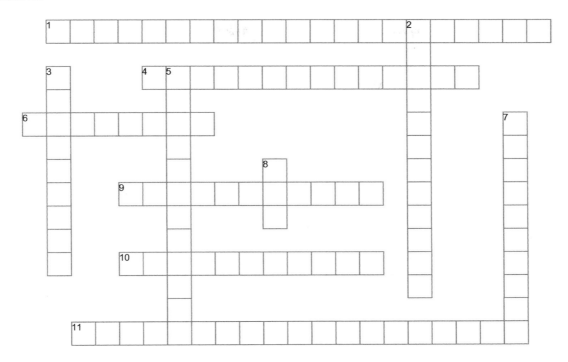

ACROSS

1. A laboratory process that determines the complete DNA sequence of an organism's genome at a single time.

4. A measure of the potential energy in water as well as the difference between the potential in a given water sample and pure water.

6. The ecological state of a species being unique to a defined geographic location, such as an island, nation, country or other defined zone, or habitat type.

9. Density is mass per volume.

10. Contraction of the protoplast of a plant cell as a result of loss of water from the cell.

11. Usually defined as a chemical reaction that involves the loss of a water molecule from the reacting molecule.

DOWN

2. The study and analysis of the patterns, causes, and effects of health and disease conditions in defined populations.

3. The complete transfer of valence electron(s) between atoms. It is a type of chemical bond that generates two oppositely charged ions.

5. a plant hormone.

7. A process in which one substance permeates another; a fluid permeates or is dissolved by a liquid or solid.

8. Stands for ribonucleic acid. It is an important molecule with long chains of nucleotides. A nucleotide contains a nitrogenous base, a ribose sugar, and a phosphate.

A. Ionic Bond
D. Whole Genome Sequencing
G. Absorption
J. Epidemiology

B. Water Potential
E. Dehydration Reaction
H. Endemism
K. Abscisic acid

C. RNA
F. Plasmolysis
I. Mass Density

31. *Using the Across and Down clues, write the correct words in the numbered grid below.*

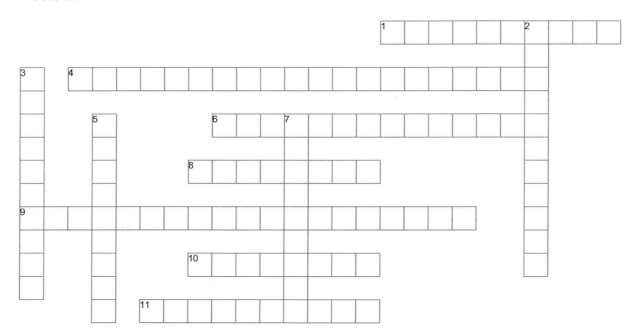

ACROSS

1. The branch of biology that studies the development of gametes (sex cells), fertilization, and development of embryos and fetuses.

4. The term used to describe what happens to an ecological community over time.

6. A cup-like sac at the beginning of the tubular component of a nephron in the mammalian kidney that performs the first step in the filtration of blood to form urine.

8. Organisms that produce an egg composed of shell and membranes that creates a protected environment in which the embryo can develop out of water

9. An evolutionary theory that explains the origin of eukaryotic cells from prokaryotes.

10. The intersection of the three medians of the triangle (each median connecting a vertex with the midpoint of the opposite side).

11. The study of insects.

DOWN

2. When two genes are close together on the same chromosome, they do not assort independently.

3. The theory that all living things are made up of cells.

5. A medical specialty that is concerned with the diagnosis of disease based on the laboratory analysis of bodily fluids such as blood and urine.

7. Any of the elongated contractile threads found in striated muscle cells.

A. Amniotes
B. Embryology
C. Ecological Succession
D. Bowmans capsule
E. Centroid
F. Myofibril
G. Cell theory
H. Linked Genes
I. Entomology
J. Endosymbiotic Theory
K. Pathology

32. *Using the Across and Down clues, write the correct words in the numbered grid below.*

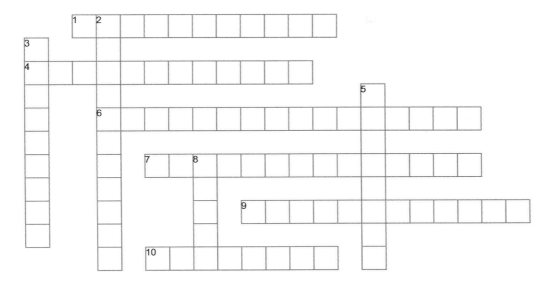

ACROSS

1. Work to convert light energy of the Sun into sugars that can be used by cells.

4. Variations in a phenotype among individuals carrying a particular genotype.

6. A chemical entity that accepts electrons transferred to it from another compound.

7. The application of concepts and methods of biology to solve real world problems.

9. The study of parasites, their hosts, and the relationship between them.

10. A short branched extension of a nerve cell, along which impulses received from other cells at synapses are transmitted to the cell body

DOWN

2. The branch of zoology concerned with reptiles and amphibians.

3. Also known as a macula adhaerens, is a cell structure specialized for cell to cell adhesion.

5. The study of heredity

8. a part of an organism that is typically self-contained and has a specific vital function, such as the heart or liver in humans.

A. Genetics
E. Organ
I. Chloroplast

B. Desmosome
F. Dendrite
J. Parasitology

C. Bioengineering
G. Herpetology

D. Expressivity
H. Electron Acceptor

33. *Using the Across and Down clues, write the correct words in the numbered grid below.*

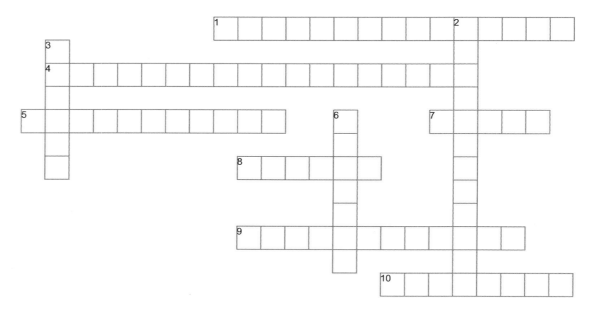

ACROSS

1. A microbially facilitated process of nitrate reduction that may ultimately produce molecular nitrogen.
4. The study of genetic variation within populations, and involves the examination and modeling of changes in the frequencies of genes and alleles.
5. Density is mass per volume.
7. The red liquid that circulates in the arteries and veins of humans and other vertebrate animals, carrying oxygen to and carbon dioxide from the tissues of the body.
8. Any particle that is made from quarks, anti
9. Plasma cells, also called plasma B cells, plasmocytes, plasmacytes, or effector B cells, are white blood cells that secrete large volumes of antibodies.
10. The study of viruses-submicroscopic, parasitic particles of genetic material contained in a protein coat and virus-like agents.

DOWN

2. The lowest theoretically attainable temperature (at which the kinetic energy of atoms and molecules is minimal)
3. Mitosis and cytokinesis together define this phase of an animal cell cycle-the division of the mother cell into two daughter cells, genetically identical to each other and the parent.
6. Application of biological methods and systems found in nature to the study and design of engineering systems and modern technology.

A. Mass Density
E. Virology
I. Bionics

B. M phase
F. Blood
J. Population Genetics

C. Denitrification
G. Hadron

D. Effector Cell
H. Absolute zero

34. *Using the Across and Down clues, write the correct words in the numbered grid below.*

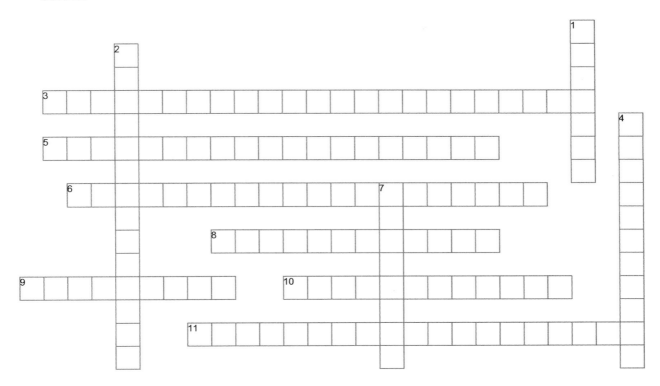

ACROSS

3. A gradient of electrochemical potential, usually for an ion that can move across a membrane.

5. An evolutionary theory that explains the origin of eukaryotic cells from prokaryotes.

6. The branch of biology concerned with the relations between organisms and their environment.

8. Giving birth to one of its kind, sexually or asexually.

9. The interaction of genes that are not alleles, in particular the suppression of the effect of one such gene by another.

10. The study of the distribution of species and ecosystems in geographic space and through time.

11. Organism which is capable of producing energy through aerobic respiration and then switching to anaerobic respiration depending on the amounts of oxygen.

DOWN

1. The branch of morphology that deals with the structure of animals

2. Evolutionary change within a species or small group of organisms, especially over a short period.

4. When two genes are close together on the same chromosome, they do not assort independently.

7. Single-cell microscopic organisms which lack a true nucleus. They represent one of the three domains.

A. Reproduction
D. Endosymbiotic Theory
G. Anatomy
J. Electrochemical Gradient

B. Linked Genes
E. Microevolution
H. Environmental Biology
K. Biogeography

C. Bacteria
F. Facultative Anaerobe
I. Epistasis

35. *Using the Across and Down clues, write the correct words in the numbered grid below.*

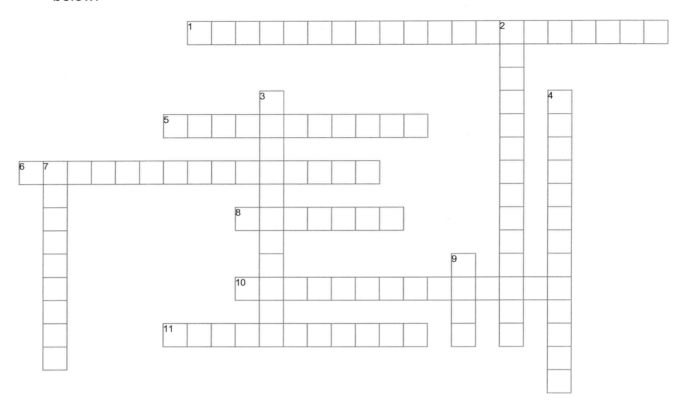

ACROSS

1. The four bases found in DNA are adenine, cytosine, guanine and thymine. These four bases are attached to the sugar

5. The study of organic particles, such as bacteria, fungal spores, very small insects, pollen grains and viruses, which are passively transported by the air.

6. Transport of a substance (as a protein or drug) across a cell membrane against the concentration gradient; requires an expenditure of energy

8. Refers to the number of elements to which it can connect.

10. A pairing between two nucleotides in RNA molecules that does not follow Watson

11. A complex organic substance present in living cells, especially DNA or RNA, whose molecules consist of many nucleotides linked in a long chain.

DOWN

2. Glands that secrete their products, hormones, directly into the blood rather than through a duct.

3. The deep sea (2000 meters or more) where there is no light.

4. Nutrients that provide calories or energy. Nutrients are substances needed for growth, metabolism, and for other body functions.

7. A branch of physical science that studies the composition, structure, properties and change of matter.

9. The structural and functional unit of all organisms; an autonomous self

A. Active Transport
D. Aerobiology
G. Macronutrient
J. Nucleic Acid

B. Deoxyribonucleic Acid
E. Abyssal zone
H. Endocrine Gland
K. Valence

C. Wobble Base Pair
F. Cell
I. Chemistry

1. *Using the Across and Down clues, write the correct words in the numbered grid below.*

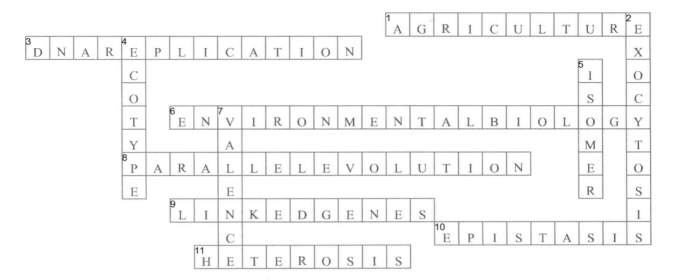

ACROSS

1. The practice of cultivating land, growing food, and raising stock.
3. The double helix is unwound and each strand acts as a template for the next strand. Bases are matched to synthesize the new partner strands.
6. The branch of biology concerned with the relations between organisms and their environment.
8. The independent evolution of similar traits, starting from a similar ancestral condition.
9. When two genes are close together on the same chromosome, they do not assort independently.
10. The interaction of genes that are not alleles, in particular the suppression of the effect of one such gene by another.
11. the tendency of a crossbred individual to show qualities superior to those of both parents.

DOWN

2. A process by which the contents of a cell vacuole are released to the exterior through fusion of the vacuole membrane with the cell membrane.
4. Describes a genetically distinct geographic variety, population or race within a species, which is adapted to specific environmental conditions.
5. A molecule with the same chemical formula as another molecule, but with a different chemical structure.
7. Refers to the number of elements to which it can connect.

A. Ecotype
D. Exocytosis
G. Linked Genes
J. Agriculture

B. Valence
E. Epistasis
H. Heterosis
K. Isomer

C. Environmental Biology
F. Parallel Evolution
I. DNA Replication

2. *Using the Across and Down clues, write the correct words in the numbered grid below.*

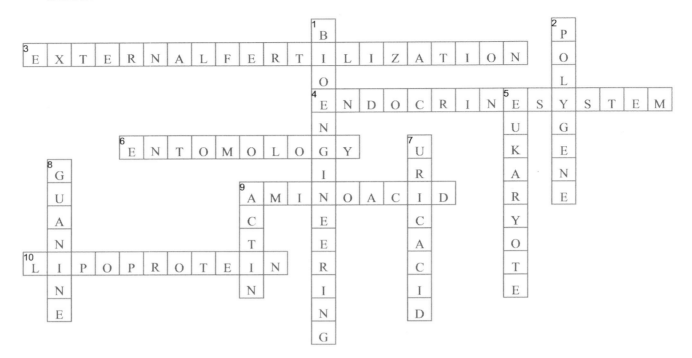

ACROSS

3. Sperm units with egg in the open, rather than inside the body of the parents

4. The collection of glands that produce hormones that regulate metabolism, growth and development, tissue function, sexual function, reproduction, sleep, and mood.

6. The study of insects.

9. A class of organic compounds containing an amino group and a carboxylic acid group

10. A biochemical assembly that contains both proteins and lipids, bound to the proteins, which allow fats to move through the water inside and outside cells.

DOWN

1. The application of concepts and methods of biology to solve real world problems.

2. A gene whose individual effect on a phenotype is too small to be observed, but which can act together with others to produce observable variation.

5. Any organism whose cells contain a nucleus and other organelles enclosed within membranes.

7. A heterocyclic compound of carbon, nitrogen, oxygen, and hydrogen. It forms ions and salts known as urates and acid urates, such as ammonium acid urate.

8. One of the four main nucleobases found in the nucleic acids DNA and RNA, the others being adenine, cytosine, and thymine.

9. One of the proteins into which actomyosin can be split; can exist in either a globular or a fibrous form.

A. Actin
B. Bioengineering
C. Polygene
D. Amino acid
E. Endocrine System
F. Uric acid
G. Entomology
H. Lipoprotein
I. External Fertilization
J. Eukaryote
K. Guanine

3. *Using the Across and Down clues, write the correct words in the numbered grid below.*

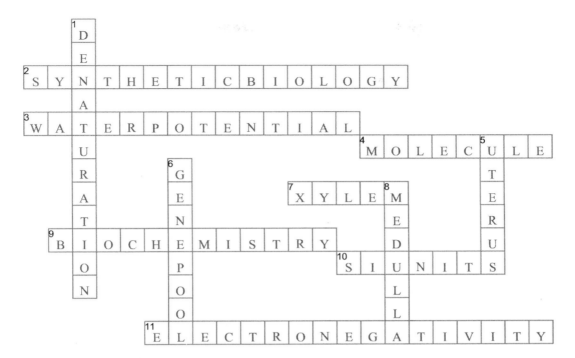

ACROSS

2. An interdisciplinary branch of biology and engineering.

3. A measure of the potential energy in water as well as the difference between the potential in a given water sample and pure water.

4. The smallest particle in a chemical element or compound that has the chemical properties of that element or compound.

7. The vascular tissue in plants that conducts water and dissolved nutrients upward from the root and also helps to form the woody element in the stem.

9. The branch of science that explores the chemical processes within and related to living organisms.

10. A system of physical units-based on the meter, kilogram, second, ampere, kelvin, candela, and mole, together with a set of prefixes.

11. A measure of the tendency of an atom to attract a bonding pair of electrons. The Pauling scale is the most commonly used.

DOWN

1. A process in which proteins or nucleic acids lose the quaternary structure, tertiary structure and secondary structure which is present in their native state.

5. The organ in the lower body of a woman or female mammal where offspring are conceived and in which they gestate before birth; the womb.

6. The stock of different genes in an interbreeding population.

8. The continuation of the spinal cord within the skull, forming the lowest part of the brainstem and containing control centers for the heart and lungs.

A. Denaturation
E. Uterus
I. Molecule
B. Synthetic Biology
F. Medulla
J. Biochemistry
C. SI units
G. Electronegativity
K. Xylem
D. Gene Pool
H. Water Potential

4. *Using the Across and Down clues, write the correct words in the numbered grid below.*

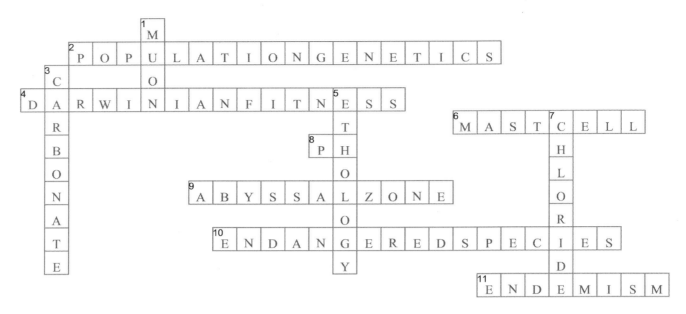

ACROSS

2. The study of genetic variation within populations, and involves the examination and modeling of changes in the frequencies of genes and alleles.

4. The genetic contribution of an individual to the next generation's gene pool relative to the average for the population.

6. A cell filled with basophil granules, found in numbers in connective tissue and releasing histamine and other substances during inflammatory and allergic reactions.

8. A numeric scale used to specify the acidity or basicity (alkalinity) of an aqueous solution. It is roughly the negative of the logarithm to base 10 of the concentration.

9. The deep sea (2000 meters or more) where there is no light.

10. Threatened by factors such as habitat loss, hunting, disease and climate change, and usually have declining populations or a very limited range.

11. The ecological state of a species being unique to a defined geographic location, such as an island, nation, country or other defined zone, or habitat type.

DOWN

1. An unstable subatomic particle. Among all known unstable subatomic particles, only the neutron (lasting around 15 minutes) and some atomic nuclei have a longer decay lifetime.

3. Any member of two classes of chemical compounds derived from carbonic acid or carbon dioxide.

5. The scientific and objective study of non-human animal behavior rather than human behavior and usually with a focus on behavior under natural conditions.

7. A compound of chlorine with another element or group, especially a salt of the anion or an organic compound with chlorine bonded to an alkyl group.

A. Carbonate
E. Endemism
I. Abyssal zone
B. Endangered Species
F. Darwinian Fitness
J. Ethology
C. Population Genetics
G. Mast Cell
K. pH
D. Chloride
H. Muon

5. *Using the Across and Down clues, write the correct words in the numbered grid below.*

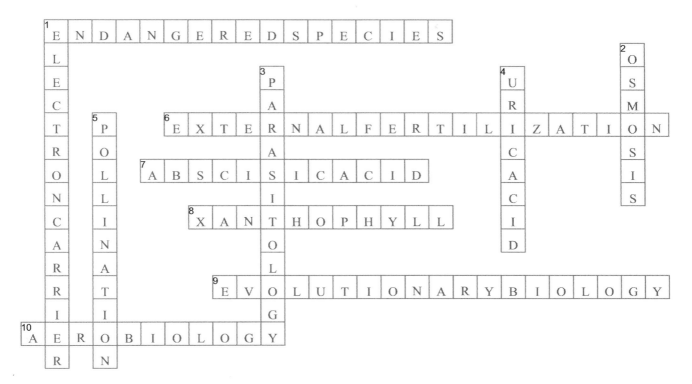

ACROSS

1. Threatened by factors such as habitat loss, hunting, disease and climate change, and usually have declining populations or a very limited range.

6. Sperm units with egg in the open, rather than inside the body of the parents

7. a plant hormone.

8. The yellow colored photosynthetic pigments.

9. The subfield of biology that studies the evolutionary processes that produced the diversity of life on Earth starting from a single origin of life.

10. The study of organic particles, such as bacteria, fungal spores, very small insects, pollen grains and viruses, which are passively transported by the air.

DOWN

1. Any of various molecules that are capable of accepting one or two electrons from one molecule and donating them to another in the process of electron transport.

2. The spontaneous net movement of solvent molecules through a semi-permeable membrane into a region of higher solute concentration.

3. The study of parasites, their hosts, and the relationship between them.

4. A heterocyclic compound of carbon, nitrogen, oxygen, and hydrogen. It forms ions and salts known as urates and acid urates, such as ammonium acid urate.

5. The act of transferring pollen grains from the male anther of a flower to the female stigma.

A. External Fertilization
D. Abscisic acid
G. Electron Carrier
J. Endangered Species

B. Uric acid
E. Osmosis
H. Xanthophyll
K. Aerobiology

C. Evolutionary Biology
F. Pollination
I. Parasitology

6. *Using the Across and Down clues, write the correct words in the numbered grid below.*

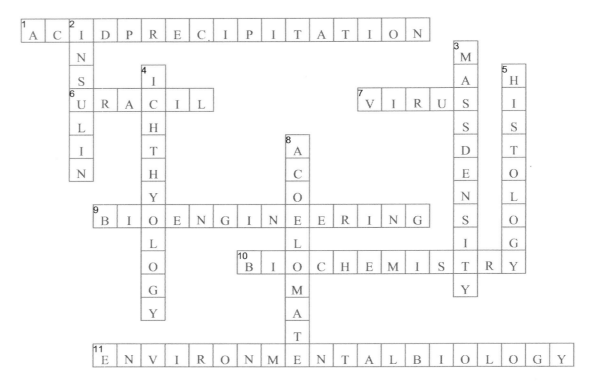

ACROSS

1. Rain containing acids that form in the atmosphere when industrial gas emissions (especially sulfur dioxide and nitrogen oxides) combine with water.

6. One of the four nucleobases in the nucleic acid of RNA that are represented by the letters A, G, C and U.

7. A biological agent that reproduces inside the cells of living hosts.

9. The application of concepts and methods of biology to solve real world problems.

10. The branch of science that explores the chemical processes within and related to living organisms.

11. The branch of biology concerned with the relations between organisms and their environment.

DOWN

2. Helps keep blood sugar level from getting too high (hyperglycemia) or too low (hypoglycemia).

3. Density is mass per volume.

4. Known as Fish Science, is the branch of biology devoted to the study of fish.

5. The study of the microscopic anatomy of cells and tissues of plants and animals.

8. Animals, like flatworms and jellyfish, that have no body cavity (coelom).

A. Acid precipitation
D. Virus
G. Mass Density
J. Bioengineering

B. Insulin
E. Biochemistry
H. Histology
K. Uracil

C. Acoelomate
F. Environmental Biology
I. Ichthyology

7. *Using the Across and Down clues, write the correct words in the numbered grid below.*

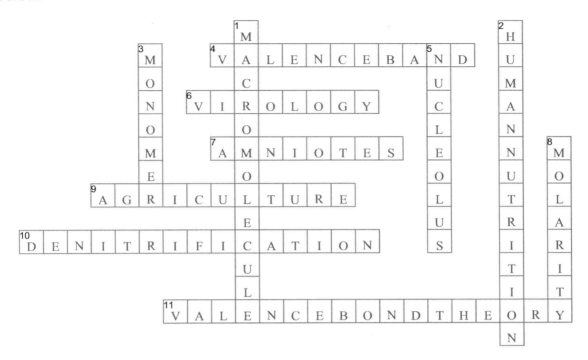

ACROSS

4. The highest range of electron energies in which electrons are normally present at absolute zero temperature.

6. The study of viruses-submicroscopic, parasitic particles of genetic material contained in a protein coat and virus-like agents.

7. Organisms that produce an egg composed of shell and membranes that creates a protected environment in which the embryo can develop out of water

9. The practice of cultivating land, growing food, and raising stock.

10. A microbially facilitated process of nitrate reduction that may ultimately produce molecular nitrogen.

11. A straightforward extension of Lewis structures. States that electrons in a covalent bond reside in a region that is the overlap of individual atomic orbitals.

DOWN

1. A very large molecule, such as protein, commonly created by polymerization of smaller subunits (monomers).

2. Refers to the provision of essential nutrients necessary to support human life and health.

3. A molecule that can be bonded to other identical molecules to form a polymer.

5. A small dense spherical structure in the nucleus of a cell during interphase.

8. A unit of concentration measuring the number of moles of a solute per liter of solution.

A. Agriculture
B. Amniotes
C. Virology
D. Nucleolus
E. Denitrification
F. Human Nutrition
G. Macromolecule
H. Molarity
I. Valence band
J. Monomer
K. Valence bond theory

8. *Using the Across and Down clues, write the correct words in the numbered grid below.*

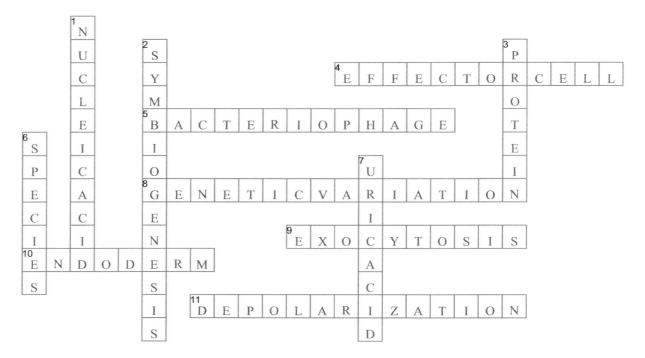

ACROSS

4. Plasma cells, also called plasma B cells, plasmocytes, plasmacytes, or effector B cells, are white blood cells that secrete large volumes of antibodies.

5. Virus that infects and multiplies within bacteria.

8. Variations of genomes between members of species, or between groups of species thriving in different parts of the world as a result of genetic mutation.

9. A process by which the contents of a cell vacuole are released to the exterior through fusion of the vacuole membrane with the cell membrane.

10. One of the three primary germ layers in the very early human embryo. The other two layers are the ectoderm (outside layer) and mesoderm (middle layer).

11. The process of reversing the charge across a cell membrane (usually a NEURON), so causing an ACTION POTENTIAL.

DOWN

1. A complex organic substance present in living cells, especially DNA or RNA, whose molecules consist of many nucleotides linked in a long chain.

2. An evolutionary theory that explains the origin of eukaryotic cells from prokaryotes.

3. Large biomolecules, or macromolecules, consisting of one or more long chains of amino acid residues.

6. Often defined as the largest group of organisms in which two individuals are capable of reproducing fertile offspring, typically using sexual reproduction.

7. A heterocyclic compound of carbon, nitrogen, oxygen, and hydrogen. It forms ions and salts known as urates and acid urates, such as ammonium acid urate.

A. Exocytosis
E. Bacteriophage
I. Nucleic Acid
B. Genetic Variation
F. Effector Cell
J. Species
C. Symbiogenesis
G. Protein
K. Depolarization
D. Endoderm
H. Uric acid

9. *Using the Across and Down clues, write the correct words in the numbered grid below.*

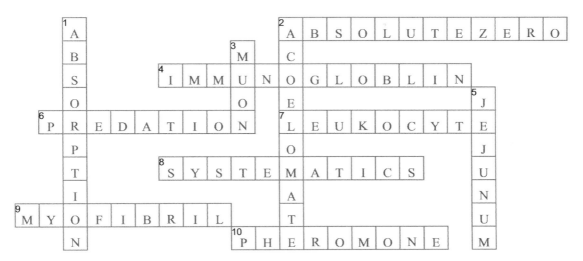

ACROSS

2. The lowest theoretically attainable temperature (at which the kinetic energy of atoms and molecules is minimal)

4. Also known as antibodies, They act as a critical part of the immune response by specifically recognizing and binding to particular antigens, and aiding in their destruction.

6. The preying of one animal on others.

7. A colorless cell which circulates in the blood and body fluids and is involved in counteracting foreign substances and disease; a white (blood) cell.

8. The branch of biology that deals with classification and nomenclature; taxonomy.

9. Any of the elongated contractile threads found in striated muscle cells.

10. A chemical substance produced and released into the environment by an animal, especially a mammal or an insect, affecting the behavior or physiology of others of its species.

DOWN

1. A process in which one substance permeates another; a fluid permeates or is dissolved by a liquid or solid.

2. Animals, like flatworms and jellyfish, that have no body cavity (coelom).

3. An unstable subatomic particle. Among all known unstable subatomic particles, only the neutron (lasting around 15 minutes) and some atomic nuclei have a longer decay lifetime.

5. The midsection of the small intestine of many higher vertebrates like mammals, birds, reptiles. It is present between the duodenum and the ileum.

A. Immunogloblin
E. Systematics
I. Absorption

B. Absolute zero
F. Pheromone
J. Muon

C. Acoelomate
G. Jejunum
K. Leukocyte

D. Myofibril
H. Predation

10. *Using the Across and Down clues, write the correct words in the numbered grid below.*

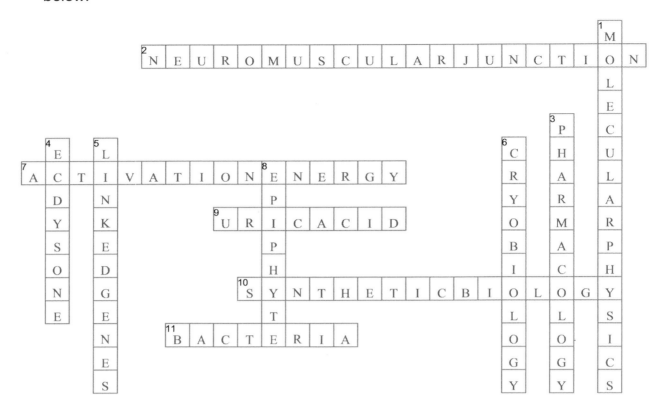

ACROSS

2. A chemical synapse formed by the contact between a motor neuron and a muscle fiber.

7. The energy that an atomic system must acquire before a process (such as an emission or reaction) can occur.

9. A heterocyclic compound of carbon, nitrogen, oxygen, and hydrogen. It forms ions and salts known as urates and acid urates, such as ammonium acid urate.

10. An interdisciplinary branch of biology and engineering.

11. Single-cell microscopic organisms which lack a true nucleus. They represent one of the three domains.

DOWN

1. The study of the physical properties of molecules, the chemical bonds between atoms as well as the molecular dynamics.

3. The science of drug action on biological systems.

4. A steroidal prohormone of the major insect molting hormone is secreted from the prothoracic glands.

5. When two genes are close together on the same chromosome, they do not assort independently.

6. The branch of biology that studies the effects of low temperatures on living things within Earth's cryosphere or in science.

8. A plant that grows harmlessly upon another plant and derives its moisture and nutrients from the air, rain, and sometimes from debris accumulating around it.

A. Molecular physics
D. Bacteria
G. Cryobiology
J. Pharmacology

B. Neuromuscular Junction
E. Activation energy
H. Epiphyte
K. Ecdysone

C. Synthetic Biology
F. Linked Genes
I. Uric acid

11. *Using the Across and Down clues, write the correct words in the numbered grid below.*

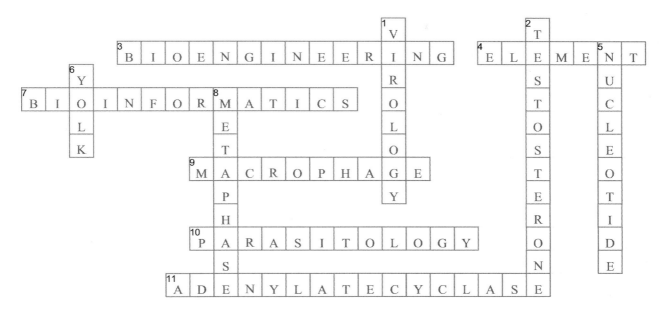

ACROSS

3. The application of concepts and methods of biology to solve real world problems.

4. A species of atoms having the same number of protons in their atomic nuclei (i.e. the same atomic number, Z).

7. The application of computer technology to the management of biological information.

9. A kind of swallowing cell, which means it functions by literally swallowing up other particles or smaller cells.

10. The study of parasites, their hosts, and the relationship between them.

11. An enzyme that catalyzes the formation of cyclic AMP from ATP.

DOWN

1. The study of viruses-submicroscopic, parasitic particles of genetic material contained in a protein coat and virus-like agents.

2. A steroid hormone from the androgen group and is found in humans and other vertebrates.

5. Organic molecules that serve as the monomers, or subunits, of nucleic acids like DNA (deoxyribonucleic acid) and RNA (ribonucleic acid).

6. The yellow internal part of a bird's egg, which is surrounded by the white, is rich in protein and fat, and nourishes the developing embryo.

8. The third phase of mitosis, the process that separates duplicated genetic material carried in the nucleus of a parent cell into two identical daughter cells.

A. Macrophage   B. Yolk   C. Bioengineering   D. Virology
E. Adenylate cyclase   F. Parasitology   G. Bioinformatics   H. Metaphase
I. Nucleotide   J. Element   K. Testosterone

12. *Using the Across and Down clues, write the correct words in the numbered grid below.*

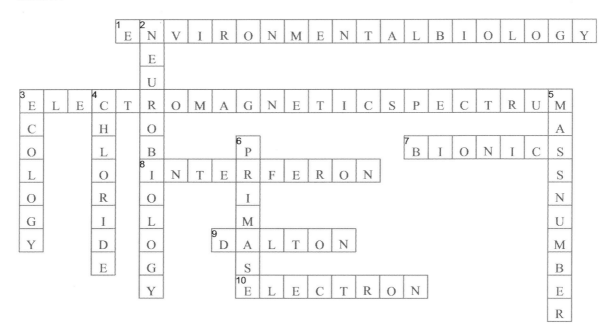

ACROSS

1. The branch of biology concerned with the relations between organisms and their environment.

3. The collective term for all possible frequencies of electromagnetic radiation.

7. Application of biological methods and systems found in nature to the study and design of engineering systems and modern technology.

8. A group of signaling proteins made and released by host cells in response to the presence of several pathogens, such as viruses, bacteria, parasites, and also tumor cells.

9. A unit of mass (also known as an atomic mass unit, amu), equal to the mass of a hydrogen atom (1.67 x 1024 g).

10. A subatomic particle with a negative elementary electric charge.

DOWN

2. The study of cells of the nervous system and the organization of these cells into functional circuits that process information and mediate behavior.

3. The scientific analysis and study of interactions among organisms and their environment. It is an interdisciplinary field that includes biology, geography and Earth science.

4. A compound of chlorine with another element or group, especially a salt of the anion or an organic compound with chlorine bonded to an alkyl group.

5. The total number of protons and neutrons (together known as nucleons) in an atomic nucleus

6. An enzyme that synthesizes short RNA sequences called primers.

A. Mass Number
D. Primase
G. Chloride
J. Electromagnetic Spectrum

B. Ecology
E. Neurobiology
H. Dalton
K. Environmental Biology

C. Electron
F. Interferon
I. Bionics

13. *Using the Across and Down clues, write the correct words in the numbered grid below.*

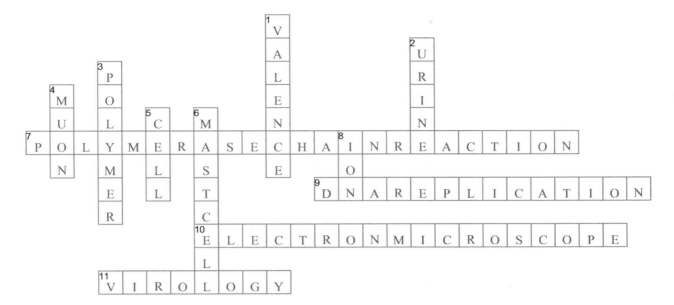

ACROSS

7. A technique used in molecular biology to amplify a single copy or a few copies of a piece of DNA across several orders of magnitude.

9. The double helix is unwound and each strand acts as a template for the next strand. Bases are matched to synthesize the new partner strands.

10. A type of microscope that uses a beam of electrons to create an image of the specimen. It is capable of much higher magnifications.

11. The study of viruses-submicroscopic, parasitic particles of genetic material contained in a protein coat and virus-like agents.

DOWN

1. Refers to the number of elements to which it can connect.

2. A liquid by-product of the body secreted by the kidneys through a process called urination (or micturition) and excreted through the urethra.

3. A large molecule, or macromolecule, composed of many repeated subunits.

4. An unstable subatomic particle. Among all known unstable subatomic particles, only the neutron (lasting around 15 minutes) and some atomic nuclei have a longer decay lifetime.

5. The structural and functional unit of all organisms; an autonomous self

6. A cell filled with basophil granules, found in numbers in connective tissue and releasing histamine and other substances during inflammatory and allergic reactions.

8. An atom or molecule with a net electric charge due to the loss or gain of one or more electrons.

A. Polymerase Chain Reaction
D. Electron Microscope
G. Urine
J. Virology

B. Polymer
E. Muon
H. DNA Replication
K. Mast Cell

C. Valence
F. Cell
I. Ion

14. *Using the Across and Down clues, write the correct words in the numbered grid below.*

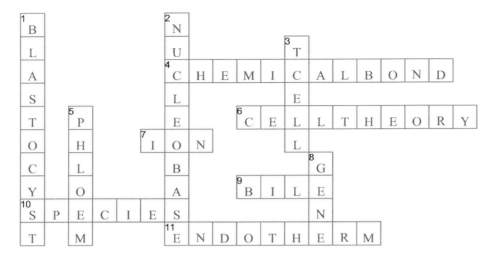

ACROSS

4. A lasting attraction between atoms that enables the formation of chemical compounds.

6. The theory that all living things are made up of cells.

7. An atom or molecule with a net electric charge due to the loss or gain of one or more electrons.

9. A dark green to yellowish brown fluid, produced by the liver of most vertebrates, that aids the digestion of lipids in the small intestine.

10. Often defined as the largest group of organisms in which two individuals are capable of reproducing fertile offspring, typically using sexual reproduction.

11. An animal that is dependent on or capable of the internal generation of heat; a warm

DOWN

1. A mammalian blastula in which some differentiation of cells has occurred.

2. Cytosine, Guanine, Adenine (which can be found in DNA and RNA), Thymine (found only in DNA), and Uracil (found only in RNA).

3. A lymphocyte of a type produced or processed by the thymus gland and actively participating in the immune response.

5. The vascular tissue in plants that conducts sugars and other metabolic products downward from the leaves.

8. A gene is a locus (or region) of DNA that encodes a functional RNA or protein product, and is the molecular unit of heredity.

A. Cell theory
B. Gene
C. Chemical bond
D. Species
E. Blastocyst
F. Nucleobase
G. Phloem
H. Endotherm
I. Ion
J. Bile
K. T Cell

15. *Using the Across and Down clues, write the correct words in the numbered grid below.*

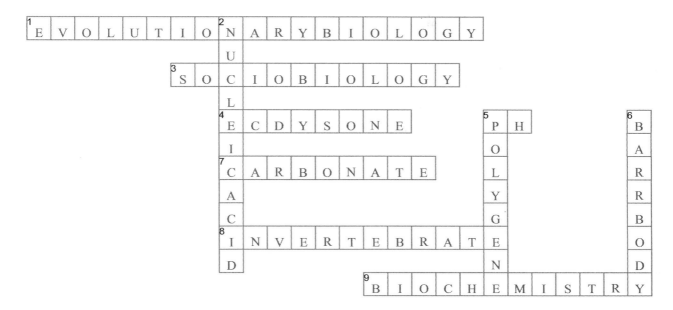

ACROSS

1. The subfield of biology that studies the evolutionary processes that produced the diversity of life on Earth starting from a single origin of life.

3. A field of scientific study that is based on the hypothesis that social behavior has resulted from evolution and attempts to explain and examine social behavior within that context.

4. A steroidal prohormone of the major insect molting hormone is secreted from the prothoracic glands.

5. A numeric scale used to specify the acidity or basicity (alkalinity) of an aqueous solution. It is roughly the negative of the logarithm to base 10 of the concentration.

7. Any member of two classes of chemical compounds derived from carbonic acid or carbon dioxide.

8. A group of animals that have no backbone, unlike animals such as reptiles, amphibians, fish, birds and mammals who all have a backbone.

9. The branch of science that explores the chemical processes within and related to living organisms.

DOWN

2. A complex organic substance present in living cells, especially DNA or RNA, whose molecules consist of many nucleotides linked in a long chain.

5. A gene whose individual effect on a phenotype is too small to be observed, but which can act together with others to produce observable variation.

6. The inactive X chromosome in a female somatic cell, rendered inactive in a process called lionization

A. Ecdysone
D. Evolutionary Biology
G. Polygene
J. Biochemistry

B. Nucleic Acid
E. Barr body
H. pH

C. Invertebrate
F. Carbonate
I. Sociobiology

16. *Using the Across and Down clues, write the correct words in the numbered grid below.*

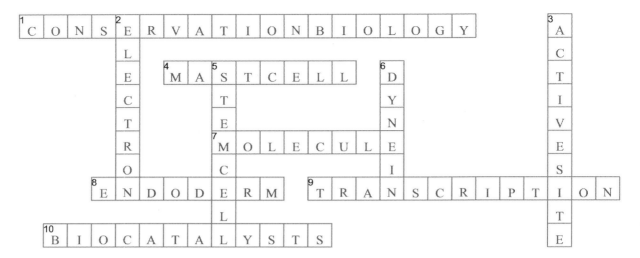

ACROSS

1. The scientific study of nature and of Earth's biodiversity with the aim of protecting species, their habitats, and ecosystems from excessive rates of extinction.

4. A cell filled with basophil granules, found in numbers in connective tissue and releasing histamine and other substances during inflammatory and allergic reactions.

7. The smallest particle in a chemical element or compound that has the chemical properties of that element or compound.

8. One of the three primary germ layers in the very early human embryo. The other two layers are the ectoderm (outside layer) and mesoderm (middle layer).

9. The first step of gene expression, in which a particular segment of DNA is copied into RNA (mRNA) by the enzyme RNA polymerase.

10. Catalysis in living systems. In biological processes, natural catalysts, such as protein enzymes, perform chemical transformations on organic compounds.

DOWN

2. A subatomic particle with a negative elementary electric charge.

3. The part of an enzyme or antibody where the chemical reaction occurs

5. An undifferentiated cell of a multicellular organism that is capable of giving rise to indefinitely more cells of the same type.

6. A motor protein in cells which converts the chemical energy contained in ATP into the mechanical energy of movement

A. Molecule
D. Mast Cell
G. Biocatalysts ·
J. Active site

B. Conservation Biology
E. Electron
H. Dynein

C. Transcription
F. Stem cell
I. Endoderm

17. *Using the Across and Down clues, write the correct words in the numbered grid below.*

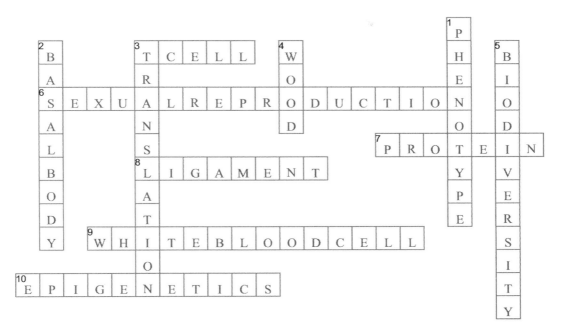

ACROSS

3. A lymphocyte of a type produced or processed by the thymus gland and actively participating in the immune response.

6. Type of reproduction in which cells from two parents unite to form the first cell of a new organism.

7. Large biomolecules, or macromolecules, consisting of one or more long chains of amino acid residues.

8. The fibrous connective tissue that connects bones to other bones.

9. Component of the blood that functions in the immune system. Also known as a leukocyte.

10. The study, in the field of genetics, of cellular and physiological phenotypic trait variations that are caused by external or environmental factors that switch genes on and off.

DOWN

1. The set of observable characteristics of an individual resulting from the interaction of its genotype with the environment.

2. An organelle formed from a centriole, and a short cylindrical array of microtubules.

3. The decoding of genetic instructions for making proteins.

4. The inner layer of the stems of woody plants; composed of xylem.

5. The variety of life in the world or in a particular habitat or ecosystem.

A. Phenotype
E. Basal body
I. Biodiversity

B. Wood
F. Epigenetics
J. Protein

C. White Blood Cell
G. T Cell
K. Sexual Reproduction

D. Ligament
H. Translation

18. *Using the Across and Down clues, write the correct words in the numbered grid below.*

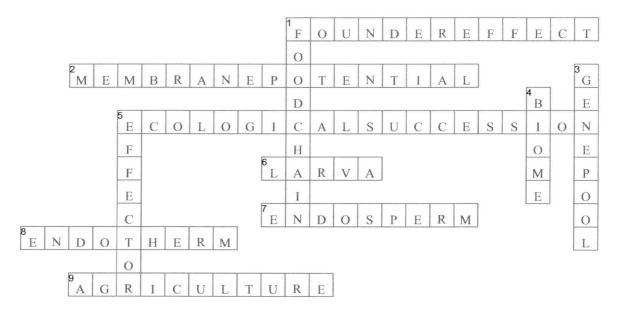

ACROSS

1. The reduced genetic diversity that results when a population is descended from a small number of colonizing ancestors.

2. When a nerve or muscle cell is at "rest", its membrane potential is called the resting membrane potential.

5. The term used to describe what happens to an ecological community over time.

6. A distinct juvenile form many animals undergo before metamorphosis into adults. Animals with indirect development such as insects, amphibians, or cnidarians.

7. A tissue produced inside the seeds of most of the flowering plants around the time of fertilization.

8. An animal that is dependent on or capable of the internal generation of heat; a warm

9. The practice of cultivating land, growing food, and raising stock.

DOWN

1. A hierarchical series of organisms each dependent on the next as a source of food.

3. The stock of different genes in an interbreeding population.

4. Very large ecological areas on the earth's surface, with fauna and flora (animals and plants) adapting to their environment.

5. An organ or cell that acts in response to a stimulus.

A. Endosperm
D. Ecological Succession
G. Membrane Potential
J. Founder Effect

B. Effector
E. Agriculture
H. Gene Pool
K. Larva

C. Endotherm
F. Food Chain
I. Biome

19. *Using the Across and Down clues, write the correct words in the numbered grid below.*

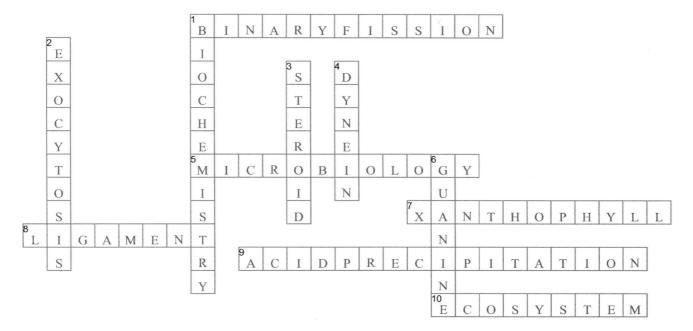

ACROSS

1. One cell dividing into two identical daughter cells.
5. The study of microscopic organisms, such as bacteria, viruses, archaea, fungi and protozoa.
7. The yellow colored photosynthetic pigments.
8. The fibrous connective tissue that connects bones to other bones.
9. Rain containing acids that form in the atmosphere when industrial gas emissions (especially sulfur dioxide and nitrogen oxides) combine with water.
10. An interaction of living things and non-living things in a physical environment.

DOWN

1. The branch of science that explores the chemical processes within and related to living organisms.
2. A process by which the contents of a cell vacuole are released to the exterior through fusion of the vacuole membrane with the cell membrane.
3. An organic compound with four rings arranged in a specific configuration. Examples include the dietary lipid cholesterol and the sex hormones.
4. A motor protein in cells which converts the chemical energy contained in ATP into the mechanical energy of movement
6. One of the four main nucleobases found in the nucleic acids DNA and RNA, the others being adenine, cytosine, and thymine.

A. Steroid
E. Exocytosis
I. Acid precipitation
B. Dynein
F. Ligament
J. Microbiology
C. Binary fission
G. Biochemistry
K. Guanine
D. Xanthophyll
H. Ecosystem

20. *Using the Across and Down clues, write the correct words in the numbered grid below.*

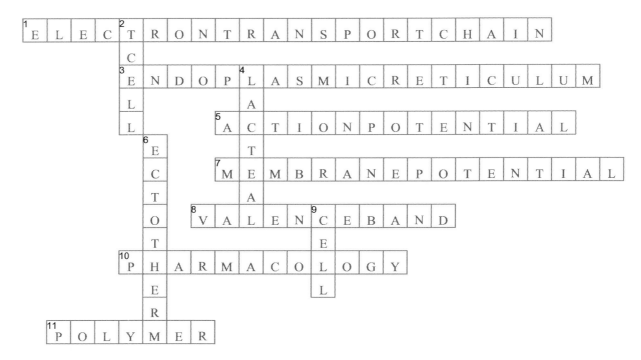

ACROSS

1. The site of oxidative phosphorylation in eukaryotes.
3. A network of membranous tubules within the cytoplasm of a eukaryotic cell, continuous with the nuclear membrane.
5. The local voltage change across the cell wall as a nerve impulse is transmitted.
7. When a nerve or muscle cell is at "rest", its membrane potential is called the resting membrane potential.
8. The highest range of electron energies in which electrons are normally present at absolute zero temperature.
10. The science of drug action on biological systems.
11. A large molecule, or macromolecule, composed of many repeated subunits.

DOWN

2. A lymphocyte of a type produced or processed by the thymus gland and actively participating in the immune response.
4. A lymphatic capillary that absorbs dietary fats in the villi of the small intestine.
6. A organism in which internal physiological sources of heat are of relatively small or quite negligible importance in controlling body temperature. "Cold blooded".
9. The structural and functional unit of all organisms; an autonomous self

A. Action potential
D. Cell
G. Endoplasmic Reticulum
J. Polymer

B. T Cell
E. Membrane Potential
H. Ectotherm
K. Electron Transport Chain

C. Valence band
F. Lacteal
I. Pharmacology

21. *Using the Across and Down clues, write the correct words in the numbered grid below.*

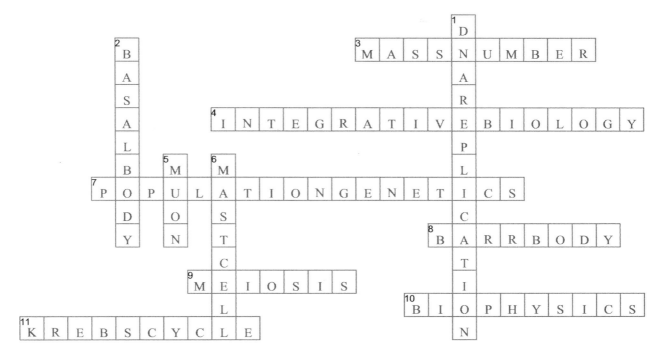

ACROSS

3. The total number of protons and neutrons (together known as nucleons) in an atomic nucleus
4. A label frequently used to describe various forms of cross-disciplinary and multitaxon research.
7. The study of genetic variation within populations, and involves the examination and modeling of changes in the frequencies of genes and alleles.
8. The inactive X chromosome in a female somatic cell, rendered inactive in a process called lionization
9. A type of cell division that reduces the number of chromosomes in the parent cell by half and produces four gamete cells.
10. An interdisciplinary science that applies the approaches and methods of physics to study biological systems.
11. A series of chemical reactions used by all aerobic organisms to generate energy through the oxidation of acetyl

DOWN

1. The double helix is unwound and each strand acts as a template for the next strand. Bases are matched to synthesize the new partner strands.
2. An organelle formed from a centriole, and a short cylindrical array of microtubules.
5. An unstable subatomic particle. Among all known unstable subatomic particles, only the neutron (lasting around 15 minutes) and some atomic nuclei have a longer decay lifetime.
6. A cell filled with basophil granules, found in numbers in connective tissue and releasing histamine and other substances during inflammatory and allergic reactions.

A. Biophysics
E. Meiosis
I. Krebs Cycle
B. Basal body
F. Integrative Biology
J. Population Genetics
C. Muon
G. Barr body
K. Mast Cell
D. Mass Number
H. DNA Replication

22. *Using the Across and Down clues, write the correct words in the numbered grid below.*

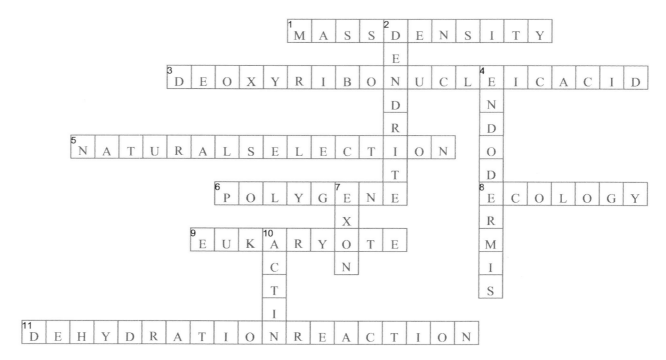

ACROSS

1. Density is mass per volume.

3. The four bases found in DNA are adenine, cytosine, guanine and thymine. These four bases are attached to the sugar

5. A process in nature in which organisms possessing certain genotypic characteristics that make them better adjusted to an environment tend to survive.

6. A gene whose individual effect on a phenotype is too small to be observed, but which can act together with others to produce observable variation.

8. The scientific analysis and study of interactions among organisms and their environment. It is an interdisciplinary field that includes biology, geography and Earth science.

9. Any organism whose cells contain a nucleus and other organelles enclosed within membranes.

11. Usually defined as a chemical reaction that involves the loss of a water molecule from the reacting molecule.

DOWN

2. A short branched extension of a nerve cell, along which impulses received from other cells at synapses are transmitted to the cell body

4. An inner layer of cells in the cortex of a root and of some stems, surrounding a vascular bundle.

7. Any part of a gene that will become a part of the final mature RNA produced by that gene after introns have been removed by RNA splicing.

10. One of the proteins into which actomyosin can be split; can exist in either a globular or a fibrous form.

A. Dehydration Reaction
D. Exon
G. Natural Selection
J. Ecology

B. Polygene
E. Deoxyribonucleic Acid
H. Actin
K. Endodermis

C. Mass Density
F. Dendrite
I. Eukaryote

23. *Using the Across and Down clues, write the correct words in the numbered grid below.*

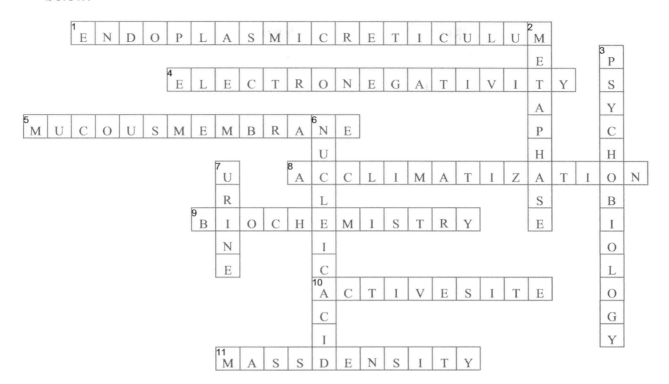

ACROSS

1. A network of membranous tubules within the cytoplasm of a eukaryotic cell, continuous with the nuclear membrane.

4. A measure of the tendency of an atom to attract a bonding pair of electrons. The Pauling scale is the most commonly used.

5. An epithelial tissue that secretes mucus and that lines many body cavities and tubular organs including the gut and respiratory passages.

8. Adaptation to a new climate (a new temperature or altitude or environment).

9. The branch of science that explores the chemical processes within and related to living organisms.

10. The part of an enzyme or antibody where the chemical reaction occurs

11. Density is mass per volume.

DOWN

2. The third phase of mitosis, the process that separates duplicated genetic material carried in the nucleus of a parent cell into two identical daughter cells.

3. The application of the principles of biology to the study of physiological, genetic, and developmental mechanisms of behavior in humans and other animals.

6. A complex organic substance present in living cells, especially DNA or RNA, whose molecules consist of many nucleotides linked in a long chain.

7. A liquid by-product of the body secreted by the kidneys through a process called urination (or micturition) and excreted through the urethra.

A. Psychobiology
D. Metaphase
G. Active site
J. Endoplasmic Reticulum

B. Mass Density
E. Acclimatization
H. Urine
K. Biochemistry

C. Electronegativity
F. Mucous Membrane
I. Nucleic Acid

24. *Using the Across and Down clues, write the correct words in the numbered grid below.*

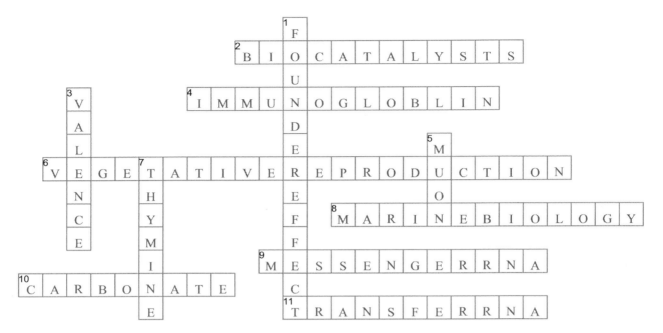

ACROSS

2. Catalysis in living systems. In biological processes, natural catalysts, such as protein enzymes, perform chemical transformations on organic compounds.

4. Also known as antibodies, They act as a critical part of the immune response by specifically recognizing and binding to particular antigens, and aiding in their destruction.

6. A form of asexual reproduction of a plant. Only one plant is involved and the offspring is the result of one parent. The new plant is genetically identical to the parent.

8. The scientific study of organisms in the ocean or other marine bodies of water.

9. The form of RNA in which genetic information transcribed from DNA as a sequence of bases is transferred to a ribosome.

10. Any member of two classes of chemical compounds derived from carbonic acid or carbon dioxide.

11. RNA consisting of folded molecules that transport amino acids from the cytoplasm of a cell to a ribosome.

DOWN

1. The reduced genetic diversity that results when a population is descended from a small number of colonizing ancestors.

3. Refers to the number of elements to which it can connect.

5. An unstable subatomic particle. Among all known unstable subatomic particles, only the neutron (lasting around 15 minutes) and some atomic nuclei have a longer decay lifetime.

7. One of the four nucleobases in the nucleic acid of DNA that are represented by the letters G–C–A–T.

A. Thymine
D. Valence
G. Muon
J. Marine Biology

B. Carbonate
E. Messenger RNA
H. Immunogloblin
K. Founder Effect

C. Transfer RNA
F. Biocatalysts
I. Vegetative reproduction

25. *Using the Across and Down clues, write the correct words in the numbered grid below.*

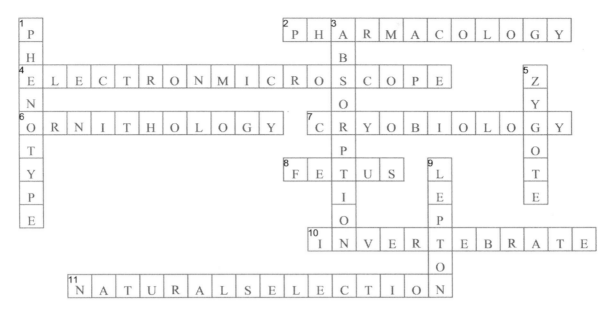

ACROSS

2. The science of drug action on biological systems.
4. A type of microscope that uses a beam of electrons to create an image of the specimen. It is capable of much higher magnifications.
6. A branch of zoology that concerns the study of birds.
7. The branch of biology that studies the effects of low temperatures on living things within Earth's cryosphere or in science.
8. A human embryo after eight weeks of development.
10. A group of animals that have no backbone, unlike animals such as reptiles, amphibians, fish, birds and mammals who all have a backbone.
11. A process in nature in which organisms possessing certain genotypic characteristics that make them better adjusted to an environment tend to survive.

DOWN

1. The set of observable characteristics of an individual resulting from the interaction of its genotype with the environment.
3. A process in which one substance permeates another; a fluid permeates or is dissolved by a liquid or solid.
5. A diploid cell resulting from the fusion of two haploid gametes; a fertilized ovum.
9. An elementary, half-integer spin particle that does not undergo strong interactions.

A. Zygote
E. Cryobiology
I. Electron Microscope

B. Invertebrate
F. Pharmacology
J. Ornithology

C. Lepton
G. Fetus
K. Absorption

D. Natural Selection
H. Phenotype

26. *Using the Across and Down clues, write the correct words in the numbered grid below.*

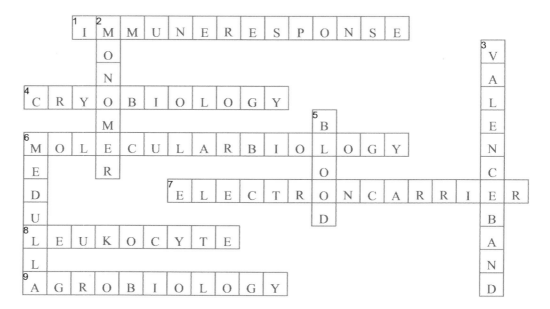

ACROSS

1. How your body recognizes and defends itself against bacteria, viruses, and substances that appear foreign and harmful.

4. The branch of biology that studies the effects of low temperatures on living things within Earth's cryosphere or in science.

6. A branch of science concerning biological activity at the molecular level.

7. Any of various molecules that are capable of accepting one or two electrons from one molecule and donating them to another in the process of electron transport.

8. A colorless cell which circulates in the blood and body fluids and is involved in counteracting foreign substances and disease; a white (blood) cell.

9. The study of plant nutrition and growth especially as a way to increase crop yield

DOWN

2. A molecule that can be bonded to other identical molecules to form a polymer.

3. The highest range of electron energies in which electrons are normally present at absolute zero temperature.

5. The red liquid that circulates in the arteries and veins of humans and other vertebrate animals, carrying oxygen to and carbon dioxide from the tissues of the body.

6. The continuation of the spinal cord within the skull, forming the lowest part of the brainstem and containing control centers for the heart and lungs.

A. Valence band
E. Medulla
I. Electron Carrier
B. Monomer
F. Blood
J. Immune Response
C. Cryobiology
G. Molecular biology
D. Leukocyte
H. Agrobiology

27. *Using the Across and Down clues, write the correct words in the numbered grid below.*

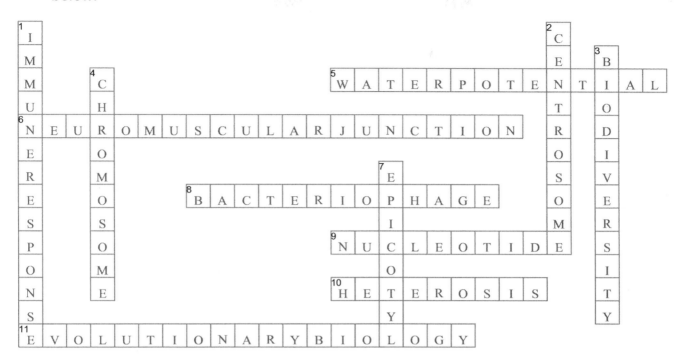

ACROSS

5. A measure of the potential energy in water as well as the difference between the potential in a given water sample and pure water.

6. A chemical synapse formed by the contact between a motor neuron and a muscle fiber.

8. Virus that infects and multiplies within bacteria.

9. Organic molecules that serve as the monomers, or subunits, of nucleic acids like DNA (deoxyribonucleic acid) and RNA (ribonucleic acid).

10. the tendency of a crossbred individual to show qualities superior to those of both parents.

11. The subfield of biology that studies the evolutionary processes that produced the diversity of life on Earth starting from a single origin of life.

DOWN

1. How your body recognizes and defends itself against bacteria, viruses, and substances that appear foreign and harmful.

2. In cell biology, an organelle that is the main place where cell microtubules get organized. They occur only in plant and animal cells.

3. The variety of life in the world or in a particular habitat or ecosystem.

4. A threadlike strand of DNA in the cell nucleus that carries the genes in a linear order.

7. The region of an embryo or seedling stem above the cotyledon.

A. Biodiversity
D. Nucleotide
G. Bacteriophage
J. Evolutionary Biology

B. Epicotyl
E. Immune Response
H. Heterosis
K. Chromosome

C. Centrosome
F. Water Potential
I. Neuromuscular Junction

28. *Using the Across and Down clues, write the correct words in the numbered grid below.*

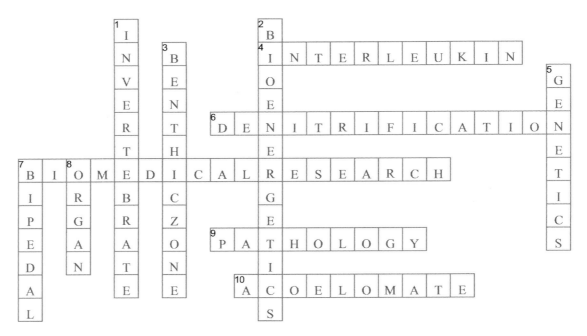

ACROSS

4. A group of cytokines (secreted proteins and signal molecules) that were first seen to be expressed by white blood cells (leukocytes)

6. A microbially facilitated process of nitrate reduction that may ultimately produce molecular nitrogen.

7. The pursuit of answers to medical questions. These investigations lead to discoveries, which in turn lead to the development of new preventions, therapies and cures.

9. A medical specialty that is concerned with the diagnosis of disease based on the laboratory analysis of bodily fluids such as blood and urine.

10. Animals, like flatworms and jellyfish, that have no body cavity (coelom).

DOWN

1. A group of animals that have no backbone, unlike animals such as reptiles, amphibians, fish, birds and mammals who all have a backbone.

2. The study of the transformation of energy in living organisms.

3. The ecological region at the lowest level of a body of water such as an ocean or a lake, including the sediment surface and some sub

5. The study of heredity

7. A form of terrestrial locomotion where an organism moves by means of its two rear limbs or legs.

8. a part of an organism that is typically self-contained and has a specific vital function, such as the heart or liver in humans.

A. Denitrification
E. Interleukin
I. Benthic zone

B. Acoelomate
F. Genetics
J. Pathology

C. Invertebrate
G. Biomedical research
K. Bipedal

D. Bioenergetics
H. Organ

29. *Using the Across and Down clues, write the correct words in the numbered grid below.*

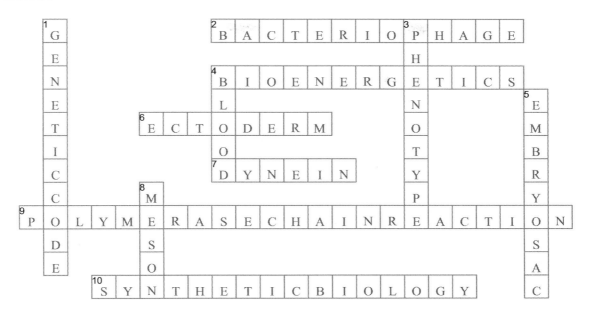

ACROSS

2. Virus that infects and multiplies within bacteria.
4. The study of the transformation of energy in living organisms.
6. The outermost layer of cells or tissue of an embryo in early development, or the parts derived from this, which include the epidermis, nerve tissue, and nephridia.
7. A motor protein in cells which converts the chemical energy contained in ATP into the mechanical energy of movement
9. A technique used in molecular biology to amplify a single copy or a few copies of a piece of DNA across several orders of magnitude.
10. An interdisciplinary branch of biology and engineering.

DOWN

1. The nucleotide triplets of DNA and RNA molecules that carry genetic information in living cells.
3. The set of observable characteristics of an individual resulting from the interaction of its genotype with the environment.
4. The red liquid that circulates in the arteries and veins of humans and other vertebrate animals, carrying oxygen to and carbon dioxide from the tissues of the body.
5. The female gametophyte of a seed plant, within which the embryo develops.
8. Hadronic subatomic particles composed of one quark and one antiquark, bound together by the strong interaction.

A. Synthetic Biology
D. Dynein
G. Embryo Sac
J. Genetic Code

B. Ectoderm
E. Polymerase Chain Reaction
H. Bioenergetics
K. Blood

C. Phenotype
F. Bacteriophage
I. Meson

30. *Using the Across and Down clues, write the correct words in the numbered grid below.*

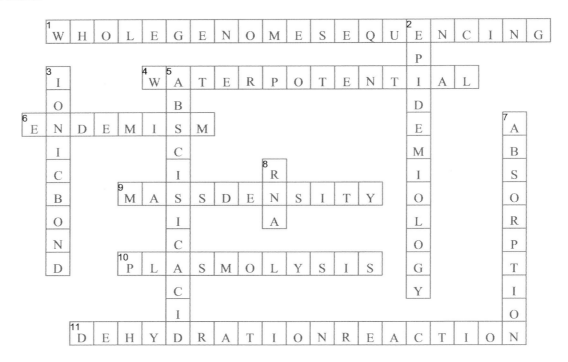

ACROSS

1. A laboratory process that determines the complete DNA sequence of an organism's genome at a single time.

4. A measure of the potential energy in water as well as the difference between the potential in a given water sample and pure water.

6. The ecological state of a species being unique to a defined geographic location, such as an island, nation, country or other defined zone, or habitat type.

9. Density is mass per volume.

10. Contraction of the protoplast of a plant cell as a result of loss of water from the cell.

11. Usually defined as a chemical reaction that involves the loss of a water molecule from the reacting molecule.

DOWN

2. The study and analysis of the patterns, causes, and effects of health and disease conditions in defined populations.

3. The complete transfer of valence electron(s) between atoms. It is a type of chemical bond that generates two oppositely charged ions.

5. a plant hormone.

7. A process in which one substance permeates another; a fluid permeates or is dissolved by a liquid or solid.

8. Stands for ribonucleic acid. It is an important molecule with long chains of nucleotides. A nucleotide contains a nitrogenous base, a ribose sugar, and a phosphate.

A. Ionic Bond
D. Whole Genome Sequencing
G. Absorption
J. Epidemiology

B. Water Potential
E. Dehydration Reaction
H. Endemism
K. Abscisic acid

C. RNA
F. Plasmolysis
I. Mass Density

31. *Using the Across and Down clues, write the correct words in the numbered grid below.*

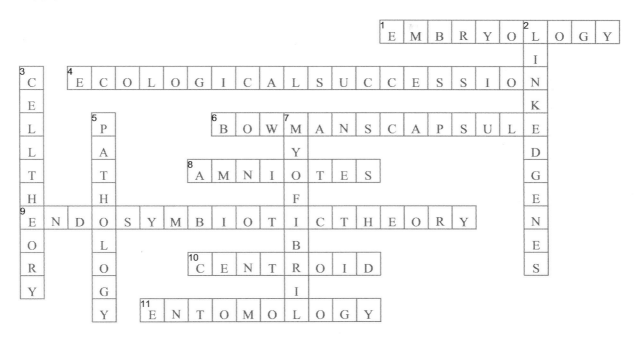

ACROSS

1. The branch of biology that studies the development of gametes (sex cells), fertilization, and development of embryos and fetuses.

4. The term used to describe what happens to an ecological community over time.

6. A cup-like sac at the beginning of the tubular component of a nephron in the mammalian kidney that performs the first step in the filtration of blood to form urine.

8. Organisms that produce an egg composed of shell and membranes that creates a protected environment in which the embryo can develop out of water

9. An evolutionary theory that explains the origin of eukaryotic cells from prokaryotes.

10. The intersection of the three medians of the triangle (each median connecting a vertex with the midpoint of the opposite side).

11. The study of insects.

DOWN

2. When two genes are close together on the same chromosome, they do not assort independently.

3. The theory that all living things are made up of cells.

5. A medical specialty that is concerned with the diagnosis of disease based on the laboratory analysis of bodily fluids such as blood and urine.

7. Any of the elongated contractile threads found in striated muscle cells.

A. Amniotes
D. Bowmans capsule
G. Cell theory
J. Endosymbiotic Theory

B. Embryology
E. Centroid
H. Linked Genes
K. Pathology

C. Ecological Succession
F. Myofibril
I. Entomology

32. *Using the Across and Down clues, write the correct words in the numbered grid below.*

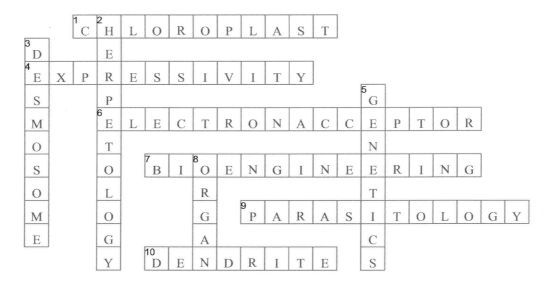

ACROSS

1. Work to convert light energy of the Sun into sugars that can be used by cells.

4. Variations in a phenotype among individuals carrying a particular genotype.

6. A chemical entity that accepts electrons transferred to it from another compound.

7. The application of concepts and methods of biology to solve real world problems.

9. The study of parasites, their hosts, and the relationship between them.

10. A short branched extension of a nerve cell, along which impulses received from other cells at synapses are transmitted to the cell body

DOWN

2. The branch of zoology concerned with reptiles and amphibians.

3. Also known as a macula adhaerens, is a cell structure specialized for cell to cell adhesion.

5. The study of heredity

8. a part of an organism that is typically self-contained and has a specific vital function, such as the heart or liver in humans.

A. Genetics
B. Desmosome
C. Bioengineering
D. Expressivity
E. Organ
F. Dendrite
G. Herpetology
H. Electron Acceptor
I. Chloroplast
J. Parasitology

33. *Using the Across and Down clues, write the correct words in the numbered grid below.*

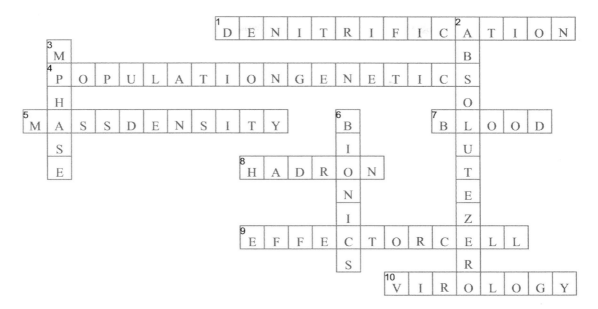

ACROSS

1. A microbially facilitated process of nitrate reduction that may ultimately produce molecular nitrogen.

4. The study of genetic variation within populations, and involves the examination and modeling of changes in the frequencies of genes and alleles.

5. Density is mass per volume.

7. The red liquid that circulates in the arteries and veins of humans and other vertebrate animals, carrying oxygen to and carbon dioxide from the tissues of the body.

8. Any particle that is made from quarks, anti

9. Plasma cells, also called plasma B cells, plasmocytes, plasmacytes, or effector B cells, are white blood cells that secrete large volumes of antibodies.

10. The study of viruses-submicroscopic, parasitic particles of genetic material contained in a protein coat and virus-like agents.

DOWN

2. The lowest theoretically attainable temperature (at which the kinetic energy of atoms and molecules is minimal)

3. Mitosis and cytokinesis together define this phase of an animal cell cycle-the division of the mother cell into two daughter cells, genetically identical to each other and the parent.

6. Application of biological methods and systems found in nature to the study and design of engineering systems and modern technology.

A. Mass Density
E. Virology
I. Bionics

B. M phase
F. Blood
J. Population Genetics

C. Denitrification
G. Hadron

D. Effector Cell
H. Absolute zero

34. *Using the Across and Down clues, write the correct words in the numbered grid below.*

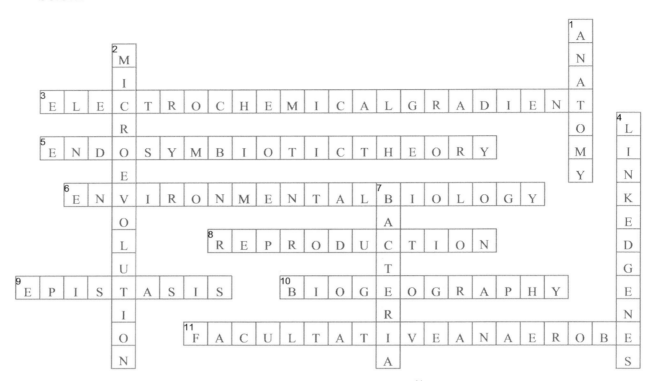

ACROSS

3. A gradient of electrochemical potential, usually for an ion that can move across a membrane.

5. An evolutionary theory that explains the origin of eukaryotic cells from prokaryotes.

6. The branch of biology concerned with the relations between organisms and their environment.

8. Giving birth to one of its kind, sexually or asexually.

9. The interaction of genes that are not alleles, in particular the suppression of the effect of one such gene by another.

10. The study of the distribution of species and ecosystems in geographic space and through time.

11. Organism which is capable of producing energy through aerobic respiration and then switching to anaerobic respiration depending on the amounts of oxygen.

DOWN

1. The branch of morphology that deals with the structure of animals

2. Evolutionary change within a species or small group of organisms, especially over a short period.

4. When two genes are close together on the same chromosome, they do not assort independently.

7. Single-cell microscopic organisms which lack a true nucleus. They represent one of the three domains.

A. Reproduction
B. Linked Genes
C. Bacteria
D. Endosymbiotic Theory
E. Microevolution
F. Facultative Anaerobe
G. Anatomy
H. Environmental Biology
I. Epistasis
J. Electrochemical Gradient
K. Biogeography

35. *Using the Across and Down clues, write the correct words in the numbered grid below.*

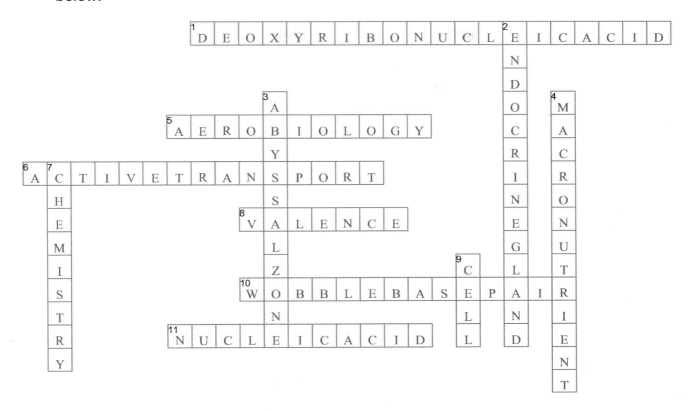

ACROSS

1. The four bases found in DNA are adenine, cytosine, guanine and thymine. These four bases are attached to the sugar

5. The study of organic particles, such as bacteria, fungal spores, very small insects, pollen grains and viruses, which are passively transported by the air.

6. Transport of a substance (as a protein or drug) across a cell membrane against the concentration gradient; requires an expenditure of energy

8. Refers to the number of elements to which it can connect.

10. A pairing between two nucleotides in RNA molecules that does not follow Watson

11. A complex organic substance present in living cells, especially DNA or RNA, whose molecules consist of many nucleotides linked in a long chain.

DOWN

2. Glands that secrete their products, hormones, directly into the blood rather than through a duct.

3. The deep sea (2000 meters or more) where there is no light.

4. Nutrients that provide calories or energy. Nutrients are substances needed for growth, metabolism, and for other body functions.

7. A branch of physical science that studies the composition, structure, properties and change of matter.

9. The structural and functional unit of all organisms; an autonomous self

A. Active Transport
D. Aerobiology
G. Macronutrient
J. Nucleic Acid

B. Deoxyribonucleic Acid
E. Abyssal zone
H. Endocrine Gland
K. Valence

C. Wobble Base Pair
F. Cell
I. Chemistry

From the words provided for each clue, provide the letter of the word which best matches the clue.

1. ____ Serves an important role in the metabolism of nitrogen-containing compounds by animals, and is the main nitrogen-containing substance in the urine of mammals.
A.polyploidy   B.urea   C.artificial selection   D.dehydration reaction

2. ____ The use of living systems and organisms to develop or make products, or "any technological application that uses biological systems, living organisms or derivatives thereof.
A.asexual reproduction   B.biotechnology   C.nucleolus   D.isomer

3. ____ The process of determining the precise order of nucleotides within a DNA molecule.
A.dna sequencing   B.valence shell   C.denitrification   D.chemical equilibrium

4. ____ The double helix is unwound and each strand acts as a template for the next strand. Bases are matched to synthesize the new partner strands.
A.parallel evolution   B.endotherm   C.dna replication   D.polymer

5. ____ The amount of work needed to move a unit charge from a reference point to a specific point against an electric field.
A.virus   B.ion   C.dehydration reaction   D.electric potential

6. ____ A small dense spherical structure in the nucleus of a cell during interphase.
A.nucleolus   B.abscisic acid   C.ectotherm   D.rna

7. ____ A branch of science concerning biological activity at the molecular level.
A.vestigiality   B.molecular biology   C.structural biology   D.molecule

8. ____ The inactive X chromosome in a female somatic cell, rendered inactive in a process called lionization
A.nucleolus   B.transcription   C.lacteal   D.barr body

9. ____ A dark green to yellowish brown fluid, produced by the liver of most vertebrates, that aids the digestion of lipids in the small intestine.
A.bile   B.ectotherm   C.structural biology   D.bacteria

10. ____ A hierarchical series of organisms each dependent on the next as a source of food.
A.food chain   B.vegetative reproduction   C.lacteal   D.dna replication

11. ____ A mammalian blastula in which some differentiation of cells has occurred.
A.zoology   B.vestigiality   C.species   D.blastocyst

12. ____ The first step of gene expression, in which a particular segment of DNA is copied into RNA (mRNA) by the enzyme RNA polymerase.
A.hermaphrodite   B.transcription   C.darwinian fitness   D.electron acceptor

13. ____ Depending on free oxygen or air.
A.aerobic   B.steroid   C.ecological niche   D.predation

14. ____ The semipermeable membrane surrounding the cytoplasm of a cell.
A.electric potential   B.cell membrane   C.molarity   D.nucleolus

15. ____ Often defined as the largest group of organisms in which two individuals are capable of reproducing fertile offspring, typically using sexual reproduction.
A.molarity   B.species   C.parallel evolution   D.abscisic acid

16. ____ An enzyme that synthesizes short RNA sequences called primers.
A.asexual reproduction   B.herpetology   C.primase   D.lipid

17. ___ A branch of physical science that studies the composition, structure, properties and change of matter.
A.human nutrition   B.rna   C.denitrification   D.chemistry

18. ___ A microbially facilitated process of nitrate reduction that may ultimately produce molecular nitrogen.
A.estrogen   B.chemistry   C.denitrification   D.endemism

19. ___ The electrons in the outermost occupied shell (or shells) determine the chemical properties of the atom; it is called the valence shell.
A.muon   B.food chain   C.valence shell   D.ion

20. ___ The process of reversing the charge across a cell membrane (usually a NEURON), so causing an ACTION POTENTIAL.
A.endotherm   B.parallel evolution   C.depolarization   D.bacteria

21. ___ Cytosine, Guanine, Adenine (which can be found in DNA and RNA), Thymine (found only in DNA), and Uracil (found only in RNA).
A.ectotherm   B.transcription   C.darwinian fitness   D.nucleobase

22. ___ Organism with both male and female reproductive organs.
A.hermaphrodite   B.ion   C.valence bond theory   D.nucleobase

23. ___ The study of genetic variation within populations, and involves the examination and modeling of changes in the frequencies of genes and alleles.
A.valence bond theory   B.population genetics   C.endemism   D.zygote

24. ___ A chemical entity that accepts electrons transferred to it from another compound.
A.electron carrier   B.autoimmunity   C.biodiversity   D.electron acceptor

25. ___ A network of membranous tubules within the cytoplasm of a eukaryotic cell, continuous with the nuclear membrane.
A.urea   B.endoplasmic reticulum   C.chemical equilibrium   D.ecological niche

26. ___ A form of asexual reproduction of a plant. Only one plant is involved and the offspring is the result of one parent. The new plant is genetically identical to the parent.
A.dna replication   B.nucleolus   C.vegetative reproduction   D.yolk

27. ___ The branch of zoology concerned with reptiles and amphibians.
A.herpetology   B.pollination   C.evolutionary biology   D.electric potential

28. ___ A short branched extension of a nerve cell, along which impulses received from other cells at synapses are transmitted to the cell body
A.dendrite   B.lepton   C.biocatalysts   D.epiphyte

29. ___ Organic molecules that serve as the monomers, or subunits, of nucleic acids like DNA (deoxyribonucleic acid) and RNA (ribonucleic acid).
A.embryo sac   B.biomedical research   C.absorption spectrum   D.nucleotide

30. ___ The independent evolution of similar traits, starting from a similar ancestral condition.
A.absorption spectrum   B.cell membrane   C.parallel evolution   D.gene

31. ___ The four bases found in DNA are adenine, cytosine, guanine and thymine. These four bases are attached to the sugar
A.deoxyribonucleic acid   B.abscisic acid   C.polygene   D.electric potential

32. ___ Single-cell microscopic organisms which lack a true nucleus. They represent one of the three domains.
A.dehydration reaction   B.plasmolysis   C.bacteria   D.denitrification

33. ___ An elementary, half-integer spin particle that does not undergo strong interactions.
A.autoimmunity B.lepton C.steroid D.nucleolus

34. ___ A pairing between two nucleotides in RNA molecules that does not follow Watson
A.wobble base pair B.evolutionary biology C.valence bond theory D.polyploidy

35. ___ An organic compound with four rings arranged in a specific configuration. Examples include the dietary lipid cholesterol and the sex hormones.
A.darwinian fitness B.steroid C.endosperm D.primase

36. ___ The state in which both reactants and products are present in concentrations which have no further tendency to change with time.
A.biocatalysts B.valence bond theory C.asexual reproduction D.chemical equilibrium

37. ___ Animals, like flatworms and jellyfish, that have no body cavity (coelom).
A.acoelomate B.invertebrate C.lacteal D.chemical equilibrium

38. ___ Refers to the provision of essential nutrients necessary to support human life and health.
A.human nutrition B.predation C.electron acceptor D.zoology

39. ___ A unit of mass (also known as an atomic mass unit, amu), equal to the mass of a hydrogen atom (1.67 x 1024 g).
A.deoxyribonucleic acid B.dalton C.nucleotide D.dna sequencing

40. ___ A chemically defined as a substance that is insoluble in water and soluble in alcohol, ether, and chloroform. The basis for fats and oils.
A.biodiversity B.lipid C.translation D.polyploidy

41. ___ An ecological niche is the role and position a species has in its environment; how it meets its needs for food and shelter, how it survives, and how it reproduces.
A.ecological niche B.polyploidy C.neuromuscular junction D.human nutrition

42. ___ Refers to genetically determined structures or attributes that have apparently lost most or all of their ancestral function in a given species.
A.predation B.biocatalysts C.vestigiality D.embryo sac

43. ___ A tissue produced inside the seeds of most of the flowering plants around the time of fertilization.
A.endosperm B.electron transport chain C.dehydration reaction D.gene

44. ___ A chemical reaction in which the standard change in free energy is positive, and energy is absorbed
A.translation B.population genetics C.absorption spectrum D.endergonic reaction

45. ___ Contraction of the protoplast of a plant cell as a result of loss of water from the cell.
A.autoimmunity B.plasmolysis C.biodiversity D.wobble base pair

46. ___ Any of various molecules that are capable of accepting one or two electrons from one molecule and donating them to another in the process of electron transport.
A.ecological niche B.incomplete dominance C.depolarization D.electron carrier

47. ___ Giving birth to one of its kind, sexually or asexually.
A.artificial selection B.water potential C.denitrification D.reproduction

48. ___ The study and discussion of chemical reactions with respect to reaction rates, effect of various variables, re
A.biomass B.transcription C.plasmolysis D.chemical kinetics

49. ____ The pursuit of answers to medical questions. These investigations lead to discoveries, which in turn lead to the development of new preventions, therapies and cures.
A.aerobic B.organism C.biomedical research D.isomer

50. ____ The region of an embryo or seedling stem above the cotyledon.
A.barr body B.primase C.epicotyl D.molecule

51. ____ A measure of the potential energy in water as well as the difference between the potential in a given water sample and pure water.
A.darwinian fitness B.steroid C.water potential D.rna

52. ____ A diploid cell resulting from the fusion of two haploid gametes; a fertilized ovum.
A.zygote B.macroevolution C.biomass D.organism

53. ____ A unit of concentration measuring the number of moles of a solute per liter of solution.
A.molarity B.dehydration reaction C.food chain D.biomedical research

54. ____ A cell filled with basophil granules, found in numbers in connective tissue and releasing histamine and other substances during inflammatory and allergic reactions.
A.absorption spectrum B.depolarization C.mast cell D.nucleolus

55. ____ Process of reproduction involving a single parent that results in offspring that are genetically identical to the parent.
A.autoimmunity B.asexual reproduction C.reproduction D.water potential

56. ____ The ecological state of a species being unique to a defined geographic location, such as an island, nation, country or other defined zone, or habitat type.
A.endemism B.molarity C.biomedical research D.epiphyte

57. ____ The site of oxidative phosphorylation in eukaryotes.
A.electron transport chain B.virus C.incomplete dominance D.endotherm

58. ____ The deep sea (2000 meters or more) where there is no light.
A.wobble base pair B.abyssal zone C.mast cell D.epiphyte

59. ____ The smallest particle in a chemical element or compound that has the chemical properties of that element or compound.
A.molecule B.bile C.structural biology D.epiphyte

60. ____ The yellow internal part of a bird's egg, which is surrounded by the white, is rich in protein and fat, and nourishes the developing embryo.
A.epiphyte B.zoology C.pheromone D.yolk

61. ____ A organism in which internal physiological sources of heat are of relatively small or quite negligible importance in controlling body temperature. "Cold blooded".
A.ectotherm B.asexual reproduction C.electric potential D.ecological niche

62. ____ Usually defined as a chemical reaction that involves the loss of a water molecule from the reacting molecule.
A.chemical equilibrium B.epiphyte C.dehydration reaction D.gene

63. ____ Organic matter derived from living, or recently living organisms.
A.electron acceptor B.molarity C.food chain D.biomass

64. ____ A gene is a locus (or region) of DNA that encodes a functional RNA or protein product, and is the molecular unit of heredity.
A.chemistry B.hermaphrodite C.gene D.bacteria

65. ____ The act of transferring pollen grains from the male anther of a flower to the female stigma.
A.evolutionary biology   B.invertebrate   C.macroevolution   D.pollination

66. ____ A form of intermediate inheritance in which one allele for a specific trait is not completely expressed over its paired allele.
A.transcription   B.macroevolution   C.incomplete dominance   D.species

67. ____ The female gametophyte of a seed plant, within which the embryo develops.
A.nucleotide   B.species   C.embryo sac   D.pollination

68. ____ The branch of biology that relates to the animal kingdom, including the structure, embryology, evolution, classification, habits, and distribution of all animals.
A.species   B.autoimmunity   C.zoology   D.dendrite

69. ____ A straightforward extension of Lewis structures. States that electrons in a covalent bond reside in a region that is the overlap of individual atomic orbitals.
A.hermaphrodite   B.organism   C.abyssal zone   D.valence bond theory

70. ____ A lymphatic capillary that absorbs dietary fats in the villi of the small intestine.
A.lacteal   B.molecule   C.dna replication   D.neuromuscular junction

71. ____ Containing more than two homologous sets of chromosomes.
A.muon   B.denitrification   C.biomass   D.polyploidy

72. ____ The variety of life in the world or in a particular habitat or ecosystem.
A.pollination   B.biotechnology   C.electron transport chain   D.biodiversity

73. ____ Any organism whose cells contain a nucleus and other organelles enclosed within membranes.
A.molecule   B.aerobic   C.eukaryote   D.blastocyst

74. ____ A group of animals that have no backbone, unlike animals such as reptiles, amphibians, fish, birds and mammals who all have a backbone.
A.valence bond theory   B.invertebrate   C.endergonic reaction   D.phenotype

75. ____ a plant hormone.
A.abscisic acid   B.dehydration reaction   C.electron transport chain   D.biomedical research

76. ____ The system of immune responses of an organism against its own healthy cells and tissues.
A.valence shell   B.autoimmunity   C.asexual reproduction   D.plasmolysis

77. ____ An atom or molecule with a net electric charge due to the loss or gain of one or more electrons.
A.phenotype   B.muon   C.gene   D.ion

78. ____ A branch of molecular biology, biochemistry, and biophysics concerned with the molecular structure of biological macromolecules, especially proteins and nucleic acids.
A.lipid   B.electron transport chain   C.structural biology   D.dna replication

79. ____ A large molecule, or macromolecule, composed of many repeated subunits.
A.aerobic   B.polymer   C.species   D.nucleotide

80. ____ Also known as selective breeding.
A.lipid   B.organism   C.artificial selection   D.chemical equilibrium

81. ____ Catalysis in living systems. In biological processes, natural catalysts, such as protein enzymes, perform chemical transformations on organic compounds.
A.biomedical research   B.bacteria   C.biocatalysts   D.pollination

82. ____ An individual animal, plant, or single-celled life form.
A.organism   B.mast cell   C.muon   D.cell membrane

83. ____ The preying of one animal on others.
A.abyssal zone   B.predation   C.eukaryote   D.wobble base pair

84. ____ A biological agent that reproduces inside the cells of living hosts.
A.dna sequencing   B.virus   C.mast cell   D.endotherm

85. ____ The decoding of genetic instructions for making proteins.
A.valence bond theory   B.pheromone   C.reproduction   D.translation

86. ____ A chemical substance produced and released into the environment by an animal, especially a mammal or an insect, affecting the behavior or physiology of others of its species.
A.biodiversity   B.eukaryote   C.species   D.pheromone

87. ____ Stands for ribonucleic acid. It is an important molecule with long chains of nucleotides. A nucleotide contains a nitrogenous base, a ribose sugar, and a phosphate.
A.aerobic   B.rna   C.herpetology   D.zygote

88. ____ An animal that is dependent on or capable of the internal generation of heat; a warm
A.endotherm   B.pollination   C.estrogen   D.ecological niche

89. ____ The subfield of biology that studies the evolutionary processes that produced the diversity of life on Earth starting from a single origin of life.
A.isomer   B.lipid   C.molecular biology   D.evolutionary biology

90. ____ A chemical synapse formed by the contact between a motor neuron and a muscle fiber.
A.neuromuscular junction   B.vegetative reproduction   C.eukaryote   D.plasmolysis

91. ____ A molecule with the same chemical formula as another molecule, but with a different chemical structure.
A.deoxyribonucleic acid   B.polygene   C.isomer   D.population genetics

92. ____ The genetic contribution of an individual to the next generation's gene pool relative to the average for the population.
A.chemical kinetics   B.dna replication   C.darwinian fitness   D.parallel evolution

93. ____ A plant that grows harmlessly upon another plant and derives its moisture and nutrients from the air, rain, and sometimes from debris accumulating around it.
A.endergonic reaction   B.muon   C.water potential   D.epiphyte

94. ____ The primary female sex hormone. It is responsible for the development and regulation of the female reproductive system and secondary sex characteristics.
A.estrogen   B.molecular biology   C.reproduction   D.hermaphrodite

95. ____ An unstable subatomic particle. Among all known unstable subatomic particles, only the neutron (lasting around 15 minutes) and some atomic nuclei have a longer decay lifetime.
A.molecular biology   B.autoimmunity   C.muon   D.endosperm

96. ____ A gene whose individual effect on a phenotype is too small to be observed, but which can act together with others to produce observable variation.
A.polyploidy   B.polygene   C.chemical equilibrium   D.estrogen

97. ____ The set of observable characteristics of an individual resulting from the interaction of its genotype with the environment.
A.species   B.phenotype   C.endosperm   D.vestigiality

98. ____ The spectrum of electromagnetic radiation that has passed through a medium that absorbed radiation of certain wavelengths.
A.asexual reproduction   B.evolutionary biology   C.population genetics   D.absorption spectrum

99. ____ Evolution on a scale of separated gene pools. Studies focus on change that occurs at or above the level of species, in contrast with microevolution.
A.dalton   B.macroevolution   C.urea   D.bile

100. ____ An epithelial tissue that secretes mucus and that lines many body cavities and tubular organs including the gut and respiratory passages.
A.dna replication   B.invertebrate   C.chemical kinetics   D.mucous membrane

From the words provided for each clue, provide the letter of the word which best matches the clue.

101. ____ The semipermeable membrane surrounding the cytoplasm of a cell.
A.cell membrane   B.population ecology   C.enantiomer   D.insulin

102. ____ The study and analysis of the patterns, causes, and effects of health and disease conditions in defined populations.
A.hermaphrodite   B.macromolecule   C.cell membrane   D.epidemiology

103. ____ The scientific study of organisms in the ocean or other marine bodies of water.
A.marine biology   B.predation   C.electron donor   D.parasitology

104. ____ a plant hormone.
A.cell membrane   B.endotherm   C.abscisic acid   D.hadron

105. ____ The study of the microscopic anatomy of cells and tissues of plants and animals.
A.structural biology   B.dehydration reaction   C.histology   D.valence shell

106. ____ A form of terrestrial locomotion where an organism moves by means of its two rear limbs or legs.
A.bipedal   B.enantiomer   C.immunogloblin   D.biology

107. ____ Usually defined as a chemical reaction that involves the loss of a water molecule from the reacting molecule.
A.meson   B.endodermis   C.enantiomer   D.dehydration reaction

108. ____ A biochemical assembly that contains both proteins and lipids, bound to the proteins, which allow fats to move through the water inside and outside cells.
A.lipoprotein   B.macromolecule   C.mass balance   D.neuron

109. ____ A steroid hormone from the androgen group and is found in humans and other vertebrates.
A.testosterone   B.epistasis   C.neuron   D.macromolecule

110. ____ The study of insects.
A.entomology   B.nucleotide   C.electromagnetic spectrum   D.neuromuscular junction

111. ____ The branch of zoology concerned with reptiles and amphibians.
A.asexual reproduction   B.denaturation   C.acid precipitation   D.herpetology

112. ____ A sub-field of ecology that deals with the dynamics of species populations and how these populations interact with the environment.
A.population genetics   B.mass balance   C.endemic species   D.population ecology

113. ____ The scientific analysis and study of interactions among organisms and their environment. It is an interdisciplinary field that includes biology, geography and Earth science.
A.ecology   B.insulin   C.genetics   D.polymerase chain reaction

114. ____ An unstable subatomic particle. Among all known unstable subatomic particles, only the neutron (lasting around 15 minutes) and some atomic nuclei have a longer decay lifetime.
A.founder effect   B.bipedal   C.muon   D.eukaryote

115. ____ Refers to two solutions having the same osmotic pressure across a semipermeable membrane.
A.endodermis   B.denaturation   C.effector cell   D.isotonic solution

116. ____ The electrons in the outermost occupied shell (or shells) determine the chemical properties of the atom; it is called the valence shell.
A.valence shell   B.genetics   C.structural biology   D.active site

117. ____ An irregularly shaped region within the cell of a prokaryote that contains all or most of the genetic material, called gonophore.
A.biology   B.aerobic   C.nucleoid   D.valence electron

118. ____ Study of living organisms.
A.valence band   B.biology   C.electrochemical gradient   D.vestigiality

119. ____ A gradient of electrochemical potential, usually for an ion that can move across a membrane.
A.isotonic solution   B.histology   C.electrochemical gradient   D.hermaphrodite

120. ____ The reduced genetic diversity that results when a population is descended from a small number of colonizing ancestors.
A.founder effect   B.cell membrane   C.vegetative reproduction   D.genetics

121. ____ The application of engineering principles and design concepts to medicine and biology for healthcare purposes (e.g. diagnostic or therapeutic).
A.immunogloblin   B.endocrine system   C.abscission   D.biomedical engineering

122. ____ Each of several hierarchical levels in an ecosystem, comprising organisms that share the same function in the food chain and the same nutritional relationship.
A.bioenergetics   B.dehydration reaction   C.marine biology   D.trophic level

123. ____ Any of the elongated contractile threads found in striated muscle cells.
A.valence band   B.neuron   C.myofibril   D.incomplete dominance

124. ____ An ecological niche is the role and position a species has in its environment; how it meets its needs for food and shelter, how it survives, and how it reproduces.
A.histology   B.ecological niche   C.macromolecule   D.hermaphrodite

125. ____ The intersection of the three medians of the triangle (each median connecting a vertex with the midpoint of the opposite side).
A.vestigiality   B.centroid   C.darwinian fitness   D.endotherm

126. ____ The study of parasites, their hosts, and the relationship between them.
A.food chain   B.hydrocarbon   C.parasitology   D.antibiotic

127. ____ A chemical substance produced and released into the environment by an animal, especially a mammal or an insect, affecting the behavior or physiology of others of its species.
A.egg   B.pheromone   C.biomedical engineering   D.effector

128. ____ A molecule that can be bonded to other identical molecules to form a polymer.
A.histology   B.predation   C.monomer   D.organism

129. ____ The study of genetic variation within populations, and involves the examination and modeling of changes in the frequencies of genes and alleles.
A.biomedical engineering B.population genetics C.macromolecule D.aerobic

130. ____ The third phase of mitosis, the process that separates duplicated genetic material carried in the nucleus of a parent cell into two identical daughter cells.
A.aerobic B.food chain C.valence band D.metaphase

131. ____ The preying of one animal on others.
A.predation B.genetics C.genetic code D.epistasis

132. ____ A class of drug used to kill bacteria.
A.neuromuscular junction B.ecological niche C.denaturation D.antibiotic

133. ____ Also known as antibodies, They act as a critical part of the immune response by specifically recognizing and binding to particular antigens, and aiding in their destruction.
A.endocytosis B.immunogloblin C.darwinian fitness D.ectotherm

134. ____ A branch of molecular biology, biochemistry, and biophysics concerned with the molecular structure of biological macromolecules, especially proteins and nucleic acids.
A.metaphase B.structural biology C.organism D.nucleolus

135. ____ Virus that infects and multiplies within bacteria.
A.active site B.abscisic acid C.bacteriophage D.electromagnetic spectrum

136. ____ Depending on free oxygen or air.
A.acid precipitation B.insulin C.aerobic D.organism

137. ____ An inner layer of cells in the cortex of a root and of some stems, surrounding a vascular bundle.
A.gene B.darwinian fitness C.aerobic D.endodermis

138. ____ The study of the transformation of energy in living organisms.
A.gene B.darwinian fitness C.bioenergetics D.atom

139. ____ An enzyme that catalyzes the formation of cyclic AMP from ATP.
A.synthetic biology B.muon C.amino acid D.adenylate cyclase

140. ____ The ecological state of a species being unique to a defined geographic location, such as an island, nation, country or other defined zone, or habitat type.
A.endemic species B.amino acid C.incomplete dominance D.nucleoid

141. ____ One of the four main nucleobases found in the nucleic acids DNA and RNA, the others being adenine, cytosine, and thymine.
A.darwinian fitness B.abscisic acid C.biomedical research D.guanine

142. ____ Stereoisomers that are non-superimposable mirror images. A molecule with 1 chiral carbon atom exists as 2 stereoisomers termed enantiomers.
A.enantiomer B.valence band C.electrochemical gradient D.acid precipitation

143. ____ Organism with both male and female reproductive organs.
A.hermaphrodite B.endocytosis C.darwinian fitness D.genetics

144. ____ The highest range of electron energies in which electrons are normally present at absolute zero temperature.
A.mass balance B.muon C.valence band D.founder effect

145. ____ The collection of glands that produce hormones that regulate metabolism, growth and development, tissue function, sexual function, reproduction, sleep, and mood.
A.embryology   B.vegetative reproduction   C.endocrine system   D.cell membrane

146. ____ A gene is a locus (or region) of DNA that encodes a functional RNA or protein product, and is the molecular unit of heredity.
A.gene   B.hydrocarbon   C.vegetative reproduction   D.mass density

147. ____ A class of organic compounds containing an amino group and a carboxylic acid group
A.hydrocarbon   B.antibiotic   C.amino acid   D.parasitology

148. ____ An electrically excitable cell that processes and transmits information through electrical and chemical signals.
A.nucleic acid   B.muon   C.lipoprotein   D.neuron

149. ____ The site of oxidative phosphorylation in eukaryotes.
A.founder effect   B.electron transport chain   C.hermaphrodite   D.biomedical engineering

150. ____ The female reproductive cell (gamete) in oogamous organisms.
A.chemical equilibrium   B.basal body   C.vestigiality   D.egg

151. ____ A organism in which internal physiological sources of heat are of relatively small or quite negligible importance in controlling body temperature. "Cold blooded".
A.ectotherm   B.founder effect   C.bacteriophage   D.mass balance

152. ____ The part of an enzyme or antibody where the chemical reaction occurs
A.active site   B.biology   C.thymine   D.cell membrane

153. ____ An organ or cell that acts in response to a stimulus.
A.egg   B.structural biology   C.biomedical research   D.effector

154. ____ Refers to genetically determined structures or attributes that have apparently lost most or all of their ancestral function in a given species.
A.vestigiality   B.ecological niche   C.neuron   D.electron donor

155. ____ A small dense spherical structure in the nucleus of a cell during interphase.
A.vestigiality   B.myofibril   C.isotonic solution   D.nucleolus

156. ____ An electron that is associated with an atom, and that can participate in the formation of a chemical bond.
A.denaturation   B.valence electron   C.active site   D.effector cell

157. ____ A very large molecule, such as protein, commonly created by polymerization of smaller subunits (monomers).
A.macromolecule   B.herpetology   C.active site   D.aerobic

158. ____ An individual animal, plant, or single-celled life form.
A.meson   B.epistasis   C.neuron   D.organism

159. ____ An application of conservation of mass to the analysis of physical systems.
A.endotherm   B.histology   C.hydrocarbon   D.mass balance

160. ____ Single-cell microscopic organisms which lack a true nucleus. They represent one of the three domains.
A.bacteria   B.ecological niche   C.effector cell   D.centroid

161. ____ The state in which both reactants and products are present in concentrations which have no further tendency to change with time.
A.chemical equilibrium B.insulin C.bioenergetics D.electrochemical gradient

162. ____ Helps keep blood sugar level from getting too high (hyperglycemia) or too low (hypoglycemia).
A.epistasis B.electromagnetic spectrum C.immunogloblin D.insulin

163. ____ A complex organic substance present in living cells, especially DNA or RNA, whose molecules consist of many nucleotides linked in a long chain.
A.binary fission B.ecology C.cell membrane D.nucleic acid

164. ____ Process of reproduction involving a single parent that results in offspring that are genetically identical to the parent.
A.asexual reproduction B.gene C.valence shell D.myofibril

165. ____ Density is mass per volume.
A.binary fission B.vegetative reproduction C.lipoprotein D.mass density

166. ____ A form of active transport in which a cell transports molecules (such as proteins) into the cell (endo
A.epistasis B.endocytosis C.chemical equilibrium D.electron transport chain

167. ____ The nucleotide triplets of DNA and RNA molecules that carry genetic information in living cells.
A.predation B.synthetic biology C.embryology D.genetic code

168. ____ A process by which the contents of a cell vacuole are released to the exterior through fusion of the vacuole membrane with the cell membrane.
A.exocytosis B.parasitology C.epistasis D.nucleotide

169. ____ Plasma cells, also called plasma B cells, plasmocytes, plasmacytes, or effector B cells, are white blood cells that secrete large volumes of antibodies.
A.effector cell B.electron transport chain C.genetic code D.exocytosis

170. ____ An interdisciplinary branch of biology and engineering.
A.structural biology B.synthetic biology C.histology D.adenylate cyclase

171. ____ A hierarchical series of organisms each dependent on the next as a source of food.
A.centroid B.food chain C.population genetics D.abscisic acid

172. ____ The pursuit of answers to medical questions. These investigations lead to discoveries, which in turn lead to the development of new preventions, therapies and cures.
A.endocytosis B.biomedical research C.cell membrane D.herpetology

173. ____ The genetic contribution of an individual to the next generation's gene pool relative to the average for the population.
A.population genetics B.exocytosis C.darwinian fitness D.vestigiality

174. ____ Shedding of flowers and leaves and fruit following formation of scar tissue in a plant.
A.macromolecule B.abscission C.exocytosis D.adenylate cyclase

175. ____ A chemical synapse formed by the contact between a motor neuron and a muscle fiber.
A.embryology B.population genetics C.neuromuscular junction D.endotherm

176. ____ A form of intermediate inheritance in which one allele for a specific trait is not completely expressed over its paired allele.
A.genetics B.binary fission C.incomplete dominance D.food chain

177. ____ Any particle that is made from quarks, anti
A.hadron B.endocrine system C.herpetology D.predation

178. ____ One cell dividing into two identical daughter cells.
A.genetics B.immunogloblin C.vegetative reproduction D.binary fission

179. ____ In organic chemistry, a hydrocarbon is an organic compound consisting entirely of hydrogen and carbon.
A.hydrocarbon B.neuromuscular junction C.structural biology D.population ecology

180. ____ The smallest component of an element having the chemical properties of the element
A.genetic code B.atom C.parasitology D.endodermis

181. ____ The deep sea (2000 meters or more) where there is no light.
A.abyssal zone B.adenylate cyclase C.eukaryote D.atom

182. ____ One of the four nucleobases in the nucleic acid of DNA that are represented by the letters G–C–A–T.
A.thymine B.nucleoid C.founder effect D.embryology

183. ____ The principle, originated by Gregor Mendel, stating that when two or more characteristics are inherited, individual hereditary factors assort independently.
A.genetic code B.population genetics C.independent assortment D.lipoprotein

184. ____ A harmless pill, medicine, or procedure prescribed more for the psychological benefit to the patient than for any physiological effect.
A.meson B.vegetative reproduction C.placebo D.macromolecule

185. ____ An electron donor is a chemical entity that donates electrons to another compound.
A.electron donor B.abscission C.antibiotic D.nucleoid

186. ____ The interaction of genes that are not alleles, in particular the suppression of the effect of one such gene by another.
A.electrochemical gradient B.aerobic C.endoplasmic reticulum D.epistasis

187. ____ Organic molecules that serve as the monomers, or subunits, of nucleic acids like DNA (deoxyribonucleic acid) and RNA (ribonucleic acid).
A.exocytosis B.endemic species C.nucleotide D.biomedical research

188. ____ A technique used in molecular biology to amplify a single copy or a few copies of a piece of DNA across several orders of magnitude.
A.electromagnetic spectrum B.polymerase chain reaction C.asexual reproduction
D.testosterone

189. ____ A process in which proteins or nucleic acids lose the quaternary structure, tertiary structure and secondary structure which is present in their native state.
A.denaturation B.placebo C.histology D.predation

190. ____ Rain containing acids that form in the atmosphere when industrial gas emissions (especially sulfur dioxide and nitrogen oxides) combine with water.
A.immunogloblin B.molecular biology C.acid precipitation D.exocytosis

191. ____ The branch of biology that studies the development of gametes (sex cells), fertilization, and development of embryos and fetuses.
A.atom B.antibiotic C.abscisic acid D.embryology

192. ____ A network of membranous tubules within the cytoplasm of a eukaryotic cell, continuous with the nuclear membrane.
A.mass balance B.embryology C.aerobic D.endoplasmic reticulum

193. ____ Hadronic subatomic particles composed of one quark and one antiquark, bound together by the strong interaction.
A.bipedal   B.abscission   C.meson   D.food chain

194. ____ The collective term for all possible frequencies of electromagnetic radiation.
A.electromagnetic spectrum   B.histology   C.testosterone   D.synthetic biology

195. ____ A form of asexual reproduction of a plant. Only one plant is involved and the offspring is the result of one parent. The new plant is genetically identical to the parent.
A.nucleolus   B.effector   C.aerobic   D.vegetative reproduction

196. ____ An animal that is dependent on or capable of the internal generation of heat; a warm
A.endotherm   B.biomedical engineering   C.exocytosis   D.valence shell

197. ____ Any organism whose cells contain a nucleus and other organelles enclosed within membranes.
A.hadron   B.eukaryote   C.isotonic solution   D.independent assortment

198. ____ An organelle formed from a centriole, and a short cylindrical array of microtubules.
A.nucleotide   B.genetics   C.basal body   D.mass density

199. ____ The study of heredity
A.abscisic acid   B.nucleoid   C.genetics   D.metaphase

200. ____ A branch of science concerning biological activity at the molecular level.
A.chemical equilibrium   B.valence shell   C.molecular biology   D.immunogloblin

From the words provided for each clue, provide the letter of the word which best matches the clue.

201. ____ A lasting attraction between atoms that enables the formation of chemical compounds.
A.chemical bond   B.cryobiology   C.myosin   D.biomass

202. ____ A branch of zoology that concerns the study of birds.
A.parallel evolution   B.effector   C.vasodilation   D.ornithology

203. ____ A steroid hormone from the androgen group and is found in humans and other vertebrates.
A.testosterone   B.cell biology   C.nucleobase   D.white blood cell

204. ____ The intersection of the three medians of the triangle (each median connecting a vertex with the midpoint of the opposite side).
A.ligament   B.gene   C.centroid   D.chemical kinetics

205. ____ When a nerve or muscle cell is at "rest", its membrane potential is called the resting membrane potential.
A.jejunum   B.membrane potential   C.chemical bond   D.absorption

206. ____ A cluster (functional group) of nerve cell bodies in a centralized nervous system.
A.parallel evolution   B.chemical compound   C.ganglion   D.chemical equilibrium

207. ____ Describes the efficiency with which energy is transferred from one trophic level to the next.
A.ecological efficiency   B.species   C.anticodon   D.centroid

208. ____ A graphical representation designed to show the biomass or bio productivity at each trophic level in a given ecosystem.
A.organ   B.phloem   C.ecological pyramid   D.si units

209. ___ The vascular tissue in plants that conducts sugars and other metabolic products downward from the leaves.
A.jejunum B.insulin C.cell biology D.phloem

210. ___ The study and discussion of chemical reactions with respect to reaction rates, effect of various variables, re
A.transfer rna B.chemical kinetics C.chemical equilibrium D.nucleobase

211. ___ A mammalian blastula in which some differentiation of cells has occurred.
A.blastocyst B.depolarization C.species D.reproduction

212. ___ RNA consisting of folded molecules that transport amino acids from the cytoplasm of a cell to a ribosome.
A.electron B.transfer rna C.gene D.organ

213. ___ A laboratory process that determines the complete DNA sequence of an organism's genome at a single time.
A.whole genome sequencing B.nucleobase C.genetic variation D.valence band

214. ___ A form of active transport in which a cell transports molecules (such as proteins) into the cell (endo
A.vegetative reproduction B.endocytosis C.b cell D.placebo

215. ___ Any organism whose cells contain a nucleus and other organelles enclosed within membranes.
A.anticodon B.cell biology C.eukaryote D.electron

216. ___ A gene is a locus (or region) of DNA that encodes a functional RNA or protein product, and is the molecular unit of heredity.
A.endocytosis B.gene C.abyssal zone D.absorption spectrum

217. ___ The vascular tissue in plants that conducts water and dissolved nutrients upward from the root and also helps to form the woody element in the stem.
A.sociobiology B.xylem C.reproduction D.mass density

218. ___ Cytosine, Guanine, Adenine (which can be found in DNA and RNA), Thymine (found only in DNA), and Uracil (found only in RNA).
A.genetic variation B.placebo C.nucleobase D.epicotyl

219. ___ The branch of biology that studies the effects of low temperatures on living things within Earth's cryosphere or in science.
A.bionics B.centroid C.cryobiology D.arachnology

220. ___ An evolutionary theory that explains the origin of eukaryotic cells from prokaryotes.
A.biogeography B.endosymbiotic theory C.arachnology D.nucleobase

221. ___ The genetic contribution of an individual to the next generation's gene pool relative to the average for the population.
A.behavioral ecology B.ganglion C.darwinian fitness D.lepton

222. ___ A type of cell division that reduces the number of chromosomes in the parent cell by half and produces four gamete cells.
A.histology B.physiology C.meiosis D.endocrine system

223. ___ A large molecule, or macromolecule, composed of many repeated subunits.
A.chemical kinetics B.zoology C.polymer D.b cell

224. ___ A measure of the tendency of an atom to attract a bonding pair of electrons. The Pauling scale is the most commonly used.
A.depolarization B.endangered species C.insulin D.electronegativity

225. ___ A lymphocyte of a type produced or processed by the thymus gland and actively participating in the immune response.
A.t cell   B.biomass   C.lepton   D.ecological efficiency

226. ___ A series of chemical reactions used by all aerobic organisms to generate energy through the oxidation of acetyl
A.testosterone   B.abscission   C.krebs cycle   D.cryobiology

227. ___ Large biomolecules, or macromolecules, consisting of one or more long chains of amino acid residues.
A.vasodilation   B.abyssal zone   C.protein   D.mass number

228. ___ The collection of glands that produce hormones that regulate metabolism, growth and development, tissue function, sexual function, reproduction, sleep, and mood.
A.testosterone   B.endocrine system   C.eukaryote   D.valence

229. ___ a part of an organism that is typically self-contained and has a specific vital function, such as the heart or liver in humans.
A.species   B.organ   C.reproduction   D.b cell

230. ___ Variation in the relative frequency of different genotypes in a small population, owing to the chance disappearance of particular genes as individuals die or do not reproduce.
A.transfer rna   B.genetic drift   C.active site   D.jejunum

231. ___ Often defined as the largest group of organisms in which two individuals are capable of reproducing fertile offspring, typically using sexual reproduction.
A.krebs cycle   B.species   C.genetic variation   D.cell nucleus

232. ___ The spectrum of electromagnetic radiation that has passed through a medium that absorbed radiation of certain wavelengths.
A.depolarization   B.absorption spectrum   C.ganglion   D.virus

233. ___ An elementary, half-integer spin particle that does not undergo strong interactions.
A.lepton   B.placebo   C.nucleobase   D.depolarization

234. ___ A gene whose individual effect on a phenotype is too small to be observed, but which can act together with others to produce observable variation.
A.endocrine system   B.anticodon   C.polygene   D.parallel evolution

235. ___ An organ or cell that acts in response to a stimulus.
A.effector   B.vasodilation   C.internal fertilization   D.membrane potential

236. ___ Threatened by factors such as habitat loss, hunting, disease and climate change, and usually have declining populations or a very limited range.
A.dalton   B.arachnology   C.genetic drift   D.endangered species

237. ___ A harmless pill, medicine, or procedure prescribed more for the psychological benefit to the patient than for any physiological effect.
A.interleukin   B.placebo   C.dna   D.electrochemical gradient

238. ___ Plasma cells, also called plasma B cells, plasmocytes, plasmacytes, or effector B cells, are white blood cells that secrete large volumes of antibodies.
A.blastocyst   B.cell biology   C.effector cell   D.jejunum

239. ___ Scientific study of spiders, scorpions, pseudo-scorpions, and harvestmen, collectively called arachnids.
A.genetic drift   B.species   C.electron   D.arachnology

240. ___ Mitosis and cytokinesis together define this phase of an animal cell cycle-the division of the mother cell into two daughter cells, genetically identical to each other and the parent.
A.dalton B.m phase C.chemical equilibrium D.vegetative reproduction

241. ___ The deep sea (2000 meters or more) where there is no light.
A.arachnology B.abyssal zone C.physiology D.endosymbiotic theory

242. ___ A gradient of electrochemical potential, usually for an ion that can move across a membrane.
A.ornithology B.electrochemical gradient C.jejunum D.chemical kinetics

243. ___ The study of the distribution of species and ecosystems in geographic space and through time.
A.reproduction B.krebs cycle C.biogeography D.membrane potential

244. ___ Variations of genomes between members of species, or between groups of species thriving in different parts of the world as a result of genetic mutation.
A.phenotype B.genetic variation C.physiology D.nucleobase

245. ___ The total number of protons and neutrons (together known as nucleons) in an atomic nucleus
A.physiology B.abscission C.mass number D.chemical reaction

246. ___ A biological agent that reproduces inside the cells of living hosts.
A.darwinian fitness B.virus C.si units D.chemical compound

247. ___ A class of organic compounds containing an amino group and a carboxylic acid group
A.blastocyst B.meiosis C.sociobiology D.amino acid

248. ___ The branch of biology that relates to the animal kingdom, including the structure, embryology, evolution, classification, habits, and distribution of all animals.
A.dalton B.zoology C.xylem D.epicotyl

249. ___ The highest range of electron energies in which electrons are normally present at absolute zero temperature.
A.vasodilation B.endocytosis C.valence band D.ligament

250. ___ Contraction of the protoplast of a plant cell as a result of loss of water from the cell.
A.ecological efficiency B.reproduction C.valence electron D.plasmolysis

251. ___ Type of lymphocyte in the humeral immunity of the adaptive immune system.
A.organ B.bionics C.b cell D.vacuole

252. ___ The dilatation of blood vessels, which decreases blood pressure.
A.vasodilation B.eukaryote C.zoology D.electron

253. ___ The part of an enzyme or antibody where the chemical reaction occurs
A.antibiotic B.organ C.electrochemical gradient D.active site

254. ___ A field of scientific study that is based on the hypothesis that social behavior has resulted from evolution and attempts to explain and examine social behavior within that context.
A.sociobiology B.xylem C.vasodilation D.transfer rna

255. ___ An electron that is associated with an atom, and that can participate in the formation of a chemical bond.
A.species B.isotonic solution C.valence electron D.darwinian fitness

256. ___ The state in which both reactants and products are present in concentrations which have no further tendency to change with time.
A.chemical equilibrium B.vasodilation C.blastocyst D.chemical kinetics

257. ____ The branch of biology dealing with the functions and activities of living organisms and their parts, including all physical and chemical processes.
A.physiology B.chemical equilibrium C.vacuole D.vasodilation

258. ____ The term used to describe what happens to an ecological community over time.
A.abyssal zone B.vegetative reproduction C.ecological succession D.testosterone

259. ____ A membrane-bound organelle which is present in all plant and fungal cells and some protist, animal and bacterial cells.
A.membrane potential B.vacuole C.abscission D.genetic variation

260. ____ Usually characterized by a chemical change, and they yield one or more products, which usually have properties different from the reactants
A.sociobiology B.chemical reaction C.reproduction D.lepton

261. ____ The study of the microscopic anatomy of cells and tissues of plants and animals.
A.histology B.mass density C.epicotyl D.cryobiology

262. ____ Shedding of flowers and leaves and fruit following formation of scar tissue in a plant.
A.abscission B.blastocyst C.organ D.chemical reaction

263. ____ The process of reversing the charge across a cell membrane (usually a NEURON), so causing an ACTION POTENTIAL.
A.genetic drift B.biomass C.whole genome sequencing D.depolarization

264. ____ Refers to the number of elements to which it can connect.
A.cell membrane B.placebo C.arachnology D.valence

265. ____ The smallest particle in a chemical element or compound that has the chemical properties of that element or compound.
A.valence electron B.absorption C.ornithology D.molecule

266. ____ A process in which one substance permeates another; a fluid permeates or is dissolved by a liquid or solid.
A.anticodon B.endocrine system C.absorption D.transfer rna

267. ____ Organic matter derived from living, or recently living organisms.
A.mass number B.biomass C.medulla D.acclimatization

268. ____ The hereditary material in humans and almost all other organisms.
A.medulla B.genetic drift C.endangered species D.dna

269. ____ A form of asexual reproduction of a plant. Only one plant is involved and the offspring is the result of one parent. The new plant is genetically identical to the parent.
A.vegetative reproduction B.protein C.internal fertilization D.ecological efficiency

270. ____ An organelle formed from a centriole, and a short cylindrical array of microtubules.
A.bionics B.basal body C.epicotyl D.si units

271. ____ The region of an embryo or seedling stem above the cotyledon.
A.cryobiology B.electrochemical gradient C.acclimatization D.epicotyl

272. ____ Helps keep blood sugar level from getting too high (hyperglycemia) or too low (hypoglycemia).
A.insulin B.valence electron C.xylem D.abyssal zone

273. ____ A class of drug used to kill bacteria.
A.cell membrane B.m phase C.antibiotic D.darwinian fitness

274. ____ The inactive X chromosome in a female somatic cell, rendered inactive in a process called lionization
A.cell nucleus   B.genetic variation   C.barr body   D.gene

275. ____ The study of the evolutionary basis for animal behavior due to ecological pressures.
A.behavioral ecology   B.darwinian fitness   C.valence   D.chemical bond

276. ____ Refers to two solutions having the same osmotic pressure across a semipermeable membrane.
A.endocytosis   B.isotonic solution   C.chemical compound   D.interleukin

277. ____ A unit of mass (also known as an atomic mass unit, amu), equal to the mass of a hydrogen atom (1.67 x 1024 g).
A.polygene   B.sociobiology   C.membrane potential   D.dalton

278. ____ Explains the structure, organization of the organelles they contain, their physiological properties, metabolic processes, signaling pathways, life cycle, and interactions.
A.white blood cell   B.meiosis   C.cell biology   D.histology

279. ____ A chemical substance consisting of two or more different chemically bonded chemical elements, with a fixed ratio determining the composition.
A.electrochemical gradient   B.chemical compound   C.chemical reaction   D.ornithology

280. ____ The "control room" for the cell. The nucleus gives out all the orders.
A.cell nucleus   B.endocrine system   C.integrative biology   D.ganglion

281. ____ A system of physical units-based on the meter, kilogram, second, ampere, kelvin, candela, and mole, together with a set of prefixes.
A.mass number   B.physiology   C.si units   D.vasodilation

282. ____ The science of diagnosing and managing plant diseases.
A.endosymbiotic theory   B.anticodon   C.physiology   D.phytopathology

283. ____ Fertilization that takes place inside the egg-producing individual.
A.internal fertilization   B.myosin   C.chemical kinetics   D.t cell

284. ____ A sequence of three nucleotides forming a unit of genetic code in a transfer RNA molecule, corresponding to a complementary codon in messenger RNA.
A.depolarization   B.effector   C.anticodon   D.histology

285. ____ The set of observable characteristics of an individual resulting from the interaction of its genotype with the environment.
A.darwinian fitness   B.nucleobase   C.chemical bond   D.phenotype

286. ____ Application of biological methods and systems found in nature to the study and design of engineering systems and modern technology.
A.bionics   B.cell nucleus   C.biomass   D.krebs cycle

287. ____ The fibrous connective tissue that connects bones to other bones.
A.absorption spectrum   B.cell membrane   C.vegetative reproduction   D.ligament

288. ____ Giving birth to one of its kind, sexually or asexually.
A.jejunum   B.effector cell   C.reproduction   D.amino acid

289. ____ Component of the blood that functions in the immune system. Also known as a leukocyte.
A.absorption   B.white blood cell   C.isotonic solution   D.species

290. ____ The independent evolution of similar traits, starting from a similar ancestral condition.
A.exon   B.parallel evolution   C.myosin   D.physiology

291. ____ A subatomic particle with a negative elementary electric charge.
A.valence band   B.interleukin   C.electron   D.polygene

292. ____ The midsection of the small intestine of many higher vertebrates like mammals, birds, reptiles. It is present between the duodenum and the ileum.
A.jejunum   B.endangered species   C.whole genome sequencing   D.chemical reaction

293. ____ The semipermeable membrane surrounding the cytoplasm of a cell.
A.chemical bond   B.ecological succession   C.cell membrane   D.nucleobase

294. ____ A group of cytokines (secreted proteins and signal molecules) that were first seen to be expressed by white blood cells (leukocytes)
A.sociobiology   B.medulla   C.interleukin   D.absorption

295. ____ Large superfamily of motor proteins that move along actin filaments, while hydrolyzing ATP.
A.cell membrane   B.myosin   C.electrochemical gradient   D.medulla

296. ____ A label frequently used to describe various forms of cross-disciplinary and multitaxon research.
A.integrative biology   B.membrane potential   C.reproduction   D.abyssal zone

297. ____ Density is mass per volume.
A.dalton   B.mass density   C.cell nucleus   D.isotonic solution

298. ____ Adaptation to a new climate (a new temperature or altitude or environment).
A.behavioral ecology   B.acclimatization   C.centroid   D.vacuole

299. ____ Any part of a gene that will become a part of the final mature RNA produced by that gene after introns have been removed by RNA splicing.
A.active site   B.endocytosis   C.exon   D.chemical kinetics

300. ____ The continuation of the spinal cord within the skull, forming the lowest part of the brainstem and containing control centers for the heart and lungs.
A.valence electron   B.phytopathology   C.active site   D.medulla

From the words provided for each clue, provide the letter of the word which best matches the clue.

1. B Serves an important role in the metabolism of nitrogen-containing compounds by animals, and is the main nitrogen-containing substance in the urine of mammals.
   A.polyploidy B.urea C.artificial selection D.dehydration reaction

2. B The use of living systems and organisms to develop or make products, or "any technological application that uses biological systems, living organisms or derivatives thereof.
   A.asexual reproduction B.biotechnology C.nucleolus D.isomer

3. A The process of determining the precise order of nucleotides within a DNA molecule.
   A.dna sequencing B.valence shell C.denitrification D.chemical equilibrium

4. C The double helix is unwound and each strand acts as a template for the next strand. Bases are matched to synthesize the new partner strands.
   A.parallel evolution B.endotherm C.dna replication D.polymer

5. D The amount of work needed to move a unit charge from a reference point to a specific point against an electric field.
   A.virus B.ion C.dehydration reaction D.electric potential

6. A A small dense spherical structure in the nucleus of a cell during interphase.
   A.nucleolus B.abscisic acid C.ectotherm D.rna

7. B A branch of science concerning biological activity at the molecular level.
   A.vestigiality B.molecular biology C.structural biology D.molecule

8. D The inactive X chromosome in a female somatic cell, rendered inactive in a process called lionization
   A.nucleolus B.transcription C.lacteal D.barr body

9. A A dark green to yellowish brown fluid, produced by the liver of most vertebrates, that aids the digestion of lipids in the small intestine.
   A.bile B.ectotherm C.structural biology D.bacteria

10. A A hierarchical series of organisms each dependent on the next as a source of food.
   A.food chain B.vegetative reproduction C.lacteal D.dna replication

11. D A mammalian blastula in which some differentiation of cells has occurred.
   A.zoology B.vestigiality C.species D.blastocyst

12. B The first step of gene expression, in which a particular segment of DNA is copied into RNA (mRNA) by the enzyme RNA polymerase.
   A.hermaphrodite B.transcription C.darwinian fitness D.electron acceptor

13. A Depending on free oxygen or air.
   A.aerobic B.steroid C.ecological niche D.predation

14. B The semipermeable membrane surrounding the cytoplasm of a cell.
   A.electric potential B.cell membrane C.molarity D.nucleolus

15. B Often defined as the largest group of organisms in which two individuals are capable of reproducing fertile offspring, typically using sexual reproduction.
   A.molarity B.species C.parallel evolution D.abscisic acid

16. C An enzyme that synthesizes short RNA sequences called primers.
   A.asexual reproduction B.herpetology C.primase D.lipid

17. D A branch of physical science that studies the composition, structure, properties and change of matter.
A.human nutrition   B.rna   C.denitrification   D.chemistry

18. C A microbially facilitated process of nitrate reduction that may ultimately produce molecular nitrogen.
A.estrogen   B.chemistry   C.denitrification   D.endemism

19. C The electrons in the outermost occupied shell (or shells) determine the chemical properties of the atom; it is called the valence shell.
A.muon   B.food chain   C.valence shell   D.ion

20. C The process of reversing the charge across a cell membrane (usually a NEURON), so causing an ACTION POTENTIAL.
A.endotherm   B.parallel evolution   C.depolarization   D.bacteria

21. D Cytosine, Guanine, Adenine (which can be found in DNA and RNA), Thymine (found only in DNA), and Uracil (found only in RNA).
A.ectotherm   B.transcription   C.darwinian fitness   D.nucleobase

22. A Organism with both male and female reproductive organs.
A.hermaphrodite   B.ion   C.valence bond theory   D.nucleobase

23. B The study of genetic variation within populations, and involves the examination and modeling of changes in the frequencies of genes and alleles.
A.valence bond theory   B.population genetics   C.endemism   D.zygote

24. D A chemical entity that accepts electrons transferred to it from another compound.
A.electron carrier   B.autoimmunity   C.biodiversity   D.electron acceptor

25. B A network of membranous tubules within the cytoplasm of a eukaryotic cell, continuous with the nuclear membrane.
A.urea   B.endoplasmic reticulum   C.chemical equilibrium   D.ecological niche

26. C A form of asexual reproduction of a plant. Only one plant is involved and the offspring is the result of one parent. The new plant is genetically identical to the parent.
A.dna replication   B.nucleolus   C.vegetative reproduction   D.yolk

27. A The branch of zoology concerned with reptiles and amphibians.
A.herpetology   B.pollination   C.evolutionary biology   D.electric potential

28. A A short branched extension of a nerve cell, along which impulses received from other cells at synapses are transmitted to the cell body
A.dendrite   B.lepton   C.biocatalysts   D.epiphyte

29. D Organic molecules that serve as the monomers, or subunits, of nucleic acids like DNA (deoxyribonucleic acid) and RNA (ribonucleic acid).
A.embryo sac   B.biomedical research   C.absorption spectrum   D.nucleotide

30. C The independent evolution of similar traits, starting from a similar ancestral condition.
A.absorption spectrum   B.cell membrane   C.parallel evolution   D.gene

31. A The four bases found in DNA are adenine, cytosine, guanine and thymine. These four bases are attached to the sugar
A.deoxyribonucleic acid   B.abscisic acid   C.polygene   D.electric potential

32. C Single-cell microscopic organisms which lack a true nucleus. They represent one of the three domains.
A.dehydration reaction   B.plasmolysis   C.bacteria   D.denitrification

33. B An elementary, half-integer spin particle that does not undergo strong interactions.
A.autoimmunity B.lepton C.steroid D.nucleolus

34. A A pairing between two nucleotides in RNA molecules that does not follow Watson
A.wobble base pair B.evolutionary biology C.valence bond theory D.polyploidy

35. B An organic compound with four rings arranged in a specific configuration. Examples include the dietary lipid cholesterol and the sex hormones.
A.darwinian fitness B.steroid C.endosperm D.primase

36. D The state in which both reactants and products are present in concentrations which have no further tendency to change with time.
A.biocatalysts B.valence bond theory C.asexual reproduction D.chemical equilibrium

37. A Animals, like flatworms and jellyfish, that have no body cavity (coelom).
A.acoelomate B.invertebrate C.lacteal D.chemical equilibrium

38. A Refers to the provision of essential nutrients necessary to support human life and health.
A.human nutrition B.predation C.electron acceptor D.zoology

39. B A unit of mass (also known as an atomic mass unit, amu), equal to the mass of a hydrogen atom (1.67 x 1024 g).
A.deoxyribonucleic acid B.dalton C.nucleotide D.dna sequencing

40. B A chemically defined as a substance that is insoluble in water and soluble in alcohol, ether, and chloroform. The basis for fats and oils.
A.biodiversity B.lipid C.translation D.polyploidy

41. A An ecological niche is the role and position a species has in its environment; how it meets its needs for food and shelter, how it survives, and how it reproduces.
A.ecological niche B.polyploidy C.neuromuscular junction D.human nutrition

42. C Refers to genetically determined structures or attributes that have apparently lost most or all of their ancestral function in a given species.
A.predation B.biocatalysts C.vestigiality D.embryo sac

43. A A tissue produced inside the seeds of most of the flowering plants around the time of fertilization.
A.endosperm B.electron transport chain C.dehydration reaction D.gene

44. D A chemical reaction in which the standard change in free energy is positive, and energy is absorbed
A.translation B.population genetics C.absorption spectrum D.endergonic reaction

45. B Contraction of the protoplast of a plant cell as a result of loss of water from the cell.
A.autoimmunity B.plasmolysis C.biodiversity D.wobble base pair

46. D Any of various molecules that are capable of accepting one or two electrons from one molecule and donating them to another in the process of electron transport.
A.ecological niche B.incomplete dominance C.depolarization D.electron carrier

47. D Giving birth to one of its kind, sexually or asexually.
A.artificial selection B.water potential C.denitrification D.reproduction

48. D The study and discussion of chemical reactions with respect to reaction rates, effect of various variables, re
A.biomass B.transcription C.plasmolysis D.chemical kinetics

49. C   The pursuit of answers to medical questions. These investigations lead to discoveries, which in turn lead to the development of new preventions, therapies and cures.
A.aerobic B.organism C.biomedical research D.isomer

50. C   The region of an embryo or seedling stem above the cotyledon.
A.barr body B.primase C.epicotyl D.molecule

51. C   A measure of the potential energy in water as well as the difference between the potential in a given water sample and pure water.
A.darwinian fitness B.steroid C.water potential D.rna

52. A   A diploid cell resulting from the fusion of two haploid gametes; a fertilized ovum.
A.zygote B.macroevolution C.biomass D.organism

53. A   A unit of concentration measuring the number of moles of a solute per liter of solution.
A.molarity B.dehydration reaction C.food chain D.biomedical research

54. C   A cell filled with basophil granules, found in numbers in connective tissue and releasing histamine and other substances during inflammatory and allergic reactions.
A.absorption spectrum B.depolarization C.mast cell D.nucleolus

55. B   Process of reproduction involving a single parent that results in offspring that are genetically identical to the parent.
A.autoimmunity B.asexual reproduction C.reproduction D.water potential

56. A   The ecological state of a species being unique to a defined geographic location, such as an island, nation, country or other defined zone, or habitat type.
A.endemism B.molarity C.biomedical research D.epiphyte

57. A   The site of oxidative phosphorylation in eukaryotes.
A.electron transport chain B.virus C.incomplete dominance D.endotherm

58. B   The deep sea (2000 meters or more) where there is no light.
A.wobble base pair B.abyssal zone C.mast cell D.epiphyte

59. A   The smallest particle in a chemical element or compound that has the chemical properties of that element or compound.
A.molecule B.bile C.structural biology D.epiphyte

60. D   The yellow internal part of a bird's egg, which is surrounded by the white, is rich in protein and fat, and nourishes the developing embryo.
A.epiphyte B.zoology C.pheromone D.yolk

61. A   A organism in which internal physiological sources of heat are of relatively small or quite negligible importance in controlling body temperature. "Cold blooded".
A.ectotherm B.asexual reproduction C.electric potential D.ecological niche

62. C   Usually defined as a chemical reaction that involves the loss of a water molecule from the reacting molecule.
A.chemical equilibrium B.epiphyte C.dehydration reaction D.gene

63. D   Organic matter derived from living, or recently living organisms.
A.electron acceptor B.molarity C.food chain D.biomass

64. C   A gene is a locus (or region) of DNA that encodes a functional RNA or protein product, and is the molecular unit of heredity.
A.chemistry B.hermaphrodite C.gene D.bacteria

65. D   The act of transferring pollen grains from the male anther of a flower to the female stigma.
        A.evolutionary biology   B.invertebrate   C.macroevolution   D.pollination

66. C   A form of intermediate inheritance in which one allele for a specific trait is not completely
        expressed over its paired allele.
        A.transcription   B.macroevolution   C.incomplete dominance   D.species

67. C   The female gametophyte of a seed plant, within which the embryo develops.
        A.nucleotide   B.species   C.embryo sac   D.pollination

68. C   The branch of biology that relates to the animal kingdom, including the structure, embryology,
        evolution, classification, habits, and distribution of all animals.
        A.species   B.autoimmunity   C.zoology   D.dendrite

69. D   A straightforward extension of Lewis structures. States that electrons in a covalent bond reside in a
        region that is the overlap of individual atomic orbitals.
        A.hermaphrodite   B.organism   C.abyssal zone   D.valence bond theory

70. A   A lymphatic capillary that absorbs dietary fats in the villi of the small intestine.
        A.lacteal   B.molecule   C.dna replication   D.neuromuscular junction

71. D   Containing more than two homologous sets of chromosomes.
        A.muon   B.denitrification   C.biomass   D.polyploidy

72. D   The variety of life in the world or in a particular habitat or ecosystem.
        A.pollination   B.biotechnology   C.electron transport chain   D.biodiversity

73. C   Any organism whose cells contain a nucleus and other organelles enclosed within membranes.
        A.molecule   B.aerobic   C.eukaryote   D.blastocyst

74. B   A group of animals that have no backbone, unlike animals such as reptiles, amphibians, fish, birds
        and mammals who all have a backbone.
        A.valence bond theory   B.invertebrate   C.endergonic reaction   D.phenotype

75. A   a plant hormone.
        A.abscisic acid   B.dehydration reaction   C.electron transport chain   D.biomedical research

76. B   The system of immune responses of an organism against its own healthy cells and tissues.
        A.valence shell   B.autoimmunity   C.asexual reproduction   D.plasmolysis

77. D   An atom or molecule with a net electric charge due to the loss or gain of one or more electrons.
        A.phenotype   B.muon   C.gene   D.ion

78. C   A branch of molecular biology, biochemistry, and biophysics concerned with the molecular structure
        of biological macromolecules, especially proteins and nucleic acids.
        A.lipid   B.electron transport chain   C.structural biology   D.dna replication

79. B   A large molecule, or macromolecule, composed of many repeated subunits.
        A.aerobic   B.polymer   C.species   D.nucleotide

80. C   Also known as selective breeding.
        A.lipid   B.organism   C.artificial selection   D.chemical equilibrium

81. C   Catalysis in living systems. In biological processes, natural catalysts, such as protein enzymes,
        perform chemical transformations on organic compounds.
        A.biomedical research   B.bacteria   C.biocatalysts   D.pollination

82. A   An individual animal, plant, or single-celled life form.
     A.organism B.mast cell C.muon D.cell membrane

83. B   The preying of one animal on others.
     A.abyssal zone B.predation C.eukaryote D.wobble base pair

84. B   A biological agent that reproduces inside the cells of living hosts.
     A.dna sequencing B.virus C.mast cell D.endotherm

85. D   The decoding of genetic instructions for making proteins.
     A.valence bond theory B.pheromone C.reproduction D.translation

86. D   A chemical substance produced and released into the environment by an animal, especially a
     mammal or an insect, affecting the behavior or physiology of others of its species.
     A.biodiversity B.eukaryote C.species D.pheromone

87. B   Stands for ribonucleic acid. It is an important molecule with long chains of nucleotides. A
     nucleotide contains a nitrogenous base, a ribose sugar, and a phosphate.
     A.aerobic B.rna C.herpetology D.zygote

88. A   An animal that is dependent on or capable of the internal generation of heat; a warm
     A.endotherm B.pollination C.estrogen D.ecological niche

89. D   The subfield of biology that studies the evolutionary processes that produced the diversity of life on
     Earth starting from a single origin of life.
     A.isomer B.lipid C.molecular biology D.evolutionary biology

90. A   A chemical synapse formed by the contact between a motor neuron and a muscle fiber.
     A.neuromuscular junction B.vegetative reproduction C.eukaryote D.plasmolysis

91. C   A molecule with the same chemical formula as another molecule, but with a different chemical
     structure.
     A.deoxyribonucleic acid B.polygene C.isomer D.population genetics

92. C   The genetic contribution of an individual to the next generation's gene pool relative to the average
     for the population.
     A.chemical kinetics B.dna replication C.darwinian fitness D.parallel evolution

93. D   A plant that grows harmlessly upon another plant and derives its moisture and nutrients from the
     air, rain, and sometimes from debris accumulating around it.
     A.endergonic reaction B.muon C.water potential D.epiphyte

94. A   The primary female sex hormone. It is responsible for the development and regulation of the
     female reproductive system and secondary sex characteristics.
     A.estrogen B.molecular biology C.reproduction D.hermaphrodite

95. C   An unstable subatomic particle. Among all known unstable subatomic particles, only the neutron
     (lasting around 15 minutes) and some atomic nuclei have a longer decay lifetime.
     A.molecular biology B.autoimmunity C.muon D.endosperm

96. B   A gene whose individual effect on a phenotype is too small to be observed, but which can act
     together with others to produce observable variation.
     A.polyploidy B.polygene C.chemical equilibrium D.estrogen

97. B   The set of observable characteristics of an individual resulting from the interaction of its genotype
     with the environment.
     A.species B.phenotype C.endosperm D.vestigiality

98. D   The spectrum of electromagnetic radiation that has passed through a medium that absorbed radiation of certain wavelengths.
A.asexual reproduction   B.evolutionary biology   C.population genetics   D.absorption spectrum

99. B   Evolution on a scale of separated gene pools. Studies focus on change that occurs at or above the level of species, in contrast with microevolution.
A.dalton   B.macroevolution   C.urea   D.bile

100. D   An epithelial tissue that secretes mucus and that lines many body cavities and tubular organs including the gut and respiratory passages.
A.dna replication   B.invertebrate   C.chemical kinetics   D.mucous membrane

From the words provided for each clue, provide the letter of the word which best matches the clue.

101. A   The semipermeable membrane surrounding the cytoplasm of a cell.
A.cell membrane   B.population ecology   C.enantiomer   D.insulin

102. D   The study and analysis of the patterns, causes, and effects of health and disease conditions in defined populations.
A.hermaphrodite   B.macromolecule   C.cell membrane   D.epidemiology

103. A   The scientific study of organisms in the ocean or other marine bodies of water.
A.marine biology   B.predation   C.electron donor   D.parasitology

104. C   a plant hormone.
A.cell membrane   B.endotherm   C.abscisic acid   D.hadron

105. C   The study of the microscopic anatomy of cells and tissues of plants and animals.
A.structural biology   B.dehydration reaction   C.histology   D.valence shell

106. A   A form of terrestrial locomotion where an organism moves by means of its two rear limbs or legs.
A.bipedal   B.enantiomer   C.immunogloblin   D.biology

107. D   Usually defined as a chemical reaction that involves the loss of a water molecule from the reacting molecule.
A.meson   B.endodermis   C.enantiomer   D.dehydration reaction

108. A   A biochemical assembly that contains both proteins and lipids, bound to the proteins, which allow fats to move through the water inside and outside cells.
A.lipoprotein   B.macromolecule   C.mass balance   D.neuron

109. A   A steroid hormone from the androgen group and is found in humans and other vertebrates.
A.testosterone   B.epistasis   C.neuron   D.macromolecule

110. A   The study of insects.
A.entomology   B.nucleotide   C.electromagnetic spectrum   D.neuromuscular junction

111. D   The branch of zoology concerned with reptiles and amphibians.
A.asexual reproduction   B.denaturation   C.acid precipitation   D.herpetology

112. D   A sub-field of ecology that deals with the dynamics of species populations and how these populations interact with the environment.
A.population genetics   B.mass balance   C.endemic species   D.population ecology

113. A   The scientific analysis and study of interactions among organisms and their environment. It is an interdisciplinary field that includes biology, geography and Earth science.
A.ecology   B.insulin   C.genetics   D.polymerase chain reaction

114. C   An unstable subatomic particle. Among all known unstable subatomic particles, only the neutron (lasting around 15 minutes) and some atomic nuclei have a longer decay lifetime.
A.founder effect   B.bipedal   C.muon   D.eukaryote

115. D   Refers to two solutions having the same osmotic pressure across a semipermeable membrane.
A.endodermis   B.denaturation   C.effector cell   D.isotonic solution

116. A   The electrons in the outermost occupied shell (or shells) determine the chemical properties of the atom; it is called the valence shell.
A.valence shell   B.genetics   C.structural biology   D.active site

117. C   An irregularly shaped region within the cell of a prokaryote that contains all or most of the genetic material, called gonophore.
A.biology   B.aerobic   C.nucleoid   D.valence electron

118. B   Study of living organisms.
A.valence band   B.biology   C.electrochemical gradient   D.vestigiality

119. C   A gradient of electrochemical potential, usually for an ion that can move across a membrane.
A.isotonic solution   B.histology   C.electrochemical gradient   D.hermaphrodite

120. A   The reduced genetic diversity that results when a population is descended from a small number of colonizing ancestors.
A.founder effect   B.cell membrane   C.vegetative reproduction   D.genetics

121. D   The application of engineering principles and design concepts to medicine and biology for healthcare purposes (e.g. diagnostic or therapeutic).
A.immunogloblin   B.endocrine system   C.abscission   D.biomedical engineering

122. D   Each of several hierarchical levels in an ecosystem, comprising organisms that share the same function in the food chain and the same nutritional relationship.
A.bioenergetics   B.dehydration reaction   C.marine biology   D.trophic level

123. C   Any of the elongated contractile threads found in striated muscle cells.
A.valence band   B.neuron   C.myofibril   D.incomplete dominance

124. B   An ecological niche is the role and position a species has in its environment; how it meets its needs for food and shelter, how it survives, and how it reproduces.
A.histology   B.ecological niche   C.macromolecule   D.hermaphrodite

125. B   The intersection of the three medians of the triangle (each median connecting a vertex with the midpoint of the opposite side).
A.vestigiality   B.centroid   C.darwinian fitness   D.endotherm

126. C   The study of parasites, their hosts, and the relationship between them.
A.food chain   B.hydrocarbon   C.parasitology   D.antibiotic

127. B   A chemical substance produced and released into the environment by an animal, especially a mammal or an insect, affecting the behavior or physiology of others of its species.
A.egg   B.pheromone   C.biomedical engineering   D.effector

128. C   A molecule that can be bonded to other identical molecules to form a polymer.
A.histology   B.predation   C.monomer   D.organism

129. B The study of genetic variation within populations, and involves the examination and modeling of changes in the frequencies of genes and alleles.
A.biomedical engineering B.population genetics C.macromolecule D.aerobic

130. D The third phase of mitosis, the process that separates duplicated genetic material carried in the nucleus of a parent cell into two identical daughter cells.
A.aerobic B.food chain C.valence band D.metaphase

131. A The preying of one animal on others.
A.predation B.genetics C.genetic code D.epistasis

132. D A class of drug used to kill bacteria.
A.neuromuscular junction B.ecological niche C.denaturation D.antibiotic

133. B Also known as antibodies, They act as a critical part of the immune response by specifically recognizing and binding to particular antigens, and aiding in their destruction.
A.endocytosis B.immungloblin C.darwinian fitness D.ectotherm

134. B A branch of molecular biology, biochemistry, and biophysics concerned with the molecular structure of biological macromolecules, especially proteins and nucleic acids.
A.metaphase B.structural biology C.organism D.nucleolus

135. C Virus that infects and multiplies within bacteria.
A.active site B.abscisic acid C.bacteriophage D.electromagnetic spectrum

136. C Depending on free oxygen or air.
A.acid precipitation B.insulin C.aerobic D.organism

137. D An inner layer of cells in the cortex of a root and of some stems, surrounding a vascular bundle.
A.gene B.darwinian fitness C.aerobic D.endodermis

138. C The study of the transformation of energy in living organisms.
A.gene B.darwinian fitness C.bioenergetics D.atom

139. D An enzyme that catalyzes the formation of cyclic AMP from ATP.
A.synthetic biology B.muon C.amino acid D.adenylate cyclase

140. A The ecological state of a species being unique to a defined geographic location, such as an island, nation, country or other defined zone, or habitat type.
A.endemic species B.amino acid C.incomplete dominance D.nucleoid

141. D One of the four main nucleobases found in the nucleic acids DNA and RNA, the others being adenine, cytosine, and thymine.
A.darwinian fitness B.abscisic acid C.biomedical research D.guanine

142. A Stereoisomers that are non-superimposable mirror images. A molecule with 1 chiral carbon atom exists as 2 stereoisomers termed enantiomers.
A.enantiomer B.valence band C.electrochemical gradient D.acid precipitation

143. A Organism with both male and female reproductive organs.
A.hermaphrodite B.endocytosis C.darwinian fitness D.genetics

144. C The highest range of electron energies in which electrons are normally present at absolute zero temperature.
A.mass balance B.muon C.valence band D.founder effect

145. C   The collection of glands that produce hormones that regulate metabolism, growth and development, tissue function, sexual function, reproduction, sleep, and mood.
A.embryology   B.vegetative reproduction   C.endocrine system   D.cell membrane

146. A   A gene is a locus (or region) of DNA that encodes a functional RNA or protein product, and is the molecular unit of heredity.
A.gene   B.hydrocarbon   C.vegetative reproduction   D.mass density

147. C   A class of organic compounds containing an amino group and a carboxylic acid group
A.hydrocarbon   B.antibiotic   C.amino acid   D.parasitology

148. D   An electrically excitable cell that processes and transmits information through electrical and chemical signals.
A.nucleic acid   B.muon   C.lipoprotein   D.neuron

149. B   The site of oxidative phosphorylation in eukaryotes.
A.founder effect   B.electron transport chain   C.hermaphrodite   D.biomedical engineering

150. D   The female reproductive cell (gamete) in oogamous organisms.
A.chemical equilibrium   B.basal body   C.vestigiality   D.egg

151. A   A organism in which internal physiological sources of heat are of relatively small or quite negligible importance in controlling body temperature. "Cold blooded".
A.ectotherm   B.founder effect   C.bacteriophage   D.mass balance

152. A   The part of an enzyme or antibody where the chemical reaction occurs
A.active site   B.biology   C.thymine   D.cell membrane

153. D   An organ or cell that acts in response to a stimulus.
A.egg   B.structural biology   C.biomedical research   D.effector

154. A   Refers to genetically determined structures or attributes that have apparently lost most or all of their ancestral function in a given species.
A.vestigiality   B.ecological niche   C.neuron   D.electron donor

155. D   A small dense spherical structure in the nucleus of a cell during interphase.
A.vestigiality   B.myofibril   C.isotonic solution   D.nucleolus

156. B   An electron that is associated with an atom, and that can participate in the formation of a chemical bond.
A.denaturation   B.valence electron   C.active site   D.effector cell

157. A   A very large molecule, such as protein, commonly created by polymerization of smaller subunits (monomers).
A.macromolecule   B.herpetology   C.active site   D.aerobic

158. D   An individual animal, plant, or single-celled life form.
A.meson   B.epistasis   C.neuron   D.organism

159. D   An application of conservation of mass to the analysis of physical systems.
A.endotherm   B.histology   C.hydrocarbon   D.mass balance

160. A   Single-cell microscopic organisms which lack a true nucleus. They represent one of the three domains.
A.bacteria   B.ecological niche   C.effector cell   D.centroid

161. A   The state in which both reactants and products are present in concentrations which have no further tendency to change with time.
A.chemical equilibrium   B.insulin   C.bioenergetics   D.electrochemical gradient

162. D   Helps keep blood sugar level from getting too high (hyperglycemia) or too low (hypoglycemia).
A.epistasis   B.electromagnetic spectrum   C.immunogloblin   D.insulin

163. D   A complex organic substance present in living cells, especially DNA or RNA, whose molecules consist of many nucleotides linked in a long chain.
A.binary fission   B.ecology   C.cell membrane   D.nucleic acid

164. A   Process of reproduction involving a single parent that results in offspring that are genetically identical to the parent.
A.asexual reproduction   B.gene   C.valence shell   D.myofibril

165. D   Density is mass per volume.
A.binary fission   B.vegetative reproduction   C.lipoprotein   D.mass density

166. B   A form of active transport in which a cell transports molecules (such as proteins) into the cell (endo
A.epistasis   B.endocytosis   C.chemical equilibrium   D.electron transport chain

167. D   The nucleotide triplets of DNA and RNA molecules that carry genetic information in living cells.
A.predation   B.synthetic biology   C.embryology   D.genetic code

168. A   A process by which the contents of a cell vacuole are released to the exterior through fusion of the vacuole membrane with the cell membrane.
A.exocytosis   B.parasitology   C.epistasis   D.nucleotide

169. A   Plasma cells, also called plasma B cells, plasmocytes, plasmacytes, or effector B cells, are white blood cells that secrete large volumes of antibodies.
A.effector cell   B.electron transport chain   C.genetic code   D.exocytosis

170. B   An interdisciplinary branch of biology and engineering.
A.structural biology   B.synthetic biology   C.histology   D.adenylate cyclase

171. B   A hierarchical series of organisms each dependent on the next as a source of food.
A.centroid   B.food chain   C.population genetics   D.abscisic acid

172. B   The pursuit of answers to medical questions. These investigations lead to discoveries, which in turn lead to the development of new preventions, therapies and cures.
A.endocytosis   B.biomedical research   C.cell membrane   D.herpetology

173. C   The genetic contribution of an individual to the next generation's gene pool relative to the average for the population.
A.population genetics   B.exocytosis   C.darwinian fitness   D.vestigiality

174. B   Shedding of flowers and leaves and fruit following formation of scar tissue in a plant.
A.macromolecule   B.abscission   C.exocytosis   D.adenylate cyclase

175. C   A chemical synapse formed by the contact between a motor neuron and a muscle fiber.
A.embryology   B.population genetics   C.neuromuscular junction   D.endotherm

176. C   A form of intermediate inheritance in which one allele for a specific trait is not completely expressed over its paired allele.
A.genetics   B.binary fission   C.incomplete dominance   D.food chain

177. A   Any particle that is made from quarks, anti
A.hadron   B.endocrine system   C.herpetology   D.predation

178. D One cell dividing into two identical daughter cells.
A.genetics B.immungloblin C.vegetative reproduction D.binary fission

179. A In organic chemistry, a hydrocarbon is an organic compound consisting entirely of hydrogen and carbon.
A.hydrocarbon B.neuromuscular junction C.structural biology D.population ecology

180. B The smallest component of an element having the chemical properties of the element
A.genetic code B.atom C.parasitology D.endodermis

181. A The deep sea (2000 meters or more) where there is no light.
A.abyssal zone B.adenylate cyclase C.eukaryote D.atom

182. A One of the four nucleobases in the nucleic acid of DNA that are represented by the letters G–C–A–T.
A.thymine B.nucleoid C.founder effect D.embryology

183. C The principle, originated by Gregor Mendel, stating that when two or more characteristics are inherited, individual hereditary factors assort independently.
A.genetic code B.population genetics C.independent assortment D.lipoprotein

184. C A harmless pill, medicine, or procedure prescribed more for the psychological benefit to the patient than for any physiological effect.
A.meson B.vegetative reproduction C.placebo D.macromolecule

185. A An electron donor is a chemical entity that donates electrons to another compound.
A.electron donor B.abscission C.antibiotic D.nucleoid

186. D The interaction of genes that are not alleles, in particular the suppression of the effect of one such gene by another.
A.electrochemical gradient B.aerobic C.endoplasmic reticulum D.epistasis

187. C Organic molecules that serve as the monomers, or subunits, of nucleic acids like DNA (deoxyribonucleic acid) and RNA (ribonucleic acid).
A.exocytosis B.endemic species C.nucleotide D.biomedical research

188. B A technique used in molecular biology to amplify a single copy or a few copies of a piece of DNA across several orders of magnitude.
A.electromagnetic spectrum B.polymerase chain reaction C.asexual reproduction
D.testosterone

189. A A process in which proteins or nucleic acids lose the quaternary structure, tertiary structure and secondary structure which is present in their native state.
A.denaturation B.placebo C.histology D.predation

190. C Rain containing acids that form in the atmosphere when industrial gas emissions (especially sulfur dioxide and nitrogen oxides) combine with water.
A.immunogloblin B.molecular biology C.acid precipitation D.exocytosis

191. D The branch of biology that studies the development of gametes (sex cells), fertilization, and development of embryos and fetuses.
A.atom B.antibiotic C.abscisic acid D.embryology

192. D A network of membranous tubules within the cytoplasm of a eukaryotic cell, continuous with the nuclear membrane.
A.mass balance B.embryology C.aerobic D.endoplasmic reticulum

193. C Hadronic subatomic particles composed of one quark and one antiquark, bound together by the strong interaction.
A.bipedal   B.abscission   C.meson   D.food chain

194. A The collective term for all possible frequencies of electromagnetic radiation.
A.electromagnetic spectrum   B.histology   C.testosterone   D.synthetic biology

195. D A form of asexual reproduction of a plant. Only one plant is involved and the offspring is the result of one parent. The new plant is genetically identical to the parent.
A.nucleolus   B.effector   C.aerobic   D.vegetative reproduction

196. A An animal that is dependent on or capable of the internal generation of heat; a warm
A.endotherm   B.biomedical engineering   C.exocytosis   D.valence shell

197. B Any organism whose cells contain a nucleus and other organelles enclosed within membranes.
A.hadron   B.eukaryote   C.isotonic solution   D.independent assortment

198. C An organelle formed from a centriole, and a short cylindrical array of microtubules.
A.nucleotide   B.genetics   C.basal body   D.mass density

199. C The study of heredity
A.abscisic acid   B.nucleoid   C.genetics   D.metaphase

200. C A branch of science concerning biological activity at the molecular level.
A.chemical equilibrium   B.valence shell   C.molecular biology   D.immunogloblin

From the words provided for each clue, provide the letter of the word which best matches the clue.

201. A A lasting attraction between atoms that enables the formation of chemical compounds.
A.chemical bond   B.cryobiology   C.myosin   D.biomass

202. D A branch of zoology that concerns the study of birds.
A.parallel evolution   B.effector   C.vasodilation   D.ornithology

203. A A steroid hormone from the androgen group and is found in humans and other vertebrates.
A.testosterone   B.cell biology   C.nucleobase   D.white blood cell

204. C The intersection of the three medians of the triangle (each median connecting a vertex with the midpoint of the opposite side).
A.ligament   B.gene   C.centroid   D.chemical kinetics

205. B When a nerve or muscle cell is at "rest", its membrane potential is called the resting membrane potential.
A.jejunum   B.membrane potential   C.chemical bond   D.absorption

206. C A cluster (functional group) of nerve cell bodies in a centralized nervous system.
A.parallel evolution   B.chemical compound   C.ganglion   D.chemical equilibrium

207. A Describes the efficiency with which energy is transferred from one trophic level to the next.
A.ecological efficiency   B.species   C.anticodon   D.centroid

208. C A graphical representation designed to show the biomass or bio productivity at each trophic level in a given ecosystem.
A.organ   B.phloem   C.ecological pyramid   D.si units

209. D   The vascular tissue in plants that conducts sugars and other metabolic products downward from the leaves.
A.jejunum   B.insulin   C.cell biology   D.phloem

210. B   The study and discussion of chemical reactions with respect to reaction rates, effect of various variables, re
A.transfer rna   B.chemical kinetics   C.chemical equilibrium   D.nucleobase

211. A   A mammalian blastula in which some differentiation of cells has occurred.
A.blastocyst   B.depolarization   C.species   D.reproduction

212. B   RNA consisting of folded molecules that transport amino acids from the cytoplasm of a cell to a ribosome.
A.electron   B.transfer rna   C.gene   D.organ

213. A   A laboratory process that determines the complete DNA sequence of an organism's genome at a single time.
A.whole genome sequencing   B.nucleobase   C.genetic variation   D.valence band

214. B   A form of active transport in which a cell transports molecules (such as proteins) into the cell (endo
A.vegetative reproduction   B.endocytosis   C.b cell   D.placebo

215. C   Any organism whose cells contain a nucleus and other organelles enclosed within membranes.
A.anticodon   B.cell biology   C.eukaryote   D.electron

216. B   A gene is a locus (or region) of DNA that encodes a functional RNA or protein product, and is the molecular unit of heredity.
A.endocytosis   B.gene   C.abyssal zone   D.absorption spectrum

217. B   The vascular tissue in plants that conducts water and dissolved nutrients upward from the root and also helps to form the woody element in the stem.
A.sociobiology   B.xylem   C.reproduction   D.mass density

218. C   Cytosine, Guanine, Adenine (which can be found in DNA and RNA), Thymine (found only in DNA), and Uracil (found only in RNA).
A.genetic variation   B.placebo   C.nucleobase   D.epicotyl

219. C   The branch of biology that studies the effects of low temperatures on living things within Earth's cryosphere or in science.
A.bionics   B.centroid   C.cryobiology   D.arachnology

220. B   An evolutionary theory that explains the origin of eukaryotic cells from prokaryotes.
A.biogeography   B.endosymbiotic theory   C.arachnology   D.nucleobase

221. C   The genetic contribution of an individual to the next generation's gene pool relative to the average for the population.
A.behavioral ecology   B.ganglion   C.darwinian fitness   D.lepton

222. C   A type of cell division that reduces the number of chromosomes in the parent cell by half and produces four gamete cells.
A.histology   B.physiology   C.meiosis   D.endocrine system

223. C   A large molecule, or macromolecule, composed of many repeated subunits.
A.chemical kinetics   B.zoology   C.polymer   D.b cell

224. D   A measure of the tendency of an atom to attract a bonding pair of electrons. The Pauling scale is the most commonly used.
A.depolarization   B.endangered species   C.insulin   D.electronegativity

225. A   A lymphocyte of a type produced or processed by the thymus gland and actively participating in the immune response.
A.t cell   B.biomass   C.lepton   D.ecological efficiency

226. C   A series of chemical reactions used by all aerobic organisms to generate energy through the oxidation of acetyl
A.testosterone   B.abscission   C.krebs cycle   D.cryobiology

227. C   Large biomolecules, or macromolecules, consisting of one or more long chains of amino acid residues.
A.vasodilation   B.abyssal zone   C.protein   D.mass number

228. B   The collection of glands that produce hormones that regulate metabolism, growth and development, tissue function, sexual function, reproduction, sleep, and mood.
A.testosterone   B.endocrine system   C.eukaryote   D.valence

229. B   a part of an organism that is typically self-contained and has a specific vital function, such as the heart or liver in humans.
A.species   B.organ   C.reproduction   D.b cell

230. B   Variation in the relative frequency of different genotypes in a small population, owing to the chance disappearance of particular genes as individuals die or do not reproduce.
A.transfer rna   B.genetic drift   C.active site   D.jejunum

231. B   Often defined as the largest group of organisms in which two individuals are capable of reproducing fertile offspring, typically using sexual reproduction.
A.krebs cycle   B.species   C.genetic variation   D.cell nucleus

232. B   The spectrum of electromagnetic radiation that has passed through a medium that absorbed radiation of certain wavelengths.
A.depolarization   B.absorption spectrum   C.ganglion   D.virus

233. A   An elementary, half-integer spin particle that does not undergo strong interactions.
A.lepton   B.placebo   C.nucleobase   D.depolarization

234. C   A gene whose individual effect on a phenotype is too small to be observed, but which can act together with others to produce observable variation.
A.endocrine system   B.anticodon   C.polygene   D.parallel evolution

235. A   An organ or cell that acts in response to a stimulus.
A.effector   B.vasodilation   C.internal fertilization   D.membrane potential

236. D   Threatened by factors such as habitat loss, hunting, disease and climate change, and usually have declining populations or a very limited range.
A.dalton   B.arachnology   C.genetic drift   D.endangered species

237. B   A harmless pill, medicine, or procedure prescribed more for the psychological benefit to the patient than for any physiological effect.
A.interleukin   B.placebo   C.dna   D.electrochemical gradient

238. C   Plasma cells, also called plasma B cells, plasmocytes, plasmacytes, or effector B cells, are white blood cells that secrete large volumes of antibodies.
A.blastocyst   B.cell biology   C.effector cell   D.jejunum

239. D   Scientific study of spiders, scorpions, pseudo-scorpions, and harvestmen, collectively called arachnids.
A.genetic drift   B.species   C.electron   D.arachnology

240. B Mitosis and cytokinesis together define this phase of an animal cell cycle-the division of the mother cell into two daughter cells, genetically identical to each other and the parent.
A.dalton B.m phase C.chemical equilibrium D.vegetative reproduction

241. B The deep sea (2000 meters or more) where there is no light.
A.arachnology B.abyssal zone C.physiology D.endosymbiotic theory

242. B A gradient of electrochemical potential, usually for an ion that can move across a membrane.
A.ornithology B.electrochemical gradient C.jejunum D.chemical kinetics

243. C The study of the distribution of species and ecosystems in geographic space and through time.
A.reproduction B.krebs cycle C.biogeography D.membrane potential

244. B Variations of genomes between members of species, or between groups of species thriving in different parts of the world as a result of genetic mutation.
A.phenotype B.genetic variation C.physiology D.nucleobase

245. C The total number of protons and neutrons (together known as nucleons) in an atomic nucleus
A.physiology B.abscission C.mass number D.chemical reaction

246. B A biological agent that reproduces inside the cells of living hosts.
A.darwinian fitness B.virus C.si units D.chemical compound

247. D A class of organic compounds containing an amino group and a carboxylic acid group
A.blastocyst B.meiosis C.sociobiology D.amino acid

248. B The branch of biology that relates to the animal kingdom, including the structure, embryology, evolution, classification, habits, and distribution of all animals.
A.dalton B.zoology C.xylem D.epicotyl

249. C The highest range of electron energies in which electrons are normally present at absolute zero temperature.
A.vasodilation B.endocytosis C.valence band D.ligament

250. D Contraction of the protoplast of a plant cell as a result of loss of water from the cell.
A.ecological efficiency B.reproduction C.valence electron D.plasmolysis

251. C Type of lymphocyte in the humeral immunity of the adaptive immune system.
A.organ B.bionics C.b cell D.vacuole

252. A The dilatation of blood vessels, which decreases blood pressure.
A.vasodilation B.eukaryote C.zoology D.electron

253. D The part of an enzyme or antibody where the chemical reaction occurs
A.antibiotic B.organ C.electrochemical gradient D.active site

254. A A field of scientific study that is based on the hypothesis that social behavior has resulted from evolution and attempts to explain and examine social behavior within that context.
A.sociobiology B.xylem C.vasodilation D.transfer rna

255. C An electron that is associated with an atom, and that can participate in the formation of a chemical bond.
A.species B.isotonic solution C.valence electron D.darwinian fitness

256. A The state in which both reactants and products are present in concentrations which have no further tendency to change with time.
A.chemical equilibrium B.vasodilation C.blastocyst D.chemical kinetics

257. A   The branch of biology dealing with the functions and activities of living organisms and their parts, including all physical and chemical processes.
A.physiology   B.chemical equilibrium   C.vacuole   D.vasodilation

258. C   The term used to describe what happens to an ecological community over time.
A.abyssal zone   B.vegetative reproduction   C.ecological succession   D.testosterone

259. B   A membrane-bound organelle which is present in all plant and fungal cells and some protist, animal and bacterial cells.
A.membrane potential   B.vacuole   C.abscission   D.genetic variation

260. B   Usually characterized by a chemical change, and they yield one or more products, which usually have properties different from the reactants
A.sociobiology   B.chemical reaction   C.reproduction   D.lepton

261. A   The study of the microscopic anatomy of cells and tissues of plants and animals.
A.histology   B.mass density   C.epicotyl   D.cryobiology

262. A   Shedding of flowers and leaves and fruit following formation of scar tissue in a plant.
A.abscission   B.blastocyst   C.organ   D.chemical reaction

263. D   The process of reversing the charge across a cell membrane (usually a NEURON), so causing an ACTION POTENTIAL.
A.genetic drift   B.biomass   C.whole genome sequencing   D.depolarization

264. D   Refers to the number of elements to which it can connect.
A.cell membrane   B.placebo   C.arachnology   D.valence

265. D   The smallest particle in a chemical element or compound that has the chemical properties of that element or compound.
A.valence electron   B.absorption   C.ornithology   D.molecule

266. C   A process in which one substance permeates another; a fluid permeates or is dissolved by a liquid or solid.
A.anticodon   B.endocrine system   C.absorption   D.transfer rna

267. B   Organic matter derived from living, or recently living organisms.
A.mass number   B.biomass   C.medulla   D.acclimatization

268. D   The hereditary material in humans and almost all other organisms.
A.medulla   B.genetic drift   C.endangered species   D.dna

269. A   A form of asexual reproduction of a plant. Only one plant is involved and the offspring is the result of one parent. The new plant is genetically identical to the parent.
A.vegetative reproduction   B.protein   C.internal fertilization   D.ecological efficiency

270. B   An organelle formed from a centriole, and a short cylindrical array of microtubules.
A.bionics   B.basal body   C.epicotyl   D.si units

271. D   The region of an embryo or seedling stem above the cotyledon.
A.cryobiology   B.electrochemical gradient   C.acclimatization   D.epicotyl

272. A   Helps keep blood sugar level from getting too high (hyperglycemia) or too low (hypoglycemia).
A.insulin   B.valence electron   C.xylem   D.abyssal zone

273. C   A class of drug used to kill bacteria.
A.cell membrane   B.m phase   C.antibiotic   D.darwinian fitness

274. C   The inactive X chromosome in a female somatic cell, rendered inactive in a process called lionization
A.cell nucleus   B.genetic variation   C.barr body   D.gene

275. A   The study of the evolutionary basis for animal behavior due to ecological pressures.
A.behavioral ecology   B.darwinian fitness   C.valence   D.chemical bond

276. B   Refers to two solutions having the same osmotic pressure across a semipermeable membrane.
A.endocytosis   B.isotonic solution   C.chemical compound   D.interleukin

277. D   A unit of mass (also known as an atomic mass unit, amu), equal to the mass of a hydrogen atom (1.67 x 1024 g).
A.polygene   B.sociobiology   C.membrane potential   D.dalton

278. C   Explains the structure, organization of the organelles they contain, their physiological properties, metabolic processes, signaling pathways, life cycle, and interactions.
A.white blood cell   B.meiosis   C.cell biology   D.histology

279. B   A chemical substance consisting of two or more different chemically bonded chemical elements, with a fixed ratio determining the composition.
A.electrochemical gradient   B.chemical compound   C.chemical reaction   D.ornithology

280. A   The "control room" for the cell. The nucleus gives out all the orders.
A.cell nucleus   B.endocrine system   C.integrative biology   D.ganglion

281. C   A system of physical units-based on the meter, kilogram, second, ampere, kelvin, candela, and mole, together with a set of prefixes.
A.mass number   B.physiology   C.si units   D.vasodilation

282. D   The science of diagnosing and managing plant diseases.
A.endosymbiotic theory   B.anticodon   C.physiology   D.phytopathology

283. A   Fertilization that takes place inside the egg-producing individual.
A.internal fertilization   B.myosin   C.chemical kinetics   D.t cell

284. C   A sequence of three nucleotides forming a unit of genetic code in a transfer RNA molecule, corresponding to a complementary codon in messenger RNA.
A.depolarization   B.effector   C.anticodon   D.histology

285. D   The set of observable characteristics of an individual resulting from the interaction of its genotype with the environment.
A.darwinian fitness   B.nucleobase   C.chemical bond   D.phenotype

286. A   Application of biological methods and systems found in nature to the study and design of engineering systems and modern technology.
A.bionics   B.cell nucleus   C.biomass   D.krebs cycle

287. D   The fibrous connective tissue that connects bones to other bones.
A.absorption spectrum   B.cell membrane   C.vegetative reproduction   D.ligament

288. C   Giving birth to one of its kind, sexually or asexually.
A.jejunum   B.effector cell   C.reproduction   D.amino acid

289. B   Component of the blood that functions in the immune system. Also known as a leukocyte.
A.absorption   B.white blood cell   C.isotonic solution   D.species

290. B   The independent evolution of similar traits, starting from a similar ancestral condition.
A.exon   B.parallel evolution   C.myosin   D.physiology

291. C   A subatomic particle with a negative elementary electric charge.
     A.valence band   B.interleukin   C.electron   D.polygene

292. A   The midsection of the small intestine of many higher vertebrates like mammals, birds, reptiles. It is present between the duodenum and the ileum.
     A.jejunum   B.endangered species   C.whole genome sequencing   D.chemical reaction

293. C   The semipermeable membrane surrounding the cytoplasm of a cell.
     A.chemical bond   B.ecological succession   C.cell membrane   D.nucleobase

294. C   A group of cytokines (secreted proteins and signal molecules) that were first seen to be expressed by white blood cells (leukocytes)
     A.sociobiology   B.medulla   C.interleukin   D.absorption

295. B   Large superfamily of motor proteins that move along actin filaments, while hydrolyzing ATP.
     A.cell membrane   B.myosin   C.electrochemical gradient   D.medulla

296. A   A label frequently used to describe various forms of cross-disciplinary and multitaxon research.
     A.integrative biology   B.membrane potential   C.reproduction   D.abyssal zone

297. B   Density is mass per volume.
     A.dalton   B.mass density   C.cell nucleus   D.isotonic solution

298. B   Adaptation to a new climate (a new temperature or altitude or environment).
     A.behavioral ecology   B.acclimatization   C.centroid   D.vacuole

299. C   Any part of a gene that will become a part of the final mature RNA produced by that gene after introns have been removed by RNA splicing.
     A.active site   B.endocytosis   C.exon   D.chemical kinetics

300. D   The continuation of the spinal cord within the skull, forming the lowest part of the brainstem and containing control centers for the heart and lungs.
     A.valence electron   B.phytopathology   C.active site   D.medulla

Provide the word that best matches each clue.

1. _____ The energy that an atomic system must acquire before a process (such as an emission or reaction) can occur.

2. _____ The genetic contribution of an individual to the next generation's gene pool relative to the average for the population.

3. _____ A network of membranous tubules within the cytoplasm of a eukaryotic cell, continuous with the nuclear membrane.

4. _____ The branch of biology that relates to the animal kingdom, including the structure, embryology, evolution, classification, habits, and distribution of all animals.

5. _____ Threatened by factors such as habitat loss, hunting, disease and climate change, and usually have declining populations or a very limited range.

6. _____ One of the four nucleobases in the nucleic acid of RNA that are represented by the letters A, G, C and U.

7. _____ The four bases found in DNA are adenine, cytosine, guanine and thymine. These four bases are attached to the sugar

8. _____ The study and discussion of chemical reactions with respect to reaction rates, effect of various variables, re

9. _____ An interaction of living things and non-living things in a physical environment.

10. _____ Variations of genomes between members of species, or between groups of species thriving in different parts of the world as a result of genetic mutation.

11. _____ The study of the history of life on Earth as reflected in the fossil record. Fossils are the remains or traces of organisms.

12. _____ The pursuit of answers to medical questions. These investigations lead to discoveries, which in turn lead to the development of new preventions, therapies and cures.

13. _____ A system of physical units-based on the meter, kilogram, second, ampere, kelvin, candela, and mole, together with a set of prefixes.

14. _____ An organelle formed from a centriole, and a short cylindrical array of microtubules.

15. _____ A sequence of three nucleotides forming a unit of genetic code in a transfer RNA molecule, corresponding to a complementary codon in messenger RNA.

16. _____ A molecule with the same chemical formula as another molecule, but with a different chemical structure.

17. _____ Virus that infects and multiplies within bacteria.

18. _____ Any particle that is made from quarks, anti

19. _____ The vascular tissue in plants that conducts sugars and other metabolic products downward from the leaves.

20. _____ The study of insects.

A. Deoxyribonucleic Acid
B. Endangered Species
C. Darwinian Fitness
D. Anticodon
E. Biomedical research
F. Isomer
G. Zoology
H. Chemical kinetics
I. Phloem
J. Genetic Variation
K. SI units
L. Entomology
M. Hadron
N. Basal body
O. Paleontology
P. Endoplasmic Reticulum
Q. Bacteriophage
R. Ecosystem
S. Uracil
T. Activation energy

Provide the word that best matches each clue.

21. _____ Transport of a substance (as a protein or drug) across a cell membrane against the concentration gradient; requires an expenditure of energy

22. _____ A field of scientific study that is based on the hypothesis that social behavior has resulted from evolution and attempts to explain and examine social behavior within that context.

23. _____ a part of an organism that is typically self-contained and has a specific vital function, such as the heart or liver in humans.

24. _____ A chemical reaction in which the standard change in free energy is positive, and energy is absorbed

25. _____ A branch of zoology that concerns the study of birds.

26. _____ A chemical entity that accepts electrons transferred to it from another compound.

27. _____ The inactive X chromosome in a female somatic cell, rendered inactive in a process called lionization

28. _____ The reduced genetic diversity that results when a population is descended from a small number of colonizing ancestors.

29. _____ The study of the chemical elements and compounds necessary for plant growth, plant metabolism and their external supply.

30. _____ Variations of genomes between members of species, or between groups of species thriving in different parts of the world as a result of genetic mutation.

31. _____ A subatomic particle with a negative elementary electric charge.

32. _____ The form of RNA in which genetic information transcribed from DNA as a sequence of bases is transferred to a ribosome.

33. _____ Study of living organisms.

34. _____ The study of plants.

35. _____ Giving birth to one of its kind, sexually or asexually.

36. _____ Any of the elongated contractile threads found in striated muscle cells.

37. _____ A steroidal prohormone of the major insect molting hormone is secreted from the prothoracic glands.

38. _____ A tissue produced inside the seeds of most of the flowering plants around the time of fertilization.

39. _____ A lymphocyte of a type produced or processed by the thymus gland and actively participating in the immune response.

40. _____ Biological molecules (proteins) that act as catalysts and help complex reactions occur everywhere in life.

A. Active Transport   B. Plant Nutrition   C. Ecdysone   D. Organ
E. Messenger RNA   F. Endosperm   G. Barr body   H. Endergonic Reaction
I. Botany   J. Reproduction   K. Enzyme   L. Genetic Variation
M. Founder Effect   N. T Cell   O. Biology   P. Electron Acceptor
Q. Sociobiology   R. Electron   S. Ornithology   T. Myofibril

Provide the word that best matches each clue.

41. _____ Means "falling off at maturity" or "tending to fall off", and it is typically used in order to refer to trees or shrubs that lose their leaves seasonally.

42. _____ An evolutionary theory that explains the origin of eukaryotic cells from prokaryotes.

43. _____ An elementary particle with half-integer spin, that interacts only via the weak subatomic force and gravity. Its mass is tiny compared to other subatomic particles.

44. _____ The smallest particle in a chemical element or compound that has the chemical properties of that element or compound.

45. _____ A cell filled with basophil granules, found in numbers in connective tissue and releasing histamine and other substances during inflammatory and allergic reactions.

46. _____ A series of chemical reactions used by all aerobic organisms to generate energy through the oxidation of acetyl

47. _____ The energy that an atomic system must acquire before a process (such as an emission or reaction) can occur.

48. _____ The branch of biology dealing with the functions and activities of living organisms and their parts, including all physical and chemical processes.

49. _____ A branch of molecular biology, biochemistry, and biophysics concerned with the molecular structure of biological macromolecules, especially proteins and nucleic acids.

50. _____ Component of the blood that functions in the immune system. Also known as a leukocyte.

51. _____ The intersection of the three medians of the triangle (each median connecting a vertex with the midpoint of the opposite side).

52. _____ A lymphocyte of a type produced or processed by the thymus gland and actively participating in the immune response.

53. _____ Work to convert light energy of the Sun into sugars that can be used by cells.

54. _____ The SI unit of measurement used to measure the number of things, usually atoms or molecules.

55. _____ A human embryo after eight weeks of development.

56. _____ An undifferentiated cell of a multicellular organism that is capable of giving rise to indefinitely more cells of the same type.

57. _____ An organelle formed from a centriole, and a short cylindrical array of microtubules.

58. _____ An interdisciplinary science that applies the approaches and methods of physics to study biological systems.

59. _____ The study of insects.

60. _____ A numeric scale used to specify the acidity or basicity (alkalinity) of an aqueous solution. It is roughly the negative of the logarithm to base 10 of the concentration.

A. Krebs Cycle   B. Basal body   C. Chloroplast   D. Activation energy
E. Mole   F. Biophysics   G. Entomology   H. Centroid
I. Structural Biology J. pH   K. Deciduous   L. Neutrino
M. Mast Cell   N. Physiology   O. Stem cell   P. Fetus
Q. Symbiogenesis   R. White Blood Cell S. Molecule   T. T Cell

Provide the word that best matches each clue.

61. _____ A branch of medicine that deals with the prevention, diagnosis and treatment of cancer.

62. _____ The continuation of the spinal cord within the skull, forming the lowest part of the brainstem and containing control centers for the heart and lungs.

63. _____ The application of the principles of biology to the study of physiological, genetic, and developmental mechanisms of behavior in humans and other animals.

64. _____ The nucleotide triplets of DNA and RNA molecules that carry genetic information in living cells.

65. _____ An ecological niche is the role and position a species has in its environment; how it meets its needs for food and shelter, how it survives, and how it reproduces.

66. _____ The study of the microscopic anatomy of cells and tissues of plants and animals.

67. _____ The amount of work needed to move a unit charge from a reference point to a specific point against an electric field.

68. _____ A gene whose individual effect on a phenotype is too small to be observed, but which can act together with others to produce observable variation.

69. _____ The "control room" for the cell. The nucleus gives out all the orders.

70. _____ The highest range of electron energies in which electrons are normally present at absolute zero temperature.

71. _____ Glands that secrete their products, hormones, directly into the blood rather than through a duct.

72. _____ The preying of one animal on others.

73. _____ An individual animal, plant, or single-celled life form.

74. _____ The process of determining the precise order of nucleotides within a DNA molecule.

75. _____ The branch of biology that studies the effects of low temperatures on living things within Earth's cryosphere or in science.

76. _____ The site of oxidative phosphorylation in eukaryotes.

77. _____ Known as Fish Science, is the branch of biology devoted to the study of fish.

78. _____ The genetic contribution of an individual to the next generation's gene pool relative to the average for the population.

79. _____ The study of the transformation of energy in living organisms.

80. _____ A series of chemical reactions used by all aerobic organisms to generate energy through the oxidation of acetyl

A. Ichthyology
B. Electron Transport Chain
C. Darwinian Fitness
D. Electric Potential
E. Oncology
F. Histology
G. Genetic Code
H. Cryobiology
I. Predation
J. Endocrine Gland
K. Valence band
L. Psychobiology
M. Polygene
N. Organism
O. Cell nucleus
P. DNA Sequencing
Q. Ecological Niche
R. Medulla
S. Bioenergetics
T. Krebs Cycle

Provide the word that best matches each clue.

81. _____ Another term for adrenaline.

82. _____ Usually defined as a chemical reaction that involves the loss of a water molecule from the reacting molecule.

83. _____ A threadlike strand of DNA in the cell nucleus that carries the genes in a linear order.

84. _____ Conducted or conducting outwards or away from something (for nerves, the central nervous system; for blood vessels, the organ supplied).

85. _____ Organism which is capable of producing energy through aerobic respiration and then switching to anaerobic respiration depending on the amounts of oxygen.

86. _____ A type of cell division that reduces the number of chromosomes in the parent cell by half and produces four gamete cells.

87. _____ A chemical entity that accepts electrons transferred to it from another compound.

88. _____ A succession of letters that indicate the order of nucleotides within a DNA (using GACT) or RNA (GACU) molecule.

89. _____ Refers to two solutions having the same osmotic pressure across a semipermeable membrane.

90. _____ The process of determining the precise order of nucleotides within a DNA molecule.

91. _____ A laboratory process that determines the complete DNA sequence of an organism's genome at a single time.

92. _____ The "control room" for the cell. The nucleus gives out all the orders.

93. _____ The complete transfer of valence electron(s) between atoms. It is a type of chemical bond that generates two oppositely charged ions.

94. _____ The application of the principles of biology to the study of physiological, genetic, and developmental mechanisms of behavior in humans and other animals.

95. _____ A form of asexual reproduction of a plant. Only one plant is involved and the offspring is the result of one parent. The new plant is genetically identical to the parent.

96. _____ A short branched extension of a nerve cell, along which impulses received from other cells at synapses are transmitted to the cell body

97. _____ In cell biology, an organelle that is the main place where cell microtubules get organized. They occur only in plant and animal cells.

98. _____ The subfield of biology that studies the evolutionary processes that produced the diversity of life on Earth starting from a single origin of life.

99. _____ An ecological niche is the role and position a species has in its environment; how it meets its needs for food and shelter, how it survives, and how it reproduces.

100. _____ The scientific analysis and study of interactions among organisms and their environment. It is an interdisciplinary field that includes biology, geography and Earth science.

A. Meiosis
B. Chromosome
C. Isotonic Solution
D. Dehydration Reaction
E. Whole Genome Sequencing
F. Psychobiology
G. Evolutionary Biology
H. Electron Acceptor
I. Efferent
J. Ecology
K. Vegetative reproduction
L. Centrosome
M. Epinephrine
N. Facultative Anaerobe
O. DNA Sequencing
P. Dendrite
Q. Cell nucleus
R. Nucleic Acid Sequence
S. Ecological Niche
T. Ionic Bond

Provide the word that best matches each clue.

101. _____ A microscopic single

102. _____ A microbially facilitated process of nitrate reduction that may ultimately produce molecular nitrogen.

103. _____ The outermost layer of cells or tissue of an embryo in early development, or the parts derived from this, which include the epidermis, nerve tissue, and nephridia.

104. _____ Sperm units with egg in the open, rather than inside the body of the parents

105. _____ An epithelial tissue that secretes mucus and that lines many body cavities and tubular organs including the gut and respiratory passages.

106. _____ The study of heredity

107. _____ A type of cell division that reduces the number of chromosomes in the parent cell by half and produces four gamete cells.

108. _____ One of the four nucleobases in the nucleic acid of RNA that are represented by the letters A, G, C and U.

109. _____ Variation in the relative frequency of different genotypes in a small population, owing to the chance disappearance of particular genes as individuals die or do not reproduce.

110. _____ An atom or molecule with a net electric charge due to the loss or gain of one or more electrons.

111. _____ A branch of physical science that studies the composition, structure, properties and change of matter.

112. _____ Single-cell microscopic organisms which lack a true nucleus. They represent one of the three domains.

113. _____ A succession of letters that indicate the order of nucleotides within a DNA (using GACT) or RNA (GACU) molecule.

114. _____ A liquid by-product of the body secreted by the kidneys through a process called urination (or micturition) and excreted through the urethra.

115. _____ The deep sea (2000 meters or more) where there is no light.

116. _____ A diploid cell resulting from the fusion of two haploid gametes; a fertilized ovum.

117. _____ The use of living systems and organisms to develop or make products, or "any technological application that uses biological systems, living organisms or derivatives thereof.

118. _____ Catalysis in living systems. In biological processes, natural catalysts, such as protein enzymes, perform chemical transformations on organic compounds.

119. _____ The part of an enzyme or antibody where the chemical reaction occurs

120. _____ The complete transfer of valence electron(s) between atoms. It is a type of chemical bond that generates two oppositely charged ions.

A. Active site	B. Prokaryote	C. Ionic Bond
D. Bacteria	E. Biocatalysts	F. Urine
G. Mucous Membrane	H. Ectoderm	I. Meiosis
J. Genetic Drift	K. Ion	L. Uracil
M. Biotechnology	N. Nucleic Acid Sequence	O. Abyssal zone
P. Denitrification	Q. External Fertilization	R. Genetics
S. Zygote	T. Chemistry	

Provide the word that best matches each clue.

121. _____ Sperm units with egg in the open, rather than inside the body of the parents

122. _____ A subatomic particle with a negative elementary electric charge.

123. _____ The branch of biology that relates to the animal kingdom, including the structure, embryology, evolution, classification, habits, and distribution of all animals.

124. _____ The SI unit of measurement used to measure the number of things, usually atoms or molecules.

125. _____ The study of the structure and function of biological systems by means of the methods of "mechanics."

126. _____ The study and analysis of the patterns, causes, and effects of health and disease conditions in defined populations.

127. _____ Density is mass per volume.

128. _____ A type of microscope that uses a beam of electrons to create an image of the specimen. It is capable of much higher magnifications.

129. _____ The independent evolution of similar traits, starting from a similar ancestral condition.

130. _____ A plant that grows harmlessly upon another plant and derives its moisture and nutrients from the air, rain, and sometimes from debris accumulating around it.

131. _____ a nerve cell (neuron) whose cell body is located in the spinal cord and whose fiber (axon) projects outside the spinal cord to directly or indirectly control effector organs.

132. _____ A chemically defined as a substance that is insoluble in water and soluble in alcohol, ether, and chloroform. The basis for fats and oils.

133. _____ An enzyme that catalyzes the formation of cyclic AMP from ATP.

134. _____ Study of living organisms.

135. _____ Application of biological methods and systems found in nature to the study and design of engineering systems and modern technology.

136. _____ The collective term for all possible frequencies of electromagnetic radiation.

137. _____ A field of scientific study that is based on the hypothesis that social behavior has resulted from evolution and attempts to explain and examine social behavior within that context.

138. _____ A place for animals, people and plants and non-living things

139. _____ The study or practice of pathology with greater emphasis on the biological than on the medical aspects.

140. _____ An evolutionary theory that explains the origin of eukaryotic cells from prokaryotes.

A. Bionics
D. Epiphyte
G. Motor Neuron
J. External Fertilization
M. Mole
P. Epidemiology
S. Electromagnetic Spectrum

B. Electron Microscope
E. Sociobiology
H. Habitat
K. Lipid
N. Symbiogenesis
Q. Electron
T. Parallel Evolution

C. Zoology
F. Biomechanics
I. Adenylate cyclase
L. Biology
O. Pathobiology
R. Mass Density

Provide the word that best matches each clue.

141. _____ The study of the distribution of species and ecosystems in geographic space and through time.

142. _____ Process of reproduction involving a single parent that results in offspring that are genetically identical to the parent.

143. _____ An irregularly shaped region within the cell of a prokaryote that contains all or most of the genetic material, called gonophore.

144. _____ A biochemical assembly that contains both proteins and lipids, bound to the proteins, which allow fats to move through the water inside and outside cells.

145. _____ Contraction of the protoplast of a plant cell as a result of loss of water from the cell.

146. _____ The yellow internal part of a bird's egg, which is surrounded by the white, is rich in protein and fat, and nourishes the developing embryo.

147. _____ The interaction of genes that are not alleles, in particular the suppression of the effect of one such gene by another.

148. _____ The preying of one animal on others.

149. _____ A membrane-bound organelle which is present in all plant and fungal cells and some protist, animal and bacterial cells.

150. _____ A colorless cell which circulates in the blood and body fluids and is involved in counteracting foreign substances and disease; a white (blood) cell.

151. _____ A human embryo after eight weeks of development.

152. _____ Any of the elongated contractile threads found in striated muscle cells.

153. _____ Often defined as the largest group of organisms in which two individuals are capable of reproducing fertile offspring, typically using sexual reproduction.

154. _____ Any member of two classes of chemical compounds derived from carbonic acid or carbon dioxide.

155. _____ A technique used in molecular biology to amplify a single copy or a few copies of a piece of DNA across several orders of magnitude.

156. _____ Refers to the provision of essential nutrients necessary to support human life and health.

157. _____ An inner layer of cells in the cortex of a root and of some stems, surrounding a vascular bundle.

158. _____ A microscopic single

159. _____ An electron that is associated with an atom, and that can participate in the formation of a chemical bond.

160. _____ A form of terrestrial locomotion where an organism moves by means of its two rear limbs or legs.

A. Predation
D. Leukocyte
G. Prokaryote
J. Nucleoid

B. Asexual Reproduction
E. Polymerase Chain Reaction
H. Epistasis
K. Lipoprotein

C. Endodermis
F. Biogeography
I. Vacuole
L. Valence electron

M. Bipedal
P. Carbonate
S. Fetus

N. Myofibril
Q. Species
T. Yolk

O. Human Nutrition
R. Plasmolysis

Provide the word that best matches each clue.

161. _____ Known as Fish Science, is the branch of biology devoted to the study of fish.

162. _____ An enzyme that synthesizes short RNA sequences called primers.

163. _____ Organic molecules that serve as the monomers, or subunits, of nucleic acids like DNA (deoxyribonucleic acid) and RNA (ribonucleic acid).

164. _____ Large biomolecules, or macromolecules, consisting of one or more long chains of amino acid residues.

165. _____ the tendency of a crossbred individual to show qualities superior to those of both parents.

166. _____ The study of the chemical elements and compounds necessary for plant growth, plant metabolism and their external supply.

167. _____ A heterocyclic compound of carbon, nitrogen, oxygen, and hydrogen. It forms ions and salts known as urates and acid urates, such as ammonium acid urate.

168. _____ The spontaneous net movement of solvent molecules through a semi-permeable membrane into a region of higher solute concentration.

169. _____ A gradient of electrochemical potential, usually for an ion that can move across a membrane.

170. _____ The study of heredity

171. _____ Rain containing acids that form in the atmosphere when industrial gas emissions (especially sulfur dioxide and nitrogen oxides) combine with water.

172. _____ The continuation of the spinal cord within the skull, forming the lowest part of the brainstem and containing control centers for the heart and lungs.

173. _____ The practice of cultivating land, growing food, and raising stock.

174. _____ The science of drug action on biological systems.

175. _____ Giving birth to one of its kind, sexually or asexually.

176. _____ The electrons in the outermost occupied shell (or shells) determine the chemical properties of the atom; it is called the valence shell.

177. _____ Describes a genetically distinct geographic variety, population or race within a species, which is adapted to specific environmental conditions.

178. _____ The study of viruses-submicroscopic, parasitic particles of genetic material contained in a protein coat and virus-like agents.

179. _____ The local voltage change across the cell wall as a nerve impulse is transmitted.

180. _____ A lasting attraction between atoms that enables the formation of chemical compounds.

A. Ichthyology
D. Electrochemical Gradient
G. Heterosis
J. Chemical bond
M. Reproduction
P. Uric acid
S. Ecotype

B. Virology
E. Valence shell
H. Primase
K. Agriculture
N. Plant Nutrition
Q. Pharmacology
T. Osmosis

C. Medulla
F. Genetics
I. Action potential
L. Nucleotide
O. Acid precipitation
R. Protein

Provide the word that best matches each clue.

181. _____ A measure of the tendency of an atom to attract a bonding pair of electrons. The Pauling scale is the most commonly used.

182. _____ The first step of gene expression, in which a particular segment of DNA is copied into RNA (mRNA) by the enzyme RNA polymerase.

183. _____ Propagate (an organism or cell) to make an identical copy of.

184. _____ The local voltage change across the cell wall as a nerve impulse is transmitted.

185. _____ A kind of swallowing cell, which means it functions by literally swallowing up other particles or smaller cells.

186. _____ An evolutionary theory that explains the origin of eukaryotic cells from prokaryotes.

187. _____ The branch of biology dealing with the functions and activities of living organisms and their parts, including all physical and chemical processes.

188. _____ A sequence of three nucleotides forming a unit of genetic code in a transfer RNA molecule, corresponding to a complementary codon in messenger RNA.

189. _____ A gene is a locus (or region) of DNA that encodes a functional RNA or protein product, and is the molecular unit of heredity.

190. _____ Refers to genetically determined structures or attributes that have apparently lost most or all of their ancestral function in a given species.

191. _____ A lasting attraction between atoms that enables the formation of chemical compounds.

192. _____ Study of living organisms.

193. _____ Explains the structure, organization of the organelles they contain, their physiological properties, metabolic processes, signaling pathways, life cycle, and interactions.

194. _____ A system of physical units-based on the meter, kilogram, second, ampere, kelvin, candela, and mole, together with a set of prefixes.

195. _____ The branch of biology that deals with classification and nomenclature; taxonomy.

196. _____ Organic matter derived from living, or recently living organisms.

197. _____ The amount of work needed to move a unit charge from a reference point to a specific point against an electric field.

198. _____ The lowest theoretically attainable temperature (at which the kinetic energy of atoms and molecules is minimal)

199. _____ A very large molecule, such as protein, commonly created by polymerization of smaller subunits (monomers).

200. _____ The branch of biology that relates to the animal kingdom, including the structure, embryology, evolution, classification, habits, and distribution of all animals.

A. Electronegativity   B. Electric Potential   C. Cell biology
D. Macrophage   E. Endosymbiotic Theory F. Zoology
G. Chemical bond   H. Gene   I. SI units
J. Action potential   K. Absolute zero   L. Cloning

M. Transcription
N. Biomass
O. Physiology
P. Anticodon
Q. Macromolecule
R. Systematics
S. Vestigiality
T. Biology

Provide the word that best matches each clue.

201. _____ Refers to two solutions having the same osmotic pressure across a semipermeable membrane.

202. _____ Shedding of flowers and leaves and fruit following formation of scar tissue in a plant.

203. _____ A sequence of three nucleotides forming a unit of genetic code in a transfer RNA molecule, corresponding to a complementary codon in messenger RNA.

204. _____ One of the three primary germ layers in the very early human embryo. The other two layers are the ectoderm (outside layer) and mesoderm (middle layer).

205. _____ The branch of biology concerned with the effects of outer space on living organisms and the search for extraterrestrial life

206. _____ A diploid cell resulting from the fusion of two haploid gametes; a fertilized ovum.

207. _____ A label frequently used to describe various forms of cross-disciplinary and multitaxon research.

208. _____ Also known as antibodies, They act as a critical part of the immune response by specifically recognizing and binding to particular antigens, and aiding in their destruction.

209. _____ The branch of biology that studies the development of gametes (sex cells), fertilization, and development of embryos and fetuses.

210. _____ A process by which the contents of a cell vacuole are released to the exterior through fusion of the vacuole membrane with the cell membrane.

211. _____ A chemical substance consisting of two or more different chemically bonded chemical elements, with a fixed ratio determining the composition.

212. _____ Any part of a gene that will become a part of the final mature RNA produced by that gene after introns have been removed by RNA splicing.

213. _____ The application of computer technology to the management of biological information.

214. _____ The set of observable characteristics of an individual resulting from the interaction of its genotype with the environment.

215. _____ Cytosine, Guanine, Adenine (which can be found in DNA and RNA), Thymine (found only in DNA), and Uracil (found only in RNA).

216. _____ Rain containing acids that form in the atmosphere when industrial gas emissions (especially sulfur dioxide and nitrogen oxides) combine with water.

217. _____ The theory that all living things are made up of cells.

218. _____ Any member of two classes of chemical compounds derived from carbonic acid or carbon dioxide.

219. _____ The process of determining the precise order of nucleotides within a DNA molecule.

220. _____ The branch of biology that deals with classification and nomenclature; taxonomy.

A. Bioinformatics   B. Immunogloblin   C. Zygote   D. Nucleobase
E. Phenotype   F. Astrobiology   G. Isotonic Solution H. Cell theory
I. Abscission   J. Systematics   K. Exon   L. Endoderm
M. Embryology   N. Exocytosis   O. Chemical compound P. DNA Sequencing
Q. Integrative Biology R. Acid precipitation S. Anticodon   T. Carbonate

Provide the word that best matches each clue.

221. _____ The theory that all living things are made up of cells.

222. _____ An organelle formed from a centriole, and a short cylindrical array of microtubules.

223. _____ Refers to genetically determined structures or attributes that have apparently lost most or all of their ancestral function in a given species.

224. _____ The science of diagnosing and managing plant diseases.

225. _____ The branch of biology that studies the development of gametes (sex cells), fertilization, and development of embryos and fetuses.

226. _____ A branch of medicine that deals with the prevention, diagnosis and treatment of cancer.

227. _____ The ecological region at the lowest level of a body of water such as an ocean or a lake, including the sediment surface and some sub

228. _____ A complex organic substance present in living cells, especially DNA or RNA, whose molecules consist of many nucleotides linked in a long chain.

229. _____ Variations of genomes between members of species, or between groups of species thriving in different parts of the world as a result of genetic mutation.

230. _____ A process in nature in which organisms possessing certain genotypic characteristics that make them better adjusted to an environment tend to survive.

231. _____ A cell filled with basophil granules, found in numbers in connective tissue and releasing histamine and other substances during inflammatory and allergic reactions.

232. _____ A medical specialty that is concerned with the diagnosis of disease based on the laboratory analysis of bodily fluids such as blood and urine.

233. _____ Any of various molecules that are capable of accepting one or two electrons from one molecule and donating them to another in the process of electron transport.

234. _____ Very large ecological areas on the earth's surface, with fauna and flora (animals and plants) adapting to their environment.

235. _____ Catalysis in living systems. In biological processes, natural catalysts, such as protein enzymes, perform chemical transformations on organic compounds.

236. _____ Means "falling off at maturity" or "tending to fall off", and it is typically used in order to refer to trees or shrubs that lose their leaves seasonally.

237. _____ Organism which is capable of producing energy through aerobic respiration and then switching to anaerobic respiration depending on the amounts of oxygen.

238. _____ Conducted or conducting outwards or away from something (for nerves, the central nervous system; for blood vessels, the organ supplied).

239. _____ Sperm units with egg in the open, rather than inside the body of the parents

240. _____ The branch of biology concerned with the study of fungi, including their genetic and biochemical properties, their taxonomy and their use to humans.

A. Phytopathology   B. Electron Carrier   C. Efferent
D. Oncology   E. Benthic zone   F. Deciduous
G. Embryology   H. Nucleic Acid   I. Mycology
J. Natural Selection   K. Basal body   L. Cell theory
M. Biocatalysts   N. Biome   O. External Fertilization
P. Genetic Variation   Q. Vestigiality   R. Mast Cell
S. Pathology   T. Facultative Anaerobe

Provide the word that best matches each clue.

241. _____ A network of membranous tubules within the cytoplasm of a eukaryotic cell, continuous with the nuclear membrane.

242. _____ The branch of biology concerned with the effects of outer space on living organisms and the search for extraterrestrial life

243. _____ RNA consisting of folded molecules that transport amino acids from the cytoplasm of a cell to a ribosome.

244. _____ Density is mass per volume.

245. _____ Hadronic subatomic particles composed of one quark and one antiquark, bound together by the strong interaction.

246. _____ Usually defined as a chemical reaction that involves the loss of a water molecule from the reacting molecule.

247. _____ An inner layer of cells in the cortex of a root and of some stems, surrounding a vascular bundle.

248. _____ A mammalian blastula in which some differentiation of cells has occurred.

249. _____ The site of oxidative phosphorylation in eukaryotes.

250. _____ The use of living systems and organisms to develop or make products, or "any technological application that uses biological systems, living organisms or derivatives thereof.

251. _____ An organelle formed from a centriole, and a short cylindrical array of microtubules.

252. _____ A branch of science concerning biological activity at the molecular level.

253. _____ The deep sea (2000 meters or more) where there is no light.

254. _____ The midsection of the small intestine of many higher vertebrates like mammals, birds, reptiles. It is present between the duodenum and the ileum.

255. _____ An elementary particle with half-integer spin, that interacts only via the weak subatomic force and gravity. Its mass is tiny compared to other subatomic particles.

256. _____ Biological molecules (proteins) that act as catalysts and help complex reactions occur everywhere in life.

257. _____ The branch of biology dealing with the functions and activities of living organisms and their parts, including all physical and chemical processes.

258. _____ A colorless cell which circulates in the blood and body fluids and is involved in counteracting foreign substances and disease; a white (blood) cell.

259. _____ An enzyme that catalyzes the formation of cyclic AMP from ATP.

260. _____ A complex organic substance present in living cells, especially DNA or RNA, whose molecules consist of many nucleotides linked in a long chain.

A. Leukocyte
D. Blastocyst
G. Mass Density
J. Endodermis
M. Astrobiology
P. Basal body
S. Biotechnology

B. Nucleic Acid
E. Dehydration Reaction
H. Adenylate cyclase
K. Endoplasmic Reticulum
N. Transfer RNA
Q. Enzyme
T. Jejunum

C. Electron Transport Chain
F. Physiology
I. Neutrino
L. Abyssal zone
O. Meson
R. Molecular biology

Provide the word that best matches each clue.

261. _____ Adaptation to a new climate (a new temperature or altitude or environment).

262. _____ A sub-field of ecology that deals with the dynamics of species populations and how these populations interact with the environment.

263. _____ The term used to describe what happens to an ecological community over time.

264. _____ A diploid cell resulting from the fusion of two haploid gametes; a fertilized ovum.

265. _____ A form of intermediate inheritance in which one allele for a specific trait is not completely expressed over its paired allele.

266. _____ Glands that secrete their products, hormones, directly into the blood rather than through a duct.

267. _____ The study of plant nutrition and growth especially as a way to increase crop yield

268. _____ Study of living organisms.

269. _____ The branch of biology that deals with classification and nomenclature; taxonomy.

270. _____ The scientific study of organisms in the ocean or other marine bodies of water.

271. _____ In cell biology, an organelle that is the main place where cell microtubules get organized. They occur only in plant and animal cells.

272. _____ An evolutionary theory that explains the origin of eukaryotic cells from prokaryotes.

273. _____ Any particle that is made from quarks, anti

274. _____ A membrane-bound organelle which is present in all plant and fungal cells and some protist, animal and bacterial cells.

275. _____ A heterocyclic compound of carbon, nitrogen, oxygen, and hydrogen. It forms ions and salts known as urates and acid urates, such as ammonium acid urate.

276. _____ The double helix is unwound and each strand acts as a template for the next strand. Bases are matched to synthesize the new partner strands.

277. _____ A distinct juvenile form many animals undergo before metamorphosis into adults. Animals with indirect development such as insects, amphibians, or cnidarians.

278. _____ The system of immune responses of an organism against its own healthy cells and tissues.

279. _____ A form of active transport in which a cell transports molecules (such as proteins) into the cell (endo

280. _____ The genetic contribution of an individual to the next generation's gene pool relative to the average for the population.

A. Endocytosis
B. DNA Replication
C. Endosymbiotic Theory
D. Darwinian Fitness
E. Acclimatization
F. Larva
G. Population Ecology
H. Autoimmunity
I. Biology
J. Marine Biology
K. Uric acid
L. Vacuole
M. Incomplete Dominance
N. Hadron
O. Endocrine Gland
P. Centrosome
Q. Ecological Succession
R. Zygote
S. Systematics
T. Agrobiology

Provide the word that best matches each clue.

281. _____ Means "falling off at maturity" or "tending to fall off", and it is typically used in order to refer to trees or shrubs that lose their leaves seasonally.

282. _____ Hadronic subatomic particles composed of one quark and one antiquark, bound together by the strong interaction.

283. _____ The process in which a eukaryotic cell nucleus splits in two, followed by division of the parent cell into two daughter cells.

284. _____ A lymphatic capillary that absorbs dietary fats in the villi of the small intestine.

285. _____ A biochemical assembly that contains both proteins and lipids, bound to the proteins, which allow fats to move through the water inside and outside cells.

286. _____ A nucleotide derived from adenosine that occurs in muscle tissue; the major source of energy for cellular reactions.

287. _____ The vascular tissue in plants that conducts water and dissolved nutrients upward from the root and also helps to form the woody element in the stem.

288. _____ A microscopic single

289. _____ A gradient of electrochemical potential, usually for an ion that can move across a membrane.

290. _____ The study of viruses-submicroscopic, parasitic particles of genetic material contained in a protein coat and virus-like agents.

291. _____ The vascular tissue in plants that conducts sugars and other metabolic products downward from the leaves.

292. _____ Known as Fish Science, is the branch of biology devoted to the study of fish.

293. _____ Known as chemical messengers, are endogenous chemicals that enable neurotransmission.

294. _____ A class of organic compounds containing an amino group and a carboxylic acid group

295. _____ A system of physical units-based on the meter, kilogram, second, ampere, kelvin, candela, and mole, together with a set of prefixes.

296. _____ The change in genetic composition of a population over successive generations, which may be caused by natural selection, inbreeding, hybridization, or mutation.

297. _____ An individual animal, plant, or single-celled life form.

298. _____ The site of oxidative phosphorylation in eukaryotes.

299. _____ When two genes are close together on the same chromosome, they do not assort independently.

300. _____ The study of insects.

A. Lacteal   B. Electrochemical Gradient   C. Lipoprotein
D. Deciduous   E. Phloem   F. Electron Transport Chain
G. Amino acid   H. Evolution   I. Prokaryote
J. Ichthyology   K. Adenosine Triphosphate   L. Mitosis
M. Virology   N. Neurotransmitter   O. Meson
P. Organism   Q. Entomology   R. Linked Genes
S. Xylem   T. SI units

Provide the word that best matches each clue.

301. _____ Stands for ribonucleic acid. It is an important molecule with long chains of nucleotides. A nucleotide contains a nitrogenous base, a ribose sugar, and a phosphate.

302. _____ The variety of life in the world or in a particular habitat or ecosystem.

303. _____ Any of various molecules that are capable of accepting one or two electrons from one molecule and donating them to another in the process of electron transport.

304. _____ The red liquid that circulates in the arteries and veins of humans and other vertebrate animals, carrying oxygen to and carbon dioxide from the tissues of the body.

305. _____ A class of drug used to kill bacteria.

306. _____ Fertilization that takes place inside the egg-producing individual.

307. _____ A large molecule, or macromolecule, composed of many repeated subunits.

308. _____ The use of living systems and organisms to develop or make products, or "any technological application that uses biological systems, living organisms or derivatives thereof.

309. _____ Any part of a gene that will become a part of the final mature RNA produced by that gene after introns have been removed by RNA splicing.

310. _____ An animal that is dependent on or capable of the internal generation of heat; a warm

311. _____ The study of plants.

312. _____ The act of transferring pollen grains from the male anther of a flower to the female stigma.

313. _____ Describes a genetically distinct geographic variety, population or race within a species, which is adapted to specific environmental conditions.

314. _____ The spectrum of electromagnetic radiation that has passed through a medium that absorbed radiation of certain wavelengths.

315. _____ The process in which a eukaryotic cell nucleus splits in two, followed by division of the parent cell into two daughter cells.

316. _____ The scientific analysis and study of interactions among organisms and their environment. It is an interdisciplinary field that includes biology, geography and Earth science.

317. _____ A cluster (functional group) of nerve cell bodies in a centralized nervous system.

318. _____ A sequence of three nucleotides forming a unit of genetic code in a transfer RNA molecule, corresponding to a complementary codon in messenger RNA.

319. _____ The energy that an atomic system must acquire before a process (such as an emission or reaction) can occur.

320. _____ An organic lipid molecule that is biosynthesized by all animal cells because it is an essential structural component of all animal cell membranes.

A. Ganglion	B. Biotechnology	C. Absorption spectrum	D. Polymer
E. Ecotype	F. Electron Carrier	G. Endotherm	H. Blood
I. Exon	J. Mitosis	K. Ecology	L. Anticodon
M. Biodiversity	N. Pollination	O. RNA	P. Antibiotic
Q. Cholesterol	R. Botany	S. Internal Fertilization	T. Activation energy

Provide the word that best matches each clue.

321. _____ Type of reproduction in which cells from two parents unite to form the first cell of a new organism.

322. _____ The study of the evolutionary basis for animal behavior due to ecological pressures.

323. _____ A branch of molecular biology, biochemistry, and biophysics concerned with the molecular structure of biological macromolecules, especially proteins and nucleic acids.

324. _____ The ecological state of a species being unique to a defined geographic location, such as an island, nation, country or other defined zone, or habitat type.

325. _____ The branch of biology that studies the effects of low temperatures on living things within Earth's cryosphere or in science.

326. _____ Threatened by factors such as habitat loss, hunting, disease and climate change, and usually have declining populations or a very limited range.

327. _____ The inactive X chromosome in a female somatic cell, rendered inactive in a process called lionization

328. _____ The double helix is unwound and each strand acts as a template for the next strand. Bases are matched to synthesize the new partner strands.

329. _____ The pursuit of answers to medical questions. These investigations lead to discoveries, which in turn lead to the development of new preventions, therapies and cures.

330. _____ Any member of two classes of chemical compounds derived from carbonic acid or carbon dioxide.

331. _____ One of the three primary germ layers in the very early human embryo. The other two layers are the ectoderm (outside layer) and mesoderm (middle layer).

332. _____ A cup-like sac at the beginning of the tubular component of a nephron in the mammalian kidney that performs the first step in the filtration of blood to form urine.

333. _____ A subatomic particle with a negative elementary electric charge.

334. _____ A medical specialty that is concerned with the diagnosis of disease based on the laboratory analysis of bodily fluids such as blood and urine.

335. _____ Also known as a macula adhaerens, is a cell structure specialized for cell to cell adhesion.

336. _____ The study and discussion of chemical reactions with respect to reaction rates, effect of various variables, re

337. _____ A chemical substance consisting of two or more different chemically bonded chemical elements, with a fixed ratio determining the composition.

338. _____ Conducted or conducting outwards or away from something (for nerves, the central nervous system; for blood vessels, the organ supplied).

339. _____ A unit of concentration measuring the number of moles of a solute per liter of solution.

340. _____ The branch of biology that deals with classification and nomenclature; taxonomy.

A. Endemism
E. Desmosome
I. Chemical kinetics
M. Molarity
Q. Endangered Species

B. Cryobiology
F. Biomedical research
J. Pathology
N. Barr body
R. Structural Biology

C. DNA Replication
G. Behavioral ecology
K. Chemical compound
O. Systematics
S. Electron

D. Efferent
H. Carbonate
L. Endoderm
P. Sexual Reproduction
T. Bowmans capsule

Provide the word that best matches each clue.

1. ACTIVATION ENERGY — The energy that an atomic system must acquire before a process (such as an emission or reaction) can occur.

2. DARWINIAN FITNESS — The genetic contribution of an individual to the next generation's gene pool relative to the average for the population.

3. ENDOPLASMIC RETICULUM — A network of membranous tubules within the cytoplasm of a eukaryotic cell, continuous with the nuclear membrane.

4. ZOOLOGY — The branch of biology that relates to the animal kingdom, including the structure, embryology, evolution, classification, habits, and distribution of all animals.

5. ENDANGERED SPECIES — Threatened by factors such as habitat loss, hunting, disease and climate change, and usually have declining populations or a very limited range.

6. URACIL — One of the four nucleobases in the nucleic acid of RNA that are represented by the letters A, G, C and U.

7. DEOXYRIBONUCLEIC ACID — The four bases found in DNA are adenine, cytosine, guanine and thymine. These four bases are attached to the sugar

8. CHEMICAL KINETICS — The study and discussion of chemical reactions with respect to reaction rates, effect of various variables, re

9. ECOSYSTEM — An interaction of living things and non-living things in a physical environment.

10. GENETIC VARIATION — Variations of genomes between members of species, or between groups of species thriving in different parts of the world as a result of genetic mutation.

11. PALEONTOLOGY — The study of the history of life on Earth as reflected in the fossil record. Fossils are the remains or traces of organisms.

12. BIOMEDICAL RESEARCH — The pursuit of answers to medical questions. These investigations lead to discoveries, which in turn lead to the development of new preventions, therapies and cures.

13. SI UNITS — A system of physical units-based on the meter, kilogram, second, ampere, kelvin, candela, and mole, together with a set of prefixes.

14. BASAL BODY — An organelle formed from a centriole, and a short cylindrical array of microtubules.

15. ANTICODON — A sequence of three nucleotides forming a unit of genetic code in a transfer RNA molecule, corresponding to a complementary codon in messenger RNA.

16. ISOMER — A molecule with the same chemical formula as another molecule, but with a different chemical structure.

17. BACTERIOPHAGE — Virus that infects and multiplies within bacteria.

18. HADRON — Any particle that is made from quarks, anti

19. PHLOEM — The vascular tissue in plants that conducts sugars and other metabolic products downward from the leaves.

20. ENTOMOLOGY — The study of insects.

A. Deoxyribonucleic Acid	B. Endangered Species	C. Darwinian Fitness
D. Anticodon	E. Biomedical research	F. Isomer
G. Zoology	H. Chemical kinetics	I. Phloem
J. Genetic Variation	K. SI units	L. Entomology
M. Hadron	N. Basal body	O. Paleontology
P. Endoplasmic Reticulum	Q. Bacteriophage	R. Ecosystem
S. Uracil	T. Activation energy	

Provide the word that best matches each clue.

21. ACTIVE TRANSPORT — Transport of a substance (as a protein or drug) across a cell membrane against the concentration gradient; requires an expenditure of energy

22. SOCIOBIOLOGY — A field of scientific study that is based on the hypothesis that social behavior has resulted from evolution and attempts to explain and examine social behavior within that context.

23. ORGAN — a part of an organism that is typically self-contained and has a specific vital function, such as the heart or liver in humans.

24. ENDERGONIC REACTION — A chemical reaction in which the standard change in free energy is positive, and energy is absorbed

25. ORNITHOLOGY — A branch of zoology that concerns the study of birds.

26. ELECTRON ACCEPTOR — A chemical entity that accepts electrons transferred to it from another compound.

27. BARR BODY — The inactive X chromosome in a female somatic cell, rendered inactive in a process called lionization

28. FOUNDER EFFECT — The reduced genetic diversity that results when a population is descended from a small number of colonizing ancestors.

29. PLANT NUTRITION _____ The study of the chemical elements and compounds necessary for plant growth, plant metabolism and their external supply.

30. GENETIC VARIATION _____ Variations of genomes between members of species, or between groups of species thriving in different parts of the world as a result of genetic mutation.

31. ELECTRON _____ A subatomic particle with a negative elementary electric charge.

32. MESSENGER RNA _____ The form of RNA in which genetic information transcribed from DNA as a sequence of bases is transferred to a ribosome.

33. BIOLOGY _____ Study of living organisms.

34. BOTANY _____ The study of plants.

35. REPRODUCTION _____ Giving birth to one of its kind, sexually or asexually.

36. MYOFIBRIL _____ Any of the elongated contractile threads found in striated muscle cells.

37. ECDYSONE _____ A steroidal prohormone of the major insect molting hormone is secreted from the prothoracic glands.

38. ENDOSPERM _____ A tissue produced inside the seeds of most of the flowering plants around the time of fertilization.

39. T CELL _____ A lymphocyte of a type produced or processed by the thymus gland and actively participating in the immune response.

40. ENZYME _____ Biological molecules (proteins) that act as catalysts and help complex reactions occur everywhere in life.

A. Active Transport   B. Plant Nutrition   C. Ecdysone   D. Organ
E. Messenger RNA   F. Endosperm   G. Barr body   H. Endergonic Reaction
I. Botany   J. Reproduction   K. Enzyme   L. Genetic Variation
M. Founder Effect   N. T Cell   O. Biology   P. Electron Acceptor
Q. Sociobiology   R. Electron   S. Ornithology   T. Myofibril

Provide the word that best matches each clue.

41. DECIDUOUS _____ Means "falling off at maturity" or "tending to fall off", and it is typically used in order to refer to trees or shrubs that lose their leaves seasonally.

42. SYMBIOGENESIS _____ An evolutionary theory that explains the origin of eukaryotic cells from prokaryotes.

43. NEUTRINO — An elementary particle with half-integer spin, that interacts only via the weak subatomic force and gravity. Its mass is tiny compared to other subatomic particles.

44. MOLECULE — The smallest particle in a chemical element or compound that has the chemical properties of that element or compound.

45. MAST CELL — A cell filled with basophil granules, found in numbers in connective tissue and releasing histamine and other substances during inflammatory and allergic reactions.

46. KREBS CYCLE — A series of chemical reactions used by all aerobic organisms to generate energy through the oxidation of acetyl

47. ACTIVATION ENERGY — The energy that an atomic system must acquire before a process (such as an emission or reaction) can occur.

48. PHYSIOLOGY — The branch of biology dealing with the functions and activities of living organisms and their parts, including all physical and chemical processes.

49. STRUCTURAL BIOLOGY — A branch of molecular biology, biochemistry, and biophysics concerned with the molecular structure of biological macromolecules, especially proteins and nucleic acids.

50. WHITE BLOOD CELL — Component of the blood that functions in the immune system. Also known as a leukocyte.

51. CENTROID — The intersection of the three medians of the triangle (each median connecting a vertex with the midpoint of the opposite side).

52. T CELL — A lymphocyte of a type produced or processed by the thymus gland and actively participating in the immune response.

53. CHLOROPLAST — Work to convert light energy of the Sun into sugars that can be used by cells.

54. MOLE — The SI unit of measurement used to measure the number of things, usually atoms or molecules.

55. FETUS — A human embryo after eight weeks of development.

56. STEM CELL — An undifferentiated cell of a multicellular organism that is capable of giving rise to indefinitely more cells of the same type.

57. BASAL BODY — An organelle formed from a centriole, and a short cylindrical array of microtubules.

58. BIOPHYSICS — An interdisciplinary science that applies the approaches and methods of physics to study biological systems.

59. ENTOMOLOGY   The study of insects.

60. PH   A numeric scale used to specify the acidity or basicity (alkalinity) of an aqueous solution. It is roughly the negative of the logarithm to base 10 of the concentration.

A. Krebs Cycle	B. Basal body	C. Chloroplast	D. Activation energy
E. Mole	F. Biophysics	G. Entomology	H. Centroid
I. Structural Biology	J. pH	K. Deciduous	L. Neutrino
M. Mast Cell	N. Physiology	O. Stem cell	P. Fetus
Q. Symbiogenesis	R. White Blood Cell	S. Molecule	T. T Cell

Provide the word that best matches each clue.

61. ONCOLOGY   A branch of medicine that deals with the prevention, diagnosis and treatment of cancer.

62. MEDULLA   The continuation of the spinal cord within the skull, forming the lowest part of the brainstem and containing control centers for the heart and lungs.

63. PSYCHOBIOLOGY   The application of the principles of biology to the study of physiological, genetic, and developmental mechanisms of behavior in humans and other animals.

64. GENETIC CODE   The nucleotide triplets of DNA and RNA molecules that carry genetic information in living cells.

65. ECOLOGICAL NICHE   An ecological niche is the role and position a species has in its environment; how it meets its needs for food and shelter, how it survives, and how it reproduces.

66. HISTOLOGY   The study of the microscopic anatomy of cells and tissues of plants and animals.

67. ELECTRIC POTENTIAL   The amount of work needed to move a unit charge from a reference point to a specific point against an electric field.

68. POLYGENE   A gene whose individual effect on a phenotype is too small to be observed, but which can act together with others to produce observable variation.

69. CELL NUCLEUS   The "control room" for the cell. The nucleus gives out all the orders.

70. VALENCE BAND   The highest range of electron energies in which electrons are normally present at absolute zero temperature.

71. ENDOCRINE GLAND _____ Glands that secrete their products, hormones, directly into the blood rather than through a duct.

72. PREDATION _____ The preying of one animal on others.

73. ORGANISM _____ An individual animal, plant, or single-celled life form.

74. DNA SEQUENCING _____ The process of determining the precise order of nucleotides within a DNA molecule.

75. CRYOBIOLOGY _____ The branch of biology that studies the effects of low temperatures on living things within Earth's cryosphere or in science.

76. ELECTRON TRANSPORT CHAIN _____ The site of oxidative phosphorylation in eukaryotes.

77. ICHTHYOLOGY _____ Known as Fish Science, is the branch of biology devoted to the study of fish.

78. DARWINIAN FITNESS _____ The genetic contribution of an individual to the next generation's gene pool relative to the average for the population.

79. BIOENERGETICS _____ The study of the transformation of energy in living organisms.

80. KREBS CYCLE _____ A series of chemical reactions used by all aerobic organisms to generate energy through the oxidation of acetyl

A. Ichthyology
D. Electric Potential
G. Genetic Code
J. Endocrine Gland
M. Polygene
P. DNA Sequencing
S. Bioenergetics

B. Electron Transport Chain
E. Oncology
H. Cryobiology
K. Valence band
N. Organism
Q. Ecological Niche
T. Krebs Cycle

C. Darwinian Fitness
F. Histology
I. Predation
L. Psychobiology
O. Cell nucleus
R. Medulla

Provide the word that best matches each clue.

81. EPINEPHRINE _____ Another term for adrenaline.

82. DEHYDRATION REACTION _____ Usually defined as a chemical reaction that involves the loss of a water molecule from the reacting molecule.

83. CHROMOSOME _____ A threadlike strand of DNA in the cell nucleus that carries the genes in a linear order.

84. EFFERENT   Conducted or conducting outwards or away from something (for nerves, the central nervous system; for blood vessels, the organ supplied).

85. FACULTATIVE ANAEROBE   Organism which is capable of producing energy through aerobic respiration and then switching to anaerobic respiration depending on the amounts of oxygen.

86. MEIOSIS   A type of cell division that reduces the number of chromosomes in the parent cell by half and produces four gamete cells.

87. ELECTRON ACCEPTOR   A chemical entity that accepts electrons transferred to it from another compound.

88. NUCLEIC ACID SEQUENCE   A succession of letters that indicate the order of nucleotides within a DNA (using GACT) or RNA (GACU) molecule.

89. ISOTONIC SOLUTION   Refers to two solutions having the same osmotic pressure across a semipermeable membrane.

90. DNA SEQUENCING   The process of determining the precise order of nucleotides within a DNA molecule.

91. WHOLE GENOME SEQUENCING   A laboratory process that determines the complete DNA sequence of an organism's genome at a single time.

92. CELL NUCLEUS   The "control room" for the cell. The nucleus gives out all the orders.

93. IONIC BOND   The complete transfer of valence electron(s) between atoms. It is a type of chemical bond that generates two oppositely charged ions.

94. PSYCHOBIOLOGY   The application of the principles of biology to the study of physiological, genetic, and developmental mechanisms of behavior in humans and other animals.

95. VEGETATIVE REPRODUCTION   A form of asexual reproduction of a plant. Only one plant is involved and the offspring is the result of one parent. The new plant is genetically identical to the parent.

96. DENDRITE   A short branched extension of a nerve cell, along which impulses received from other cells at synapses are transmitted to the cell body

97. CENTROSOME _____ In cell biology, an organelle that is the main place where cell microtubules get organized. They occur only in plant and animal cells.

98. EVOLUTIONARY BIOLOGY _____ The subfield of biology that studies the evolutionary processes that produced the diversity of life on Earth starting from a single origin of life.

99. ECOLOGICAL NICHE _____ An ecological niche is the role and position a species has in its environment; how it meets its needs for food and shelter, how it survives, and how it reproduces.

100. ECOLOGY _____ The scientific analysis and study of interactions among organisms and their environment. It is an interdisciplinary field that includes biology, geography and Earth science.

A. Meiosis	B. Chromosome	C. Isotonic Solution
D. Dehydration Reaction	E. Whole Genome Sequencing	F. Psychobiology
G. Evolutionary Biology	H. Electron Acceptor	I. Efferent
J. Ecology	K. Vegetative reproduction	L. Centrosome
M. Epinephrine	N. Facultative Anaerobe	O. DNA Sequencing
P. Dendrite	Q. Cell nucleus	R. Nucleic Acid Sequence
S. Ecological Niche	T. Ionic Bond	

Provide the word that best matches each clue.

101. PROKARYOTE _____ A microscopic single

102. DENITRIFICATION _____ A microbially facilitated process of nitrate reduction that may ultimately produce molecular nitrogen.

103. ECTODERM _____ The outermost layer of cells or tissue of an embryo in early development, or the parts derived from this, which include the epidermis, nerve tissue, and nephridia.

104. EXTERNAL FERTILIZATION Sperm units with egg in the open, rather than inside the body of the parents

105. MUCOUS MEMBRANE _____ An epithelial tissue that secretes mucus and that lines many body cavities and tubular organs including the gut and respiratory passages.

106. GENETICS _____ The study of heredity

107. MEIOSIS _____ A type of cell division that reduces the number of chromosomes in the parent cell by half and produces four gamete cells.

108. URACIL _____ One of the four nucleobases in the nucleic acid of RNA that are represented by the letters A, G, C and U.

109. GENETIC DRIFT _____ Variation in the relative frequency of different genotypes in a small population, owing to the chance disappearance of particular genes as individuals die or do not reproduce.

110. ION _____ An atom or molecule with a net electric charge due to the loss or gain of one or more electrons.

111. CHEMISTRY _____ A branch of physical science that studies the composition, structure, properties and change of matter.

112. BACTERIA _____ Single-cell microscopic organisms which lack a true nucleus. They represent one of the three domains.

113. NUCLEIC ACID SEQUENCE _____ A succession of letters that indicate the order of nucleotides within a DNA (using GACT) or RNA (GACU) molecule.

114. URINE _____ A liquid by-product of the body secreted by the kidneys through a process called urination (or micturition) and excreted through the urethra.

115. ABYSSAL ZONE _____ The deep sea (2000 meters or more) where there is no light.

116. ZYGOTE _____ A diploid cell resulting from the fusion of two haploid gametes; a fertilized ovum.

117. BIOTECHNOLOGY _____ The use of living systems and organisms to develop or make products, or "any technological application that uses biological systems, living organisms or derivatives thereof.

118. BIOCATALYSTS _____ Catalysis in living systems. In biological processes, natural catalysts, such as protein enzymes, perform chemical transformations on organic compounds.

119. ACTIVE SITE _____ The part of an enzyme or antibody where the chemical reaction occurs

120. IONIC BOND _____ The complete transfer of valence electron(s) between atoms. It is a type of chemical bond that generates two oppositely charged ions.

A. Active site	B. Prokaryote	C. Ionic Bond
D. Bacteria	E. Biocatalysts	F. Urine
G. Mucous Membrane	H. Ectoderm	I. Meiosis
J. Genetic Drift	K. Ion	L. Uracil
M. Biotechnology	N. Nucleic Acid Sequence	O. Abyssal zone
P. Denitrification	Q. External Fertilization	R. Genetics
S. Zygote	T. Chemistry	

Provide the word that best matches each clue.

121. EXTERNAL FERTILIZATION — Sperm units with egg in the open, rather than inside the body of the parents

122. ELECTRON — A subatomic particle with a negative elementary electric charge.

123. ZOOLOGY — The branch of biology that relates to the animal kingdom, including the structure, embryology, evolution, classification, habits, and distribution of all animals.

124. MOLE — The SI unit of measurement used to measure the number of things, usually atoms or molecules.

125. BIOMECHANICS — The study of the structure and function of biological systems by means of the methods of "mechanics."

126. EPIDEMIOLOGY — The study and analysis of the patterns, causes, and effects of health and disease conditions in defined populations.

127. MASS DENSITY — Density is mass per volume.

128. ELECTRON MICROSCOPE — A type of microscope that uses a beam of electrons to create an image of the specimen. It is capable of much higher magnifications.

129. PARALLEL EVOLUTION — The independent evolution of similar traits, starting from a similar ancestral condition.

130. EPIPHYTE — A plant that grows harmlessly upon another plant and derives its moisture and nutrients from the air, rain, and sometimes from debris accumulating around it.

131. MOTOR NEURON — a nerve cell (neuron) whose cell body is located in the spinal cord and whose fiber (axon) projects outside the spinal cord to directly or indirectly control effector organs.

132. LIPID — A chemically defined as a substance that is insoluble in water and soluble in alcohol, ether, and chloroform. The basis for fats and oils.

133. ADENYLATE CYCLASE — An enzyme that catalyzes the formation of cyclic AMP from ATP.

134. BIOLOGY — Study of living organisms.

135. BIONICS _____ Application of biological methods and systems found in nature to the study and design of engineering systems and modern technology.

136. ELECTROMAGNETIC SPECTRUM The collective term for all possible frequencies of electromagnetic radiation.

137. SOCIOBIOLOGY _____ A field of scientific study that is based on the hypothesis that social behavior has resulted from evolution and attempts to explain and examine social behavior within that context.

138. HABITAT _____ A place for animals, people and plants and non-living things

139. PATHOBIOLOGY _____ The study or practice of pathology with greater emphasis on the biological than on the medical aspects.

140. SYMBIOGENESIS _____ An evolutionary theory that explains the origin of eukaryotic cells from prokaryotes.

A. Bionics
B. Electron Microscope
C. Zoology
D. Epiphyte
E. Sociobiology
F. Biomechanics
G. Motor Neuron
H. Habitat
I. Adenylate cyclase
J. External Fertilization
K. Lipid
L. Biology
M. Mole
N. Symbiogenesis
O. Pathobiology
P. Epidemiology
Q. Electron
R. Mass Density
S. Electromagnetic Spectrum
T. Parallel Evolution

Provide the word that best matches each clue.

141. BIOGEOGRAPHY _____ The study of the distribution of species and ecosystems in geographic space and through time.

142. ASEXUAL REPRODUCTION _____ Process of reproduction involving a single parent that results in offspring that are genetically identical to the parent.

143. NUCLEOID _____ An irregularly shaped region within the cell of a prokaryote that contains all or most of the genetic material, called gonophore.

144. LIPOPROTEIN _____ A biochemical assembly that contains both proteins and lipids, bound to the proteins, which allow fats to move through the water inside and outside cells.

145. PLASMOLYSIS _____ Contraction of the protoplast of a plant cell as a result of loss of water from the cell.

146. YOLK _____ The yellow internal part of a bird's egg, which is surrounded by the white, is rich in protein and fat, and nourishes the developing embryo.

147. EPISTASIS _____ The interaction of genes that are not alleles, in particular the suppression of the effect of one such gene by another.

148. PREDATION _____ The preying of one animal on others.

149. VACUOLE _____ A membrane-bound organelle which is present in all plant and fungal cells and some protist, animal and bacterial cells.

150. LEUKOCYTE _____ A colorless cell which circulates in the blood and body fluids and is involved in counteracting foreign substances and disease; a white (blood) cell.

151. FETUS _____ A human embryo after eight weeks of development.

152. MYOFIBRIL _____ Any of the elongated contractile threads found in striated muscle cells.

153. SPECIES _____ Often defined as the largest group of organisms in which two individuals are capable of reproducing fertile offspring, typically using sexual reproduction.

154. CARBONATE _____ Any member of two classes of chemical compounds derived from carbonic acid or carbon dioxide.

155. POLYMERASE CHAIN REACTION _____ A technique used in molecular biology to amplify a single copy or a few copies of a piece of DNA across several orders of magnitude.

156. HUMAN NUTRITION _____ Refers to the provision of essential nutrients necessary to support human life and health.

157. ENDODERMIS _____ An inner layer of cells in the cortex of a root and of some stems, surrounding a vascular bundle.

158. PROKARYOTE _____ A microscopic single

159. VALENCE ELECTRON _____ An electron that is associated with an atom, and that can participate in the formation of a chemical bond.

160. BIPEDAL _____ A form of terrestrial locomotion where an organism moves by means of its two rear limbs or legs.

A. Predation
D. Leukocyte
G. Prokaryote
J. Nucleoid

B. Asexual Reproduction
E. Polymerase Chain Reaction
H. Epistasis
K. Lipoprotein

C. Endodermis
F. Biogeography
I. Vacuole
L. Valence electron

M. Bipedal   N. Myofibril   O. Human Nutrition
P. Carbonate   Q. Species   R. Plasmolysis
S. Fetus   T. Yolk

Provide the word that best matches each clue.

161. ICHTHYOLOGY   Known as Fish Science, is the branch of biology devoted to the study of fish.

162. PRIMASE   An enzyme that synthesizes short RNA sequences called primers.

163. NUCLEOTIDE   Organic molecules that serve as the monomers, or subunits, of nucleic acids like DNA (deoxyribonucleic acid) and RNA (ribonucleic acid).

164. PROTEIN   Large biomolecules, or macromolecules, consisting of one or more long chains of amino acid residues.

165. HETEROSIS   the tendency of a crossbred individual to show qualities superior to those of both parents.

166. PLANT NUTRITION   The study of the chemical elements and compounds necessary for plant growth, plant metabolism and their external supply.

167. URIC ACID   A heterocyclic compound of carbon, nitrogen, oxygen, and hydrogen. It forms ions and salts known as urates and acid urates, such as ammonium acid urate.

168. OSMOSIS   The spontaneous net movement of solvent molecules through a semi-permeable membrane into a region of higher solute concentration.

169. ELECTROCHEMICAL GRADIENT   A gradient of electrochemical potential, usually for an ion that can move across a membrane.

170. GENETICS   The study of heredity

171. ACID PRECIPITATION   Rain containing acids that form in the atmosphere when industrial gas emissions (especially sulfur dioxide and nitrogen oxides) combine with water.

172. MEDULLA   The continuation of the spinal cord within the skull, forming the lowest part of the brainstem and containing control centers for the heart and lungs.

173. AGRICULTURE   The practice of cultivating land, growing food, and raising stock.

174. PHARMACOLOGY   The science of drug action on biological systems.

175. REPRODUCTION _____ Giving birth to one of its kind, sexually or asexually.

176. VALENCE SHELL _____ The electrons in the outermost occupied shell (or shells) determine the chemical properties of the atom; it is called the valence shell.

177. ECOTYPE _____ Describes a genetically distinct geographic variety, population or race within a species, which is adapted to specific environmental conditions.

178. VIROLOGY _____ The study of viruses-submicroscopic, parasitic particles of genetic material contained in a protein coat and virus-like agents.

179. ACTION POTENTIAL _____ The local voltage change across the cell wall as a nerve impulse is transmitted.

180. CHEMICAL BOND _____ A lasting attraction between atoms that enables the formation of chemical compounds.

A. Ichthyology
B. Virology
C. Medulla
D. Electrochemical Gradient
E. Valence shell
F. Genetics
G. Heterosis
H. Primase
I. Action potential
J. Chemical bond
K. Agriculture
L. Nucleotide
M. Reproduction
N. Plant Nutrition
O. Acid precipitation
P. Uric acid
Q. Pharmacology
R. Protein
S. Ecotype
T. Osmosis

Provide the word that best matches each clue.

181. ELECTRONEGATIVITY _____ A measure of the tendency of an atom to attract a bonding pair of electrons. The Pauling scale is the most commonly used.

182. TRANSCRIPTION _____ The first step of gene expression, in which a particular segment of DNA is copied into RNA (mRNA) by the enzyme RNA polymerase.

183. CLONING _____ Propagate (an organism or cell) to make an identical copy of.

184. ACTION POTENTIAL _____ The local voltage change across the cell wall as a nerve impulse is transmitted.

185. MACROPHAGE _____ A kind of swallowing cell, which means it functions by literally swallowing up other particles or smaller cells.

186. ENDOSYMBIOTIC THEORY _____ An evolutionary theory that explains the origin of eukaryotic cells from prokaryotes.

187. PHYSIOLOGY _____ The branch of biology dealing with the functions and activities of living organisms and their parts, including all physical and chemical processes.

188. ANTICODON _____ A sequence of three nucleotides forming a unit of genetic code in a transfer RNA molecule, corresponding to a complementary codon in messenger RNA.

189. GENE _____ A gene is a locus (or region) of DNA that encodes a functional RNA or protein product, and is the molecular unit of heredity.

190. VESTIGIALITY _____ Refers to genetically determined structures or attributes that have apparently lost most or all of their ancestral function in a given species.

191. CHEMICAL BOND _____ A lasting attraction between atoms that enables the formation of chemical compounds.

192. BIOLOGY _____ Study of living organisms.

193. CELL BIOLOGY _____ Explains the structure, organization of the organelles they contain, their physiological properties, metabolic processes, signaling pathways, life cycle, and interactions.

194. SI UNITS _____ A system of physical units-based on the meter, kilogram, second, ampere, kelvin, candela, and mole, together with a set of prefixes.

195. SYSTEMATICS _____ The branch of biology that deals with classification and nomenclature; taxonomy.

196. BIOMASS _____ Organic matter derived from living, or recently living organisms.

197. ELECTRIC POTENTIAL _____ The amount of work needed to move a unit charge from a reference point to a specific point against an electric field.

198. ABSOLUTE ZERO _____ The lowest theoretically attainable temperature (at which the kinetic energy of atoms and molecules is minimal)

199. MACROMOLECULE _____ A very large molecule, such as protein, commonly created by polymerization of smaller subunits (monomers).

200. ZOOLOGY _____ The branch of biology that relates to the animal kingdom, including the structure, embryology, evolution, classification, habits, and distribution of all animals.

A. Electronegativity
B. Electric Potential
C. Cell biology
D. Macrophage
E. Endosymbiotic Theory
F. Zoology
G. Chemical bond
H. Gene
I. SI units
J. Action potential
K. Absolute zero
L. Cloning

M. Transcription   N. Biomass   O. Physiology
P. Anticodon   Q. Macromolecule   R. Systematics
S. Vestigiality   T. Biology

Provide the word that best matches each clue.

201. ISOTONIC SOLUTION — Refers to two solutions having the same osmotic pressure across a semipermeable membrane.

202. ABSCISSION — Shedding of flowers and leaves and fruit following formation of scar tissue in a plant.

203. ANTICODON — A sequence of three nucleotides forming a unit of genetic code in a transfer RNA molecule, corresponding to a complementary codon in messenger RNA.

204. ENDODERM — One of the three primary germ layers in the very early human embryo. The other two layers are the ectoderm (outside layer) and mesoderm (middle layer).

205. ASTROBIOLOGY — The branch of biology concerned with the effects of outer space on living organisms and the search for extraterrestrial life

206. ZYGOTE — A diploid cell resulting from the fusion of two haploid gametes; a fertilized ovum.

207. INTEGRATIVE BIOLOGY — A label frequently used to describe various forms of cross-disciplinary and multitaxon research.

208. IMMUNOGLOBLIN — Also known as antibodies, They act as a critical part of the immune response by specifically recognizing and binding to particular antigens, and aiding in their destruction.

209. EMBRYOLOGY — The branch of biology that studies the development of gametes (sex cells), fertilization, and development of embryos and fetuses.

210. EXOCYTOSIS — A process by which the contents of a cell vacuole are released to the exterior through fusion of the vacuole membrane with the cell membrane.

211. CHEMICAL COMPOUND — A chemical substance consisting of two or more different chemically bonded chemical elements, with a fixed ratio determining the composition.

212. EXON — Any part of a gene that will become a part of the final mature RNA produced by that gene after introns have been removed by RNA splicing.

213. BIOINFORMATICS _____ The application of computer technology to the management of biological information.

214. PHENOTYPE _____ The set of observable characteristics of an individual resulting from the interaction of its genotype with the environment.

215. NUCLEOBASE _____ Cytosine, Guanine, Adenine (which can be found in DNA and RNA), Thymine (found only in DNA), and Uracil (found only in RNA).

216. ACID PRECIPITATION _____ Rain containing acids that form in the atmosphere when industrial gas emissions (especially sulfur dioxide and nitrogen oxides) combine with water.

217. CELL THEORY _____ The theory that all living things are made up of cells.

218. CARBONATE _____ Any member of two classes of chemical compounds derived from carbonic acid or carbon dioxide.

219. DNA SEQUENCING _____ The process of determining the precise order of nucleotides within a DNA molecule.

220. SYSTEMATICS _____ The branch of biology that deals with classification and nomenclature; taxonomy.

A. Bioinformatics   B. Immunogloblin   C. Zygote   D. Nucleobase
E. Phenotype   F. Astrobiology   G. Isotonic Solution   H. Cell theory
I. Abscission   J. Systematics   K. Exon   L. Endoderm
M. Embryology   N. Exocytosis   O. Chemical compound   P. DNA Sequencing
Q. Integrative Biology   R. Acid precipitation S. Anticodon   T. Carbonate

Provide the word that best matches each clue.

221. CELL THEORY _____ The theory that all living things are made up of cells.

222. BASAL BODY _____ An organelle formed from a centriole, and a short cylindrical array of microtubules.

223. VESTIGIALITY _____ Refers to genetically determined structures or attributes that have apparently lost most or all of their ancestral function in a given species.

224. PHYTOPATHOLOGY _____ The science of diagnosing and managing plant diseases.

225. EMBRYOLOGY _____ The branch of biology that studies the development of gametes (sex cells), fertilization, and development of embryos and fetuses.

226. ONCOLOGY _____ A branch of medicine that deals with the prevention, diagnosis and treatment of cancer.

227. BENTHIC ZONE — The ecological region at the lowest level of a body of water such as an ocean or a lake, including the sediment surface and some sub

228. NUCLEIC ACID — A complex organic substance present in living cells, especially DNA or RNA, whose molecules consist of many nucleotides linked in a long chain.

229. GENETIC VARIATION — Variations of genomes between members of species, or between groups of species thriving in different parts of the world as a result of genetic mutation.

230. NATURAL SELECTION — A process in nature in which organisms possessing certain genotypic characteristics that make them better adjusted to an environment tend to survive.

231. MAST CELL — A cell filled with basophil granules, found in numbers in connective tissue and releasing histamine and other substances during inflammatory and allergic reactions.

232. PATHOLOGY — A medical specialty that is concerned with the diagnosis of disease based on the laboratory analysis of bodily fluids such as blood and urine.

233. ELECTRON CARRIER — Any of various molecules that are capable of accepting one or two electrons from one molecule and donating them to another in the process of electron transport.

234. BIOME — Very large ecological areas on the earth's surface, with fauna and flora (animals and plants) adapting to their environment.

235. BIOCATALYSTS — Catalysis in living systems. In biological processes, natural catalysts, such as protein enzymes, perform chemical transformations on organic compounds.

236. DECIDUOUS — Means "falling off at maturity" or "tending to fall off", and it is typically used in order to refer to trees or shrubs that lose their leaves seasonally.

237. FACULTATIVE ANAEROBE — Organism which is capable of producing energy through aerobic respiration and then switching to anaerobic respiration depending on the amounts of oxygen.

238. EFFERENT — Conducted or conducting outwards or away from something (for nerves, the central nervous system; for blood vessels, the organ supplied).

239. EXTERNAL FERTILIZATION — Sperm units with egg in the open, rather than inside the body of the parents

240. MYCOLOGY _____ The branch of biology concerned with the study of fungi, including their genetic and biochemical properties, their taxonomy and their use to humans.

A. Phytopathology	B. Electron Carrier	C. Efferent
D. Oncology	E. Benthic zone	F. Deciduous
G. Embryology	H. Nucleic Acid	I. Mycology
J. Natural Selection	K. Basal body	L. Cell theory
M. Biocatalysts	N. Biome	O. External Fertilization
P. Genetic Variation	Q. Vestigiality	R. Mast Cell
S. Pathology	T. Facultative Anaerobe	

Provide the word that best matches each clue.

241. ENDOPLASMIC RETICULUM _____ A network of membranous tubules within the cytoplasm of a eukaryotic cell, continuous with the nuclear membrane.

242. ASTROBIOLOGY _____ The branch of biology concerned with the effects of outer space on living organisms and the search for extraterrestrial life

243. TRANSFER RNA _____ RNA consisting of folded molecules that transport amino acids from the cytoplasm of a cell to a ribosome.

244. MASS DENSITY _____ Density is mass per volume.

245. MESON _____ Hadronic subatomic particles composed of one quark and one antiquark, bound together by the strong interaction.

246. DEHYDRATION REACTION _____ Usually defined as a chemical reaction that involves the loss of a water molecule from the reacting molecule.

247. ENDODERMIS _____ An inner layer of cells in the cortex of a root and of some stems, surrounding a vascular bundle.

248. BLASTOCYST _____ A mammalian blastula in which some differentiation of cells has occurred.

249. ELECTRON TRANSPORT CHAIN The site of oxidative phosphorylation in eukaryotes.

250. BIOTECHNOLOGY _____ The use of living systems and organisms to develop or make products, or "any technological application that uses biological systems, living organisms or derivatives thereof.

251. BASAL BODY _____ An organelle formed from a centriole, and a short cylindrical array of microtubules.

252. MOLECULAR BIOLOGY _____ A branch of science concerning biological activity at the molecular level.

253. ABYSSAL ZONE _____ The deep sea (2000 meters or more) where there is no light.

254. JEJUNUM _____ The midsection of the small intestine of many higher vertebrates like mammals, birds, reptiles. It is present between the duodenum and the ileum.

255. NEUTRINO _____ An elementary particle with half-integer spin, that interacts only via the weak subatomic force and gravity. Its mass is tiny compared to other subatomic particles.

256. ENZYME _____ Biological molecules (proteins) that act as catalysts and help complex reactions occur everywhere in life.

257. PHYSIOLOGY _____ The branch of biology dealing with the functions and activities of living organisms and their parts, including all physical and chemical processes.

258. LEUKOCYTE _____ A colorless cell which circulates in the blood and body fluids and is involved in counteracting foreign substances and disease; a white (blood) cell.

259. ADENYLATE CYCLASE _____ An enzyme that catalyzes the formation of cyclic AMP from ATP.

260. NUCLEIC ACID _____ A complex organic substance present in living cells, especially DNA or RNA, whose molecules consist of many nucleotides linked in a long chain.

A. Leukocyte
B. Nucleic Acid
C. Electron Transport Chain
D. Blastocyst
E. Dehydration Reaction
F. Physiology
G. Mass Density
H. Adenylate cyclase
I. Neutrino
J. Endodermis
K. Endoplasmic Reticulum
L. Abyssal zone
M. Astrobiology
N. Transfer RNA
O. Meson
P. Basal body
Q. Enzyme
R. Molecular biology
S. Biotechnology
T. Jejunum

Provide the word that best matches each clue.

261. ACCLIMATIZATION _____ Adaptation to a new climate (a new temperature or altitude or environment).

262. POPULATION ECOLOGY _____ A sub-field of ecology that deals with the dynamics of species populations and how these populations interact with the environment.

263. ECOLOGICAL SUCCESSION   The term used to describe what happens to an ecological community over time.

264. ZYGOTE   A diploid cell resulting from the fusion of two haploid gametes; a fertilized ovum.

265. INCOMPLETE DOMINANCE   A form of intermediate inheritance in which one allele for a specific trait is not completely expressed over its paired allele.

266. ENDOCRINE GLAND   Glands that secrete their products, hormones, directly into the blood rather than through a duct.

267. AGROBIOLOGY   The study of plant nutrition and growth especially as a way to increase crop yield

268. BIOLOGY   Study of living organisms.

269. SYSTEMATICS   The branch of biology that deals with classification and nomenclature; taxonomy.

270. MARINE BIOLOGY   The scientific study of organisms in the ocean or other marine bodies of water.

271. CENTROSOME   In cell biology, an organelle that is the main place where cell microtubules get organized. They occur only in plant and animal cells.

272. ENDOSYMBIOTIC THEORY   An evolutionary theory that explains the origin of eukaryotic cells from prokaryotes.

273. HADRON   Any particle that is made from quarks, anti

274. VACUOLE   A membrane-bound organelle which is present in all plant and fungal cells and some protist, animal and bacterial cells.

275. URIC ACID   A heterocyclic compound of carbon, nitrogen, oxygen, and hydrogen. It forms ions and salts known as urates and acid urates, such as ammonium acid urate.

276. DNA REPLICATION   The double helix is unwound and each strand acts as a template for the next strand. Bases are matched to synthesize the new partner strands.

277. LARVA   A distinct juvenile form many animals undergo before metamorphosis into adults. Animals with indirect development such as insects, amphibians, or cnidarians.

278. AUTOIMMUNITY   The system of immune responses of an organism against its own healthy cells and tissues.

279. ENDOCYTOSIS _____ A form of active transport in which a cell transports molecules (such as proteins) into the cell (endo

280. DARWINIAN FITNESS _____ The genetic contribution of an individual to the next generation's gene pool relative to the average for the population.

A. Endocytosis	B. DNA Replication	C. Endosymbiotic Theory
D. Darwinian Fitness	E. Acclimatization	F. Larva
G. Population Ecology	H. Autoimmunity	I. Biology
J. Marine Biology	K. Uric acid	L. Vacuole
M. Incomplete Dominance	N. Hadron	O. Endocrine Gland
P. Centrosome	Q. Ecological Succession	R. Zygote
S. Systematics	T. Agrobiology	

Provide the word that best matches each clue.

281. DECIDUOUS _____ Means "falling off at maturity" or "tending to fall off", and it is typically used in order to refer to trees or shrubs that lose their leaves seasonally.

282. MESON _____ Hadronic subatomic particles composed of one quark and one antiquark, bound together by the strong interaction.

283. MITOSIS _____ The process in which a eukaryotic cell nucleus splits in two, followed by division of the parent cell into two daughter cells.

284. LACTEAL _____ A lymphatic capillary that absorbs dietary fats in the villi of the small intestine.

285. LIPOPROTEIN _____ A biochemical assembly that contains both proteins and lipids, bound to the proteins, which allow fats to move through the water inside and outside cells.

286. ADENOSINE TRIPHOSPHATE _____ A nucleotide derived from adenosine that occurs in muscle tissue; the major source of energy for cellular reactions.

287. XYLEM _____ The vascular tissue in plants that conducts water and dissolved nutrients upward from the root and also helps to form the woody element in the stem.

288. PROKARYOTE _____ A microscopic single

289. ELECTROCHEMICAL GRADIENT A gradient of electrochemical potential, usually for an ion that can move across a membrane.

290. VIROLOGY _____ The study of viruses-submicroscopic, parasitic particles of genetic material contained in a protein coat and virus-like agents.

291. PHLOEM _____ The vascular tissue in plants that conducts sugars and other metabolic products downward from the leaves.

292. ICHTHYOLOGY _____ Known as Fish Science, is the branch of biology devoted to the study of fish.

293. NEUROTRANSMITTER _____ Known as chemical messengers, are endogenous chemicals that enable neurotransmission.

294. AMINO ACID _____ A class of organic compounds containing an amino group and a carboxylic acid group

295. SI UNITS _____ A system of physical units-based on the meter, kilogram, second, ampere, kelvin, candela, and mole, together with a set of prefixes.

296. EVOLUTION _____ The change in genetic composition of a population over successive generations, which may be caused by natural selection, inbreeding, hybridization, or mutation.

297. ORGANISM _____ An individual animal, plant, or single-celled life form.

298. ELECTRON TRANSPORT CHAIN _____ The site of oxidative phosphorylation in eukaryotes.

299. LINKED GENES _____ When two genes are close together on the same chromosome, they do not assort independently.

300. ENTOMOLOGY _____ The study of insects.

A. Lacteal	B. Electrochemical Gradient	C. Lipoprotein
D. Deciduous	E. Phloem	F. Electron Transport Chain
G. Amino acid	H. Evolution	I. Prokaryote
J. Ichthyology	K. Adenosine Triphosphate	L. Mitosis
M. Virology	N. Neurotransmitter	O. Meson
P. Organism	Q. Entomology	R. Linked Genes
S. Xylem	T. SI units	

Provide the word that best matches each clue.

301. RNA _____ Stands for ribonucleic acid. It is an important molecule with long chains of nucleotides. A nucleotide contains a nitrogenous base, a ribose sugar, and a phosphate.

302. BIODIVERSITY _____ The variety of life in the world or in a particular habitat or ecosystem.

303. ELECTRON CARRIER — Any of various molecules that are capable of accepting one or two electrons from one molecule and donating them to another in the process of electron transport.

304. BLOOD — The red liquid that circulates in the arteries and veins of humans and other vertebrate animals, carrying oxygen to and carbon dioxide from the tissues of the body.

305. ANTIBIOTIC — A class of drug used to kill bacteria.

306. INTERNAL FERTILIZATION — Fertilization that takes place inside the egg-producing individual.

307. POLYMER — A large molecule, or macromolecule, composed of many repeated subunits.

308. BIOTECHNOLOGY — The use of living systems and organisms to develop or make products, or "any technological application that uses biological systems, living organisms or derivatives thereof.

309. EXON — Any part of a gene that will become a part of the final mature RNA produced by that gene after introns have been removed by RNA splicing.

310. ENDOTHERM — An animal that is dependent on or capable of the internal generation of heat; a warm

311. BOTANY — The study of plants.

312. POLLINATION — The act of transferring pollen grains from the male anther of a flower to the female stigma.

313. ECOTYPE — Describes a genetically distinct geographic variety, population or race within a species, which is adapted to specific environmental conditions.

314. ABSORPTION SPECTRUM — The spectrum of electromagnetic radiation that has passed through a medium that absorbed radiation of certain wavelengths.

315. MITOSIS — The process in which a eukaryotic cell nucleus splits in two, followed by division of the parent cell into two daughter cells.

316. ECOLOGY — The scientific analysis and study of interactions among organisms and their environment. It is an interdisciplinary field that includes biology, geography and Earth science.

317. GANGLION — A cluster (functional group) of nerve cell bodies in a centralized nervous system.

318. ANTICODON   A sequence of three nucleotides forming a unit of genetic code in a transfer RNA molecule, corresponding to a complementary codon in messenger RNA.

319. ACTIVATION ENERGY   The energy that an atomic system must acquire before a process (such as an emission or reaction) can occur.

320. CHOLESTEROL   An organic lipid molecule that is biosynthesized by all animal cells because it is an essential structural component of all animal cell membranes.

A. Ganglion	B. Biotechnology	C. Absorption spectrum	D. Polymer
E. Ecotype	F. Electron Carrier	G. Endotherm	H. Blood
I. Exon	J. Mitosis	K. Ecology	L. Anticodon
M. Biodiversity	N. Pollination	O. RNA	P. Antibiotic
Q. Cholesterol	R. Botany	S. Internal Fertilization	T. Activation energy

Provide the word that best matches each clue.

321. SEXUAL REPRODUCTION   Type of reproduction in which cells from two parents unite to form the first cell of a new organism.

322. BEHAVIORAL ECOLOGY   The study of the evolutionary basis for animal behavior due to ecological pressures.

323. STRUCTURAL BIOLOGY   A branch of molecular biology, biochemistry, and biophysics concerned with the molecular structure of biological macromolecules, especially proteins and nucleic acids.

324. ENDEMISM   The ecological state of a species being unique to a defined geographic location, such as an island, nation, country or other defined zone, or habitat type.

325. CRYOBIOLOGY   The branch of biology that studies the effects of low temperatures on living things within Earth's cryosphere or in science.

326. ENDANGERED SPECIES   Threatened by factors such as habitat loss, hunting, disease and climate change, and usually have declining populations or a very limited range.

327. BARR BODY   The inactive X chromosome in a female somatic cell, rendered inactive in a process called lionization

328. DNA REPLICATION   The double helix is unwound and each strand acts as a template for the next strand. Bases are matched to synthesize the new partner strands.

329. BIOMEDICAL RESEARCH — The pursuit of answers to medical questions. These investigations lead to discoveries, which in turn lead to the development of new preventions, therapies and cures.

330. CARBONATE — Any member of two classes of chemical compounds derived from carbonic acid or carbon dioxide.

331. ENDODERM — One of the three primary germ layers in the very early human embryo. The other two layers are the ectoderm (outside layer) and mesoderm (middle layer).

332. BOWMANS CAPSULE — A cup-like sac at the beginning of the tubular component of a nephron in the mammalian kidney that performs the first step in the filtration of blood to form urine.

333. ELECTRON — A subatomic particle with a negative elementary electric charge.

334. PATHOLOGY — A medical specialty that is concerned with the diagnosis of disease based on the laboratory analysis of bodily fluids such as blood and urine.

335. DESMOSOME — Also known as a macula adhaerens, is a cell structure specialized for cell to cell adhesion.

336. CHEMICAL KINETICS — The study and discussion of chemical reactions with respect to reaction rates, effect of various variables, re

337. CHEMICAL COMPOUND — A chemical substance consisting of two or more different chemically bonded chemical elements, with a fixed ratio determining the composition.

338. EFFERENT — Conducted or conducting outwards or away from something (for nerves, the central nervous system; for blood vessels, the organ supplied).

339. MOLARITY — A unit of concentration measuring the number of moles of a solute per liter of solution.

340. SYSTEMATICS — The branch of biology that deals with classification and nomenclature; taxonomy.

A. Endemism
B. Cryobiology
C. DNA Replication
D. Efferent
E. Desmosome
F. Biomedical research
G. Behavioral ecology
H. Carbonate
I. Chemical kinetics
J. Pathology
K. Chemical compound
L. Endoderm
M. Molarity
N. Barr body
O. Systematics
P. Sexual Reproduction
Q. Endangered Species
R. Structural Biology
S. Electron
T. Bowmans capsule

1. *Find the hidden words. The words have been placed horizontally, vertically, or diagonally. When you locate a word, draw a circle around it.*

Y	K	W	I	Q	C	A	C	O	E	L	O	M	A	T	E	A	T	N	O
A	B	S	O	L	U	T	E	Z	E	R	O	P	O	L	Y	M	E	R	N
Q	A	B	S	O	R	P	T	I	O	N	S	P	E	C	T	R	U	M	C
B	M	F	B	I	O	I	N	F	O	R	M	A	T	I	C	S	D	Y	O
Q	R	R	Q	G	E	M	E	I	O	S	I	S	M	X	Y	X	E	S	L
Z	K	R	A	U	T	O	I	M	M	U	N	I	T	Y	O	B	C	T	O
O	R	G	A	N	B	C	E	L	L	B	I	P	E	D	A	L	I	E	G
D	M	I	C	R	O	E	V	O	L	U	T	I	O	N	C	A	D	R	Y
A	B	Y	S	S	A	L	Z	O	N	E	J	X	U	S	T	U	U	O	W
A	E	A	W	C	H	O	L	E	S	T	E	R	O	L	M	A	O	I	E
Y	N	E	U	R	O	T	R	A	N	S	M	I	T	T	E	R	U	D	K
E	L	E	C	T	R	I	C	P	O	T	E	N	T	I	A	L	S	E	N

1. The deep sea (2000 meters or more) where there is no light.
2. An organic lipid molecule that is biosynthesized by all animal cells because it is an essential structural component of all animal cell membranes.
3. Means "falling off at maturity" or "tending to fall off", and it is typically used in order to refer to trees or shrubs that lose their leaves seasonally.
4. Animals, like flatworms and jellyfish, that have no body cavity (coelom).
5. A type of cell division that reduces the number of chromosomes in the parent cell by half and produces four gamete cells.
6. The amount of work needed to move a unit charge from a reference point to a specific point against an electric field.
7. An organic compound with four rings arranged in a specific configuration. Examples include the dietary lipid cholesterol and the sex hormones.
8. The lowest theoretically attainable temperature (at which the kinetic energy of atoms and molecules is minimal)
9. A branch of medicine that deals with the prevention, diagnosis and treatment of cancer.
10. A form of terrestrial locomotion where an organism moves by means of its two rear limbs or legs.
11. The spectrum of electromagnetic radiation that has passed through a medium that absorbed radiation of certain wavelengths.
12. The application of computer technology to the management of biological information.
13. Type of lymphocyte in the humeral immunity of the adaptive immune system.
14. Evolutionary change within a species or small group of organisms, especially over a short period.
15. Known as chemical messengers, are endogenous chemicals that enable neurotransmission.
16. A large molecule, or macromolecule, composed of many repeated subunits.
17. The system of immune responses of an organism against its own healthy cells and tissues.
18. Adaptation to a new climate (a new temperature or altitude or environment).
19. a part of an organism that is typically self-contained and has a specific vital function, such as the heart or liver in humans.

A. Cholesterol
B. Bipedal
C. Absolute zero
D. Meiosis
E. Acclimatization
F. Bioinformatics
G. Steroid
H. Absorption spectrum
I. Microevolution
J. Acoelomate
K. Abyssal zone
L. Electric Potential
M. B cell
N. Organ
O. Deciduous
P. Autoimmunity
Q. Polymer
R. Oncology
S. Neurotransmitter

2. *Find the hidden words. The words have been placed horizontally, vertically, or diagonally. When you locate a word, draw a circle around it.*

Z	S	J	E	A	P	M	Y	O	S	I	N	P	L	A	C	E	B	O	I
M	D	E	H	Y	D	R	A	T	I	O	N	R	E	A	C	T	I	O	N
A	N	A	T	O	M	Y	Q	C	E	L	L	M	E	M	B	R	A	N	E
W	G	Q	Y	N	T	A	R	A	C	H	N	O	L	O	G	Y	D	S	U
O	B	W	A	T	E	R	P	O	T	E	N	T	I	A	L	X	B	C	G
C	N	Z	E	K	G	A	M	A	S	S	N	U	M	B	E	R	A	Y	N
W	K	L	D	E	S	T	R	O	G	E	N	E	N	D	E	M	I	S	M
E	L	G	R	O	A	O	S	D	C	E	L	L	T	H	E	O	R	Y	I
D	E	O	X	Y	R	I	B	O	N	U	C	L	E	I	C	A	C	I	D
E	P	I	D	E	M	I	O	L	O	G	Y	Y	B	I	O	M	E	X	W
Z	T	N	S	Y	H	Y	D	R	O	C	A	R	B	O	N	Q	C	C	M
P	D	B	K	W	H	I	T	E	B	L	O	O	D	C	E	L	L	V	F

1. Large superfamily of motor proteins that move along actin filaments, while hydrolyzing ATP.
2. The total number of protons and neutrons (together known as nucleons) in an atomic nucleus
3. Usually defined as a chemical reaction that involves the loss of a water molecule from the reacting molecule.
4. In organic chemistry, a hydrocarbon is an organic compound consisting entirely of hydrogen and carbon.
5. The primary female sex hormone. It is responsible for the development and regulation of the female reproductive system and secondary sex characteristics.
6. A harmless pill, medicine, or procedure prescribed more for the psychological benefit to the patient than for any physiological effect.
7. The study and analysis of the patterns, causes, and effects of health and disease conditions in defined populations.
8. A measure of the potential energy in water as well as the difference between the potential in a given water sample and pure water.
9. Scientific study of spiders, scorpions, pseudo-scorpions, and harvestmen, collectively called arachnids.
10. Very large ecological areas on the earth's surface, with fauna and flora (animals and plants) adapting to their environment.
11. The semipermeable membrane surrounding the cytoplasm of a cell.
12. Component of the blood that functions in the immune system. Also known as a leukocyte.
13. The four bases found in DNA are adenine, cytosine, guanine and thymine. These four bases are attached to the sugar
14. The theory that all living things are made up of cells.
15. The branch of morphology that deals with the structure of animals
16. The ecological state of a species being unique to a defined geographic location, such as an island, nation, country or other defined zone, or habitat type.
17. Refers to the provision of essential nutrients necessary to support human life and health.
18. How your body recognizes and defends itself against bacteria, viruses, and substances that appear foreign and harmful.
19. a nerve cell (neuron) whose cell body is located in the spinal cord and whose fiber (axon) projects outside the spinal cord to directly or indirectly control effector organs.

A. Hydrocarbon
B. Biome
C. Myosin
D. Endemism
E. Arachnology
F. Anatomy
G. Motor Neuron
H. Immune Response
I. Human Nutrition
J. Deoxyribonucleic Acid
K. Cell membrane
L. White Blood Cell
M. Dehydration Reaction
N. Mass Number
O. Cell theory
P. Placebo
Q. Water Potential
R. Epidemiology
S. Estrogen

3. *Find the hidden words. The words have been placed horizontally, vertically, or diagonally. When you locate a word, draw a circle around it.*

P	U	J	J	D	N	A	R	E	P	L	I	C	A	T	I	O	N	B	W
A	E	C	G	U	L	A	R	P	O	L	Y	P	L	O	I	D	Y	R	C
R	F	K	C	H	L	O	R	O	P	L	A	S	T	D	A	L	T	O	N
A	F	E	X	O	N	L	Z	V	X	A	N	T	H	O	P	H	Y	L	L
S	E	Z	H	D	E	N	A	T	U	R	A	T	I	O	N	Y	B	G	
I	C	Y	Q	G	G	K	M	C	E	N	D	O	D	E	R	M	I	S	F
T	T	G	K	K	N	O	E	U	E	X	O	C	Y	T	O	S	I	S	M
O	O	O	X	P	O	A	R	O	M	I	I	I	P	M	J	M	V	Y	D
L	R	T	X	X	U	F	I	L	E	A	N	T	I	C	O	D	O	N	C
O	W	E	S	O	I	O	Z	E	A	B	Y	S	S	A	L	Z	O	N	E
G	Y	L	I	P	O	P	R	O	T	E	I	N	O	H	Y	F	E	U	W
Y	Y	B	I	O	M	E	D	I	C	A	L	R	E	S	E	A	R	C	H

1. A biochemical assembly that contains both proteins and lipids, bound to the proteins, which allow fats to move through the water inside and outside cells.
2. Containing more than two homologous sets of chromosomes.
3. Work to convert light energy of the Sun into sugars that can be used by cells.
4. A membrane-bound organelle which is present in all plant and fungal cells and some protist, animal and bacterial cells.
5. Of or pertaining to the throat.
6. An inner layer of cells in the cortex of a root and of some stems, surrounding a vascular bundle.
7. The pursuit of answers to medical questions. These investigations lead to discoveries, which in turn lead to the development of new preventions, therapies and cures.
8. A process by which the contents of a cell vacuole are released to the exterior through fusion of the vacuole membrane with the cell membrane.
9. A process in which proteins or nucleic acids lose the quaternary structure, tertiary structure and secondary structure which is present in their native state.
10. The double helix is unwound and each strand acts as a template for the next strand. Bases are matched to synthesize the new partner strands.
11. A diploid cell resulting from the fusion of two haploid gametes; a fertilized ovum.
12. The study of parasites, their hosts, and the relationship between them.
13. A unit of mass (also known as an atomic mass unit, amu), equal to the mass of a hydrogen atom (1.67 x 1024 g).
14. The deep sea (2000 meters or more) where there is no light.
15. Component of the blood that functions in the immune system. Also known as a leukocyte.
16. An organ or cell that acts in response to a stimulus.
17. Any part of a gene that will become a part of the final mature RNA produced by that gene after introns have been removed by RNA splicing.
18. The yellow colored photosynthetic pigments.
19. An electron that is associated with an atom, and that can participate in the formation of a chemical bond.
20. A sequence of three nucleotides forming a unit of genetic code in a transfer RNA molecule, corresponding to a complementary codon in messenger RNA.

A. White Blood Cell
E. Parasitology
I. Gular
M. Exon
Q. DNA Replication

B. Anticodon
F. Abyssal zone
J. Lipoprotein
N. Polyploidy
R. Chloroplast

C. Xanthophyll
G. Biomedical research
K. Effector
O. Zygote
S. Vacuole

D. Exocytosis
H. Endodermis
L. Valence electron
P. Denaturation
T. Dalton

4. *Find the hidden words. The words have been placed horizontally, vertically, or diagonally. When you locate a word, draw a circle around it.*

D	N	A	C	P	H	E	R	O	M	O	N	E	J	L	Y	S	J	M	L
F	M	E	M	B	R	A	N	E	P	O	T	E	N	T	I	A	L	L	I
G	E	P	X	M	A	J	J	Q	Q	E	P	L	D	A	L	T	O	N	G
C	N	R	C	O	Z	T	K	I	Z	P	R	E	D	A	T	I	O	N	A
U	A	O	M	A	R	I	N	E	B	I	O	L	O	G	Y	B	Z	P	M
I	N	K	J	A	P	E	L	E	C	T	R	O	N	S	H	E	L	L	E
J	T	A	E	N	Z	S	O	N	U	C	L	E	O	B	A	S	E	A	N
R	I	R	J	Z	C	R	Y	O	B	I	O	L	O	G	Y	E	U	C	T
Y	O	Y	U	C	W	L	I	P	I	D	S	C	Q	F	S	U	R	E	T
D	M	O	N	A	L	A	R	V	A	U	L	F	H	A	N	L	J	B	H
P	E	T	U	L	K	A	E	N	D	O	C	Y	T	O	S	I	S	O	W
Q	R	E	M	M	Y	C	O	L	O	G	Y	X	P	Y	L	Y	I	Q	X

1. The scientific study of organisms in the ocean or other marine bodies of water.
2. The midsection of the small intestine of many higher vertebrates like mammals, birds, reptiles. It is present between the duodenum and the ileum.
3. The fibrous connective tissue that connects bones to other bones.
4. A chemically defined as a substance that is insoluble in water and soluble in alcohol, ether, and chloroform. The basis for fats and oils.
5. An electron shell is the outside part of an atom around the atomic nucleus. It is a group of atomic orbitals with the same value of the principal quantum number n.
6. When a nerve or muscle cell is at "rest", its membrane potential is called the resting membrane potential.
7. Stereoisomers that are non-superimposable mirror images. A molecule with 1 chiral carbon atom exists as 2 stereoisomers termed enantiomers.
8. A distinct juvenile form many animals undergo before metamorphosis into adults. Animals with indirect development such as insects, amphibians, or cnidarians.
9. A chemical substance produced and released into the environment by an animal, especially a mammal or an insect, affecting the behavior or physiology of others of its species.
10. A unit of mass (also known as an atomic mass unit, amu), equal to the mass of a hydrogen atom (1.67 x 1024 g).
11. A microscopic single
12. A harmless pill, medicine, or procedure prescribed more for the psychological benefit to the patient than for any physiological effect.
13. The branch of biology concerned with the study of fungi, including their genetic and biochemical properties, their taxonomy and their use to humans.
14. The branch of biology that studies the effects of low temperatures on living things within Earth's cryosphere or in science.
15. The preying of one animal on others.
16. A form of active transport in which a cell transports molecules (such as proteins) into the cell (endo
17. Cytosine, Guanine, Adenine (which can be found in DNA and RNA), Thymine (found only in DNA), and Uracil (found only in RNA).
18. Also known as antibodies, They act as a critical part of the immune response by specifically recognizing and binding to particular antigens, and aiding in their destruction.
19. The hereditary material in humans and almost all other organisms.

A. Mycology
B. Dalton
C. Ligament
D. Jejunum
E. DNA
F. Pheromone
G. Lipid
H. Electron Shell
I. Endocytosis
J. Membrane Potential
K. Placebo
L. Cryobiology
M. Nucleobase
N. Predation
O. Enantiomer
P. Larva
Q. Prokaryote
R. Marine Biology
S. Immunogloblin

5. *Find the hidden words. The words have been placed horizontally, vertically, or diagonally. When you locate a word, draw a circle around it.*

U	T	E	R	U	S	C	E	L	L	T	H	E	O	R	Y	L	O	N	D
U	K	N	E	U	R	O	N	E	U	M	Y	O	F	I	B	R	I	L	E
D	R	D	H	P	M	A	C	R	O	N	U	T	R	I	E	N	T	U	S
D	E	N	I	T	R	I	F	I	C	A	T	I	O	N	D	X	U	L	M
R	D	G	C	C	L	I	P	O	P	R	O	T	E	I	N	D	W	C	O
C	A	G	R	I	C	U	L	T	U	R	E	A	E	R	O	B	I	C	S
O	C	H	E	M	I	S	T	R	Y	M	O	S	M	O	S	I	S	G	O
O	N	A	T	U	R	A	L	S	E	L	E	C	T	I	O	N	D	B	M
T	P	E	P	H	E	R	M	A	P	H	R	O	D	I	T	E	H	D	E
S	T	E	R	O	I	D	C	H	R	O	M	O	S	O	M	E	T	D	M
L	I	P	I	D	B	I	O	G	E	O	G	R	A	P	H	Y	U	B	Z
E	S	O	W	V	G	E	N	E	T	I	C	C	O	D	E	D	S	A	R

1. Organism with both male and female reproductive organs.
2. Nutrients that provide calories or energy. Nutrients are substances needed for growth, metabolism, and for other body functions.
3. A threadlike strand of DNA in the cell nucleus that carries the genes in a linear order.
4. An electrically excitable cell that processes and transmits information through electrical and chemical signals.
5. The theory that all living things are made up of cells.
6. The practice of cultivating land, growing food, and raising stock.
7. Any of the elongated contractile threads found in striated muscle cells.
8. A branch of physical science that studies the composition, structure, properties and change of matter.
9. The nucleotide triplets of DNA and RNA molecules that carry genetic information in living cells.
10. Depending on free oxygen or air.
11. The study of the distribution of species and ecosystems in geographic space and through time.
12. A biochemical assembly that contains both proteins and lipids, bound to the proteins, which allow fats to move through the water inside and outside cells.
13. A microbially facilitated process of nitrate reduction that may ultimately produce molecular nitrogen.
14. Also known as a macula adhaerens, is a cell structure specialized for cell to cell adhesion.
15. A chemically defined as a substance that is insoluble in water and soluble in alcohol, ether, and chloroform. The basis for fats and oils.
16. An organic compound with four rings arranged in a specific configuration. Examples include the dietary lipid cholesterol and the sex hormones.
17. A process in nature in which organisms possessing certain genotypic characteristics that make them better adjusted to an environment tend to survive.
18. The spontaneous net movement of solvent molecules through a semi-permeable membrane into a region of higher solute concentration.
19. The organ in the lower body of a woman or female mammal where offspring are conceived and in which they gestate before birth; the womb.

A. Denitrification
B. Desmosome
C. Hermaphrodite
D. Genetic Code
E. Cell theory
F. Chromosome
G. Steroid
H. Aerobic
I. Biogeography
J. Neuron
K. Macronutrient
L. Osmosis
M. Chemistry
N. Agriculture
O. Uterus
P. Lipid
Q. Myofibril
R. Natural Selection
S. Lipoprotein

6.

Find the hidden words. The words have been placed horizontally, vertically, or diagonally. When you locate a word, draw a circle around it.

M	P	B	I	O	I	N	F	O	R	M	A	T	I	C	S	J	C	D	T
M	F	O	U	D	M	M	N	A	B	S	O	R	P	T	I	O	N	Z	S
H	T	R	O	X	O	R	C	E	L	L	T	H	E	O	R	Y	B	Q	P
M	D	G	T	C	L	C	E	D	D	U	Q	U	A	R	K	K	T	K	Q
E	G	A	X	F	E	C	E	E	W	A	O	D	O	I	S	X	E	G	G
D	L	N	L	N	F	F	X	S	C	E	L	L	N	U	C	L	E	U	S
W	B	I	O	N	I	C	S	M	X	R	C	G	I	B	R	I	C	A	S
T	C	S	J	O	B	W	J	O	V	O	N	E	C	M	Y	U	A	E	Z
S	R	M	H	E	N	N	U	S	G	B	D	Q	Z	Y	G	O	T	E	W
H	A	B	I	T	A	T	B	O	L	I	P	O	P	R	O	T	E	I	N
E	N	D	O	P	L	A	S	M	I	C	R	E	T	I	C	U	L	U	M
N	M	E	M	B	R	A	N	E	P	O	T	E	N	T	I	A	L	N	M

1. Also known as a macula adhaerens, is a cell structure specialized for cell to cell adhesion.
2. Application of biological methods and systems found in nature to the study and design of engineering systems and modern technology.
3. The "control room" for the cell. The nucleus gives out all the orders.
4. The application of computer technology to the management of biological information.
5. The female reproductive cell (gamete) in oogamous organisms.
6. Depending on free oxygen or air.
7. A process in which one substance permeates another; a fluid permeates or is dissolved by a liquid or solid.
8. The scientific study of nature and of Earth's biodiversity with the aim of protecting species, their habitats, and ecosystems from excessive rates of extinction.
9. An individual animal, plant, or single-celled life form.
10. When a nerve or muscle cell is at "rest", its membrane potential is called the resting membrane potential.
11. A network of membranous tubules within the cytoplasm of a eukaryotic cell, continuous with the nuclear membrane.
12. The SI unit of measurement used to measure the number of things, usually atoms or molecules.
13. An elementary particle and a fundamental constituent of matter; combine to form composite particles called hadrons, the most stable of which are protons and neutrons.
14. The theory that all living things are made up of cells.
15. A group of cytokines (secreted proteins and signal molecules) that were first seen to be expressed by white blood cells (leukocytes)
16. A biochemical assembly that contains both proteins and lipids, bound to the proteins, which allow fats to move through the water inside and outside cells.
17. A diploid cell resulting from the fusion of two haploid gametes; a fertilized ovum.
18. A place for animals, people and plants and non-living things

A. Endoplasmic Reticulum
B. Desmosome
C. Lipoprotein
D. Absorption
E. Habitat
F. Interleukin
G. Bionics
H. Bioinformatics
I. Egg
J. Cell theory
K. Aerobic
L. Conservation Biology
M. Organism
N. Mole
O. Cell nucleus
P. Membrane Potential
Q. Zygote
R. Quark

7. *Find the hidden words. The words have been placed horizontally, vertically, or diagonally. When you locate a word, draw a circle around it.*

H	U	P	H	Y	S	I	O	L	O	G	Y	H	A	D	E	N	I	N	E
Z	X	Y	P	O	J	P	B	F	K	D	E	S	M	O	S	O	M	E	M
Q	R	Q	E	N	R	F	E	T	U	S	E	L	E	M	E	N	T	H	N
I	I	O	N	I	C	B	O	N	D	E	N	T	O	M	O	L	O	G	Y
E	N	D	O	P	L	A	S	M	I	C	R	E	T	I	C	U	L	U	M
V	N	P	K	C	T	R	O	P	H	I	C	L	E	V	E	L	T	R	P
Y	F	E	S	T	R	O	G	E	N	J	V	V	C	E	S	Q	W	M	E
W	U	B	I	O	E	N	G	I	N	E	E	R	I	N	G	E	Z	F	N
K	C	P	Y	S	X	C	E	L	L	T	H	E	O	R	Y	M	C	U	Z
M	B	I	O	M	E	D	I	C	A	L	R	E	S	E	A	R	C	H	Y
D	A	R	W	I	N	I	A	N	F	I	T	N	E	S	S	M	M	H	M
O	N	V	S	L	I	N	K	E	D	G	E	N	E	S	A	C	Z	A	E

1. The complete transfer of valence electron(s) between atoms. It is a type of chemical bond that generates two oppositely charged ions.
2. The genetic contribution of an individual to the next generation's gene pool relative to the average for the population.
3. A network of membranous tubules within the cytoplasm of a eukaryotic cell, continuous with the nuclear membrane.
4. The branch of biology dealing with the functions and activities of living organisms and their parts, including all physical and chemical processes.
5. A human embryo after eight weeks of development.
6. Each of several hierarchical levels in an ecosystem, comprising organisms that share the same function in the food chain and the same nutritional relationship.
7. Also known as a macula adhaerens, is a cell structure specialized for cell to cell adhesion.
8. The theory that all living things are made up of cells.
9. Biological molecules (proteins) that act as catalysts and help complex reactions occur everywhere in life.
10. The pursuit of answers to medical questions. These investigations lead to discoveries, which in turn lead to the development of new preventions, therapies and cures.
11. When two genes are close together on the same chromosome, they do not assort independently.
12. The primary female sex hormone. It is responsible for the development and regulation of the female reproductive system and secondary sex characteristics.
13. The application of concepts and methods of biology to solve real world problems.
14. The study of insects.
15. A species of atoms having the same number of protons in their atomic nuclei (i.e. the same atomic number, Z).
16. One of the two purine nucleobases (the other being guanine) used in forming nucleotides of the nucleic acids.
17. The application of computer technology to the management of biological information.
18. A type of microscope that uses a beam of electrons to create an image of the specimen. It is capable of much higher magnifications.

A. Estrogen
E. Biomedical research
I. Entomology
M. Electron Microscope
Q. Desmosome

B. Bioinformatics
F. Cell theory
J. Fetus
N. Adenine
R. Physiology

C. Element
G. Darwinian Fitness
K. Linked Genes
O. Trophic level

D. Endoplasmic Reticulum
H. Ionic Bond
L. Enzyme
P. Bioengineering

8. *Find the hidden words. The words have been placed horizontally, vertically, or diagonally. When you locate a word, draw a circle around it.*

T	B	D	C	P	L	A	S	M	O	L	Y	S	I	S	R	E	G	E	F
C	R	E	E	D	G	P	M	S	H	U	O	T	K	A	F	S	S	P	C
E	C	O	L	N	G	R	R	F	I	B	I	O	N	I	C	S	C	I	M
O	T	X	L	T	S	O	C	S	P	E	C	I	E	S	A	B	G	S	O
O	N	Y	M	C	U	K	E	M	B	R	Y	O	L	O	G	Y	E	T	L
W	Y	R	Y	E	G	A	H	A	B	S	O	R	P	T	I	O	N	A	A
O	G	I	O	L	V	R	D	E	S	M	O	S	O	M	E	G	O	S	R
B	K	B	S	L	K	Y	G	A	O	T	L	Q	W	P	R	Z	M	I	I
N	W	O	I	J	P	O	L	L	I	N	A	T	I	O	N	B	E	S	T
S	S	S	N	Z	E	T	T	M	E	N	E	U	T	R	I	N	O	X	Y
F	J	E	U	M	V	E	Q	V	S	Z	Q	M	O	N	O	M	E	R	V
X	A	R	T	I	F	I	C	I	A	L	S	E	L	E	C	T	I	O	N

1. Often defined as the largest group of organisms in which two individuals are capable of reproducing fertile offspring, typically using sexual reproduction.
2. Contraction of the protoplast of a plant cell as a result of loss of water from the cell.
3. A lymphocyte of a type produced or processed by the thymus gland and actively participating in the immune response.
4. A process in which one substance permeates another; a fluid permeates or is dissolved by a liquid or solid.
5. Also known as selective breeding.
6. A microscopic single
7. The haploid set of chromosomes in a gamete or microorganism, or in each cell of a multicellular organism.
8. An elementary particle with half-integer spin, that interacts only via the weak subatomic force and gravity. Its mass is tiny compared to other subatomic particles.
9. A molecule that can be bonded to other identical molecules to form a polymer.
10. A monosaccharide. Its name indicates that it is a deoxy sugar, meaning that it is derived from the sugar ribose by loss of an oxygen atom.
11. The interaction of genes that are not alleles, in particular the suppression of the effect of one such gene by another.
12. Large superfamily of motor proteins that move along actin filaments, while hydrolyzing ATP.
13. Also known as a macula adhaerens, is a cell structure specialized for cell to cell adhesion.
14. The collection of glands that produce hormones that regulate metabolism, growth and development, tissue function, sexual function, reproduction, sleep, and mood.
15. Application of biological methods and systems found in nature to the study and design of engineering systems and modern technology.
16. The act of transferring pollen grains from the male anther of a flower to the female stigma.
17. The branch of biology that studies the development of gametes (sex cells), fertilization, and development of embryos and fetuses.
18. The structural and functional unit of all organisms; an autonomous self
19. Rain containing acids that form in the atmosphere when industrial gas emissions (especially sulfur dioxide and nitrogen oxides) combine with water.
20. A unit of concentration measuring the number of moles of a solute per liter of solution.

A. Deoxyribose
F. Myosin
K. Monomer
P. Neutrino

B. Pollination
G. Absorption
L. Genome
Q. Species

C. Embryology
H. Epistasis
M. Prokaryote
R. T Cell

D. Acid precipitation
I. Desmosome
N. Bionics
S. Endocrine System

E. Plasmolysis
J. Cell
O. Molarity
T. Artificial Selection

9. *Find the hidden words. The words have been placed horizontally, vertically, or diagonally. When you locate a word, draw a circle around it.*

A	G	M	B	D	B	I	O	I	N	F	O	R	M	A	T	I	C	S	U
P	P	E	N	G	B	I	O	E	N	G	I	N	E	E	R	I	N	G	S
K	E	S	U	A	S	E	N	A	N	T	I	O	M	E	R	D	T	D	N
C	U	O	C	E	F	F	E	C	T	O	R	C	E	L	L	H	M	P	X
P	T	N	L	N	E	H	I	S	T	O	L	O	G	Y	I	X	T	R	M
L	C	F	E	Z	A	G	R	O	B	I	O	L	O	G	Y	V	W	H	P
A	E	K	O	Y	A	E	R	O	B	I	C	B	O	I	S	O	M	E	R
C	L	B	I	M	O	F	O	R	G	A	N	C	B	O	U	R	E	A	B
E	L	P	D	E	U	O	R	G	A	N	I	S	M	A	S	F	M	U	D
B	Q	D	E	N	I	T	R	I	F	I	C	A	T	I	O	N	M	G	K
O	C	H	E	M	I	C	A	L	R	E	A	C	T	I	O	N	J	X	U
W	L	E	P	T	O	N	I	M	M	U	N	O	G	L	O	B	L	I	N

1. A microbially facilitated process of nitrate reduction that may ultimately produce molecular nitrogen.
2. An irregularly shaped region within the cell of a prokaryote that contains all or most of the genetic material, called gonophore.
3. A lymphocyte of a type produced or processed by the thymus gland and actively participating in the immune response.
4. The study of the microscopic anatomy of cells and tissues of plants and animals.
5. Stereoisomers that are non-superimposable mirror images. A molecule with 1 chiral carbon atom exists as 2 stereoisomers termed enantiomers.
6. An elementary, half-integer spin particle that does not undergo strong interactions.
7. Plasma cells, also called plasma B cells, plasmocytes, plasmacytes, or effector B cells, are white blood cells that secrete large volumes of antibodies.
8. Serves an important role in the metabolism of nitrogen-containing compounds by animals, and is the main nitrogen-containing substance in the urine of mammals.
9. Also known as antibodies, They act as a critical part of the immune response by specifically recognizing and binding to particular antigens, and aiding in their destruction.
10. The study of plant nutrition and growth especially as a way to increase crop yield
11. a part of an organism that is typically self-contained and has a specific vital function, such as the heart or liver in humans.
12. Depending on free oxygen or air.
13. Hadronic subatomic particles composed of one quark and one antiquark, bound together by the strong interaction.
14. The application of concepts and methods of biology to solve real world problems.
15. Usually characterized by a chemical change, and they yield one or more products, which usually have properties different from the reactants
16. Biological molecules (proteins) that act as catalysts and help complex reactions occur everywhere in life.
17. A molecule with the same chemical formula as another molecule, but with a different chemical structure.
18. The application of computer technology to the management of biological information.
19. A harmless pill, medicine, or procedure prescribed more for the psychological benefit to the patient than for any physiological effect.
20. An individual animal, plant, or single-celled life form.

A. Meson
F. T Cell
K. Isomer
P. Bioinformatics

B. Enantiomer
G. Immunogloblin
L. Aerobic
Q. Effector Cell

C. Denitrification
H. Lepton
M. Nucleoid
R. Chemical reaction

D. Agrobiology
I. Organ
N. Bioengineering
S. Placebo

E. Enzyme
J. Organism
O. Urea
T. Histology

10. *Find the hidden words. The words have been placed horizontally, vertically, or diagonally. When you locate a word, draw a circle around it.*

U	T	Z	Y	F	B	I	O	M	A	S	S	W	G	A	E	A	J	H	V
M	A	A	P	H	Y	T	O	P	A	T	H	O	L	O	G	Y	A	X	A
E	L	E	C	T	R	O	N	M	I	C	R	O	S	C	O	P	E	E	S
D	C	D	B	I	O	P	H	Y	S	I	C	S	D	F	N	N	R	C	O
E	A	U	T	O	I	M	M	U	N	I	T	Y	Q	D	J	A	O	T	D
N	S	W	H	I	T	E	B	L	O	O	D	C	E	L	L	O	B	O	I
D	R	N	Z	Q	G	E	F	O	O	D	C	H	A	I	N	B	I	T	L
R	H	O	C	H	E	M	I	C	A	L	B	O	N	D	Z	C	O	H	A
I	S	U	H	Q	I	E	F	F	E	C	T	O	R	C	E	L	L	E	T
T	P	A	T	H	O	B	I	O	L	O	G	Y	F	A	U	Z	O	R	I
E	U	M	E	T	A	P	H	A	S	E	P	R	X	S	V	J	G	M	O
C	H	R	O	M	O	S	O	M	E	V	A	L	E	N	C	E	Y	H	N

1. A hierarchical series of organisms each dependent on the next as a source of food.
2. The study or practice of pathology with greater emphasis on the biological than on the medical aspects.
3. A lasting attraction between atoms that enables the formation of chemical compounds.
4. The study of organic particles, such as bacteria, fungal spores, very small insects, pollen grains and viruses, which are passively transported by the air.
5. An interdisciplinary science that applies the approaches and methods of physics to study biological systems.
6. The science of diagnosing and managing plant diseases.
7. A type of microscope that uses a beam of electrons to create an image of the specimen. It is capable of much higher magnifications.
8. A short branched extension of a nerve cell, along which impulses received from other cells at synapses are transmitted to the cell body
9. Refers to the number of elements to which it can connect.
10. Plasma cells, also called plasma B cells, plasmocytes, plasmacytes, or effector B cells, are white blood cells that secrete large volumes of antibodies.
11. The dilatation of blood vessels, which decreases blood pressure.
12. A threadlike strand of DNA in the cell nucleus that carries the genes in a linear order.
13. A organism in which internal physiological sources of heat are of relatively small or quite negligible importance in controlling body temperature. "Cold blooded".
14. The third phase of mitosis, the process that separates duplicated genetic material carried in the nucleus of a parent cell into two identical daughter cells.
15. The system of immune responses of an organism against its own healthy cells and tissues.
16. Organic matter derived from living, or recently living organisms.
17. Component of the blood that functions in the immune system. Also known as a leukocyte.
18. Giving birth to one of its kind, sexually or asexually.
19. A kind of swallowing cell, which means it functions by literally swallowing up other particles or smaller cells.

A. Electron Microscope
E. Chemical bond
I. Autoimmunity
M. Dendrite
Q. Phytopathology
B. Pathobiology
F. Chromosome
J. Macrophage
N. Vasodilation
R. Aerobiology
C. Biophysics
G. Valence
K. White Blood Cell
O. Effector Cell
S. Reproduction
D. Food Chain
H. Biomass
L. Metaphase
P. Ectotherm

11. *Find the hidden words. The words have been placed horizontally, vertically, or diagonally. When you locate a word, draw a circle around it.*

N	E	D	A	R	W	I	N	I	A	N	F	I	T	N	E	S	S	O	P
S	E	G	L	M	O	L	E	C	U	L	A	R	P	H	Y	S	I	C	S
X	H	E	I	I	Y	E	U	K	A	R	Y	O	T	E	A	M	J	S	S
S	V	N	P	H	F	M	E	Q	A	W	Q	J	J	V	G	W	A	C	F
S	D	O	O	I	R	B	N	L	Y	O	W	M	Q	V	S	J	T	D	N
V	M	M	P	J	M	R	D	U	K	O	V	H	S	F	J	N	O	T	E
D	O	E	R	E	I	Y	O	W	U	D	F	U	M	I	V	C	M	P	U
U	R	U	O	J	T	O	S	Y	U	W	F	E	L	L	I	P	I	D	R
M	H	W	T	U	O	L	P	K	R	E	B	S	C	Y	C	L	E	V	O
X	O	L	E	N	S	O	E	B	A	R	R	B	O	D	Y	K	O	J	N
Z	J	Q	I	U	I	G	R	B	I	O	C	H	E	M	I	S	T	R	Y
P	N	W	N	M	S	Y	M	N	U	C	L	E	I	C	A	C	I	D	B

1. A tissue produced inside the seeds of most of the flowering plants around the time of fertilization.
2. A chemically defined as a substance that is insoluble in water and soluble in alcohol, ether, and chloroform. The basis for fats and oils.
3. A series of chemical reactions used by all aerobic organisms to generate energy through the oxidation of acetyl
4. The branch of biology that studies the development of gametes (sex cells), fertilization, and development of embryos and fetuses.
5. The genetic contribution of an individual to the next generation's gene pool relative to the average for the population.
6. The inactive X chromosome in a female somatic cell, rendered inactive in a process called lionization
7. The study of the physical properties of molecules, the chemical bonds between atoms as well as the molecular dynamics.
8. The midsection of the small intestine of many higher vertebrates like mammals, birds, reptiles. It is present between the duodenum and the ileum.
9. Rain containing acids that form in the atmosphere when industrial gas emissions (especially sulfur dioxide and nitrogen oxides) combine with water.
10. The inner layer of the stems of woody plants; composed of xylem.
11. A biochemical assembly that contains both proteins and lipids, bound to the proteins, which allow fats to move through the water inside and outside cells.
12. The haploid set of chromosomes in a gamete or microorganism, or in each cell of a multicellular organism.
13. A succession of letters that indicate the order of nucleotides within a DNA (using GACT) or RNA (GACU) molecule.
14. A complex organic substance present in living cells, especially DNA or RNA, whose molecules consist of many nucleotides linked in a long chain.
15. The smallest component of an element having the chemical properties of the element
16. The branch of science that explores the chemical processes within and related to living organisms.
17. The branch of biology concerned with the relations between organisms and their environment.
18. The process in which a eukaryotic cell nucleus splits in two, followed by division of the parent cell into two daughter cells.
19. Any organism whose cells contain a nucleus and other organelles enclosed within membranes.
20. An electrically excitable cell that processes and transmits information through electrical and chemical signals.

A. Nucleic Acid Sequence
E. Jejunum
I. Eukaryote
M. Lipid
Q. Embryology

B. Genome
F. Atom
J. Nucleic Acid
N. Endosperm
R. Neuron

C. Darwinian Fitness
G. Krebs Cycle
K. Molecular physics
O. Mitosis
S. Lipoprotein

D. Acid precipitation
H. Biochemistry
L. Environmental Biology
P. Barr body
T. Wood

12. Find the hidden words. The words have been placed horizontally, vertically, or diagonally. When you locate a word, draw a circle around it.

C	H	B	E	N	T	H	I	C	Z	O	N	E	W	J	J	N	B	A	G
S	D	P	X	N	W	Z	O	N	C	O	L	O	G	Y	E	A	B	M	G
W	V	A	L	E	N	C	E	B	A	N	D	S	B	W	Q	M	I	I	C
C	B	I	O	T	E	C	H	N	O	L	O	G	Y	U	M	N	C	N	E
G	E	E	L	E	C	T	R	O	N	D	O	N	O	R	C	I	H	O	N
S	E	X	U	A	L	R	E	P	R	O	D	U	C	T	I	O	N	A	T
C	S	U	Y	I	C	D	T	U	D	A	L	T	O	N	P	T	F	C	R
L	V	B	I	O	E	N	E	R	G	E	T	I	C	S	M	E	B	I	O
M	A	E	O	B	I	O	D	I	V	E	R	S	I	T	Y	S	I	D	S
R	C	E	L	L	T	H	E	O	R	Y	D	A	F	R	N	H	P	B	O
E	P	I	D	E	M	I	O	L	O	G	Y	B	I	P	E	D	A	L	M
T	R	A	N	S	C	R	I	P	T	I	O	N	Z	L	A	R	V	A	E

1. A unit of mass (also known as an atomic mass unit, amu), equal to the mass of a hydrogen atom (1.67 x 1024 g).
2. The first step of gene expression, in which a particular segment of DNA is copied into RNA (mRNA) by the enzyme RNA polymerase.
3. The variety of life in the world or in a particular habitat or ecosystem.
4. A branch of medicine that deals with the prevention, diagnosis and treatment of cancer.
5. Type of reproduction in which cells from two parents unite to form the first cell of a new organism.
6. A class of organic compounds containing an amino group and a carboxylic acid group
7. The study of the transformation of energy in living organisms.
8. In cell biology, an organelle that is the main place where cell microtubules get organized. They occur only in plant and animal cells.
9. The theory that all living things are made up of cells.
10. The highest range of electron energies in which electrons are normally present at absolute zero temperature.
11. A form of terrestrial locomotion where an organism moves by means of its two rear limbs or legs.
12. An electron donor is a chemical entity that donates electrons to another compound.
13. The ecological region at the lowest level of a body of water such as an ocean or a lake, including the sediment surface and some sub
14. A distinct juvenile form many animals undergo before metamorphosis into adults. Animals with indirect development such as insects, amphibians, or cnidarians.
15. The use of living systems and organisms to develop or make products, or "any technological application that uses biological systems, living organisms or derivatives thereof.
16. The modern form of the metric system, and is the most widely used system of measurement.
17. Also known as antibodies, They act as a critical part of the immune response by specifically recognizing and binding to particular antigens, and aiding in their destruction.
18. The study and analysis of the patterns, causes, and effects of health and disease conditions in defined populations.
19. A microbially facilitated process of nitrate reduction that may ultimately produce molecular nitrogen.
20. Organisms that produce an egg composed of shell and membranes that creates a protected environment in which the embryo can develop out of water

A. Bioenergetics
E. Electron Donor
I. Benthic zone
M. Biotechnology
Q. Larva

B. Denitrification
F. International System
J. Valence band
N. Biodiversity
R. Centrosome

C. Bipedal
G. Sexual Reproduction
K. Transcription
O. Epidemiology
S. Amino acid

D. Amniotes
H. Cell theory
L. Oncology
P. Dalton
T. Immunogloblin

13. *Find the hidden words. The words have been placed horizontally, vertically, or diagonally. When you locate a word, draw a circle around it.*

Z	N	B	B	I	V	A	G	V	C	S	A	P	E	W	Z	M	D	M	C
X	L	I	R	L	E	G	E	N	P	T	S	A	X	Z	B	E	C	A	P
T	Q	L	Y	A	R	R	N	O	E	E	H	R	P	U	U	S	O	S	R
V	C	E	P	C	R	I	E	J	F	R	N	A	R	Q	A	S	G	S	K
Z	A	M	H	T	P	C	P	E	F	O	O	S	E	F	M	E	P	D	N
M	R	Y	A	E	S	U	O	W	E	I	C	I	S	X	N	N	X	E	Y
H	B	C	S	A	X	L	O	D	C	D	N	T	S	T	I	G	B	N	E
P	O	O	L	L	C	T	L	V	T	A	V	O	I	Z	O	E	Z	S	M
P	N	L	C	U	Z	U	P	B	O	S	B	L	V	B	T	R	V	I	U
C	A	O	R	P	X	R	R	S	R	B	V	O	I	T	E	R	C	T	W
G	T	G	F	K	V	E	S	I	C	L	E	G	T	P	S	N	D	Y	D
U	E	Y	B	A	R	R	B	O	D	Y	N	Y	Y	R	A	A	S	K	N

1. The branch of biology concerned with the study of fungi, including their genetic and biochemical properties, their taxonomy and their use to humans.
2. Variations in a phenotype among individuals carrying a particular genotype.
3. Density is mass per volume.
4. The practice of cultivating land, growing food, and raising stock.
5. The stock of different genes in an interbreeding population.
6. Organisms that produce an egg composed of shell and membranes that creates a protected environment in which the embryo can develop out of water
7. The study of parasites, their hosts, and the relationship between them.
8. Any of various molecules that are capable of accepting one or two electrons from one molecule and donating them to another in the process of electron transport.
9. An organic compound with four rings arranged in a specific configuration. Examples include the dietary lipid cholesterol and the sex hormones.
10. The inactive X chromosome in a female somatic cell, rendered inactive in a process called lionization
11. A lymphatic capillary that absorbs dietary fats in the villi of the small intestine.
12. Any member of two classes of chemical compounds derived from carbonic acid or carbon dioxide.
13. Glands that secrete their products, hormones, directly into the blood rather than through a duct.
14. A fluid or air-filled cavity or sac.
15. A very large molecule, such as protein, commonly created by polymerization of smaller subunits (monomers).
16. An organ or cell that acts in response to a stimulus.
17. Also known as antibodies, They act as a critical part of the immune response by specifically recognizing and binding to particular antigens, and aiding in their destruction.
18. The form of RNA in which genetic information transcribed from DNA as a sequence of bases is transferred to a ribosome.
19. A dark green to yellowish brown fluid, produced by the liver of most vertebrates, that aids the digestion of lipids in the small intestine.
20. Organism which is capable of producing energy through aerobic respiration and then switching to anaerobic respiration depending on the amounts of oxygen.

A. Gene Pool
E. Endocrine Gland
I. Amniotes
M. Lacteal
Q. Bile
B. Effector
F. Parasitology
J. Carbonate
N. Macromolecule
R. Mycology
C. Agriculture
G. Barr body
K. Steroid
O. Facultative Anaerobe
S. Expressivity
D. Mass Density
H. Immunoglobin
L. Electron Carrier
P. Vesicle
T. Messenger RNA

14. *Find the hidden words. The words have been placed horizontally, vertically, or diagonally. When you locate a word, draw a circle around it.*

E	N	D	O	C	Y	T	O	S	I	S	V	X	D	Z	S	Q	E	B	N
P	H	E	N	O	T	Y	P	E	M	Y	B	A	R	R	B	O	D	Y	U
D	A	R	W	I	N	I	A	N	F	I	T	N	E	S	S	H	C	X	C
M	W	P	L	A	N	T	N	U	T	R	I	T	I	O	N	F	D	H	L
A	B	I	O	P	H	Y	S	I	C	S	T	H	E	G	J	S	B	W	E
M	P	O	Z	Y	P	H	E	R	P	E	T	O	L	O	G	Y	O	H	O
M	N	E	T	B	A	C	T	E	R	I	O	P	H	A	G	E	T	J	T
A	H	B	C	E	N	T	R	O	I	D	B	H	A	O	T	J	A	E	I
L	O	C	E	L	L	B	I	O	L	O	G	Y	C	A	K	H	N	E	D
O	X	I	S	G	M	Y	O	S	I	N	X	L	T	R	F	X	Y	X	E
G	A	C	T	I	V	E	S	I	T	E	V	L	I	M	A	V	Z	O	O
Y	M	O	L	A	R	I	T	Y	K	T	R	P	N	U	Y	U	N	N	S

1. The yellow colored photosynthetic pigments.
2. A unit of concentration measuring the number of moles of a solute per liter of solution.
3. The study of plants.
4. The study of the chemical elements and compounds necessary for plant growth, plant metabolism and their external supply.
5. The set of observable characteristics of an individual resulting from the interaction of its genotype with the environment.
6. The part of an enzyme or antibody where the chemical reaction occurs
7. A chemical reaction in which the standard change in free energy is positive, and energy is absorbed
8. Any part of a gene that will become a part of the final mature RNA produced by that gene after introns have been removed by RNA splicing.
9. The inactive X chromosome in a female somatic cell, rendered inactive in a process called lionization
10. A measure of the tendency of an atom to attract a bonding pair of electrons. The Pauling scale is the most commonly used.
11. The genetic contribution of an individual to the next generation's gene pool relative to the average for the population.
12. Large superfamily of motor proteins that move along actin filaments, while hydrolyzing ATP.
13. Organic molecules that serve as the monomers, or subunits, of nucleic acids like DNA (deoxyribonucleic acid) and RNA (ribonucleic acid).
14. The intersection of the three medians of the triangle (each median connecting a vertex with the midpoint of the opposite side).
15. The branch of zoology concerned with reptiles and amphibians.
16. One of the proteins into which actomyosin can be split; can exist in either a globular or a fibrous form.
17. An interdisciplinary science that applies the approaches and methods of physics to study biological systems.
18. Virus that infects and multiplies within bacteria.
19. A form of active transport in which a cell transports molecules (such as proteins) into the cell (endo
20. The study of mammals. A class of vertebrates with characteristics such as homeothermic metabolism, fur, four
21. Explains the structure, organization of the organelles they contain, their physiological properties, metabolic processes, signaling pathways, life cycle, and interactions.

A. Xanthophyll
E. Cell biology
I. Myosin
M. Electronegativity
Q. Phenotype
U. Bacteriophage

B. Herpetology
F. Barr body
J. Darwinian Fitness
N. Centroid
R. Mammalogy

C. Active site
G. Exon
K. Endocytosis
O. Nucleotide
S. Endergonic Reaction

D. Plant Nutrition
H. Botany
L. Biophysics
P. Molarity
T. Actin

15.

Find the hidden words. The words have been placed horizontally, vertically, or diagonally. When you locate a word, draw a circle around it.

O	T	Q	D	E	P	H	A	R	M	A	C	O	L	O	G	Y	D	N	A
P	H	Y	T	O	P	A	T	H	O	L	O	G	Y	C	W	Z	U	N	P
O	R	G	A	N	I	S	M	E	N	D	O	S	P	E	R	M	U	E	O
A	D	E	N	Y	L	A	T	E	C	Y	C	L	A	S	E	R	X	U	L
Z	O	O	L	O	G	Y	L	I	P	O	P	R	O	T	E	I	N	T	Y
Q	O	A	B	S	C	I	S	I	C	A	C	I	D	M	T	J	B	R	P
P	H	E	T	E	R	O	S	I	S	R	K	P	O	G	U	A	Q	I	L
Z	V	N	T	V	U	N	U	C	L	E	O	L	U	S	M	K	B	N	O
Q	Z	T	A	Z	B	M	P	H	A	S	E	N	V	N	H	G	Z	O	I
D	E	C	T	O	T	H	E	R	M	Z	T	C	L	O	N	I	N	G	D
B	B	E	H	A	V	I	O	R	A	L	E	C	O	L	O	G	Y	Y	Y
P	O	P	U	L	A	T	I	O	N	G	E	N	E	T	I	C	S	C	F

1. A organism in which internal physiological sources of heat are of relatively small or quite negligible importance in controlling body temperature. "Cold blooded".
2. A biochemical assembly that contains both proteins and lipids, bound to the proteins, which allow fats to move through the water inside and outside cells.
3. The study of the evolutionary basis for animal behavior due to ecological pressures.
4. a plant hormone.
5. A small dense spherical structure in the nucleus of a cell during interphase.
6. The study of genetic variation within populations, and involves the examination and modeling of changes in the frequencies of genes and alleles.
7. Containing more than two homologous sets of chromosomes.
8. The science of drug action on biological systems.
9. Propagate (an organism or cell) to make an identical copy of.
10. An individual animal, plant, or single-celled life form.
11. An enzyme that catalyzes the formation of cyclic AMP from ATP.
12. An elementary particle with half-integer spin, that interacts only via the weak subatomic force and gravity. Its mass is tiny compared to other subatomic particles.
13. the tendency of a crossbred individual to show qualities superior to those of both parents.
14. The science of diagnosing and managing plant diseases.
15. A tissue produced inside the seeds of most of the flowering plants around the time of fertilization.
16. Mitosis and cytokinesis together define this phase of an animal cell cycle-the division of the mother cell into two daughter cells, genetically identical to each other and the parent.
17. The study of the history of life on Earth as reflected in the fossil record. Fossils are the remains or traces of organisms.
18. The branch of biology that relates to the animal kingdom, including the structure, embryology, evolution, classification, habits, and distribution of all animals.
19. An inner layer of cells in the cortex of a root and of some stems, surrounding a vascular bundle.
20. Nutrients that provide calories or energy. Nutrients are substances needed for growth, metabolism, and for other body functions.

A. Ectotherm
F. Polyploidy
K. Organism
P. Phytopathology

B. Zoology
G. Lipoprotein
L. Population Genetics
Q. Pharmacology

C. Neutrino
H. Endosperm
M. Adenylate cyclase
R. Cloning

D. Heterosis
I. Macronutrient
N. Paleontology
S. Endodermis

E. Abscisic acid
J. Nucleolus
O. Behavioral ecology
T. M phase

16.

Find the hidden words. The words have been placed horizontally, vertically, or diagonally. When you locate a word, draw a circle around it.

V	A	N	H	J	H	C	L	O	N	I	N	G	G	E	N	E	C	S	F
E	M	L	X	U	E	C	T	O	D	E	R	M	Q	M	E	A	W	G	C
S	I	Q	B	D	B	I	O	E	N	E	R	G	E	T	I	C	S	T	P
I	N	R	K	W	E	N	D	O	C	Y	T	O	S	I	S	G	G	B	M
C	O	E	L	E	M	E	N	T	B	I	O	P	H	Y	S	I	C	S	O
L	A	N	P	L	A	N	T	N	U	T	R	I	T	I	O	N	M	R	K
E	C	A	Q	N	A	B	S	O	R	P	T	I	O	N	E	Z	S	H	Q
R	I	C	T	F	W	Z	J	M	E	S	S	E	N	G	E	R	R	N	A
D	D	V	L	V	A	L	E	N	C	E	E	L	E	C	T	R	O	N	K
P	R	E	D	A	T	I	O	N	B	A	R	R	B	O	D	Y	I	U	X
P	Z	H	A	D	R	O	N	V	A	S	O	D	I	L	A	T	I	O	N
L	V	M	L	E	U	K	O	C	Y	T	E	D	Y	I	G	D	V	U	Z

1. Any particle that is made from quarks, anti
2. The inactive X chromosome in a female somatic cell, rendered inactive in a process called lionization
3. The study of the transformation of energy in living organisms.
4. The form of RNA in which genetic information transcribed from DNA as a sequence of bases is transferred to a ribosome.
5. The outermost layer of cells or tissue of an embryo in early development, or the parts derived from this, which include the epidermis, nerve tissue, and nephridia.
6. A colorless cell which circulates in the blood and body fluids and is involved in counteracting foreign substances and disease; a white (blood) cell.
7. A form of active transport in which a cell transports molecules (such as proteins) into the cell (endo
8. An interdisciplinary science that applies the approaches and methods of physics to study biological systems.
9. A gene is a locus (or region) of DNA that encodes a functional RNA or protein product, and is the molecular unit of heredity.
10. A species of atoms having the same number of protons in their atomic nuclei (i.e. the same atomic number, Z).
11. The preying of one animal on others.
12. A class of organic compounds containing an amino group and a carboxylic acid group
13. The study of the chemical elements and compounds necessary for plant growth, plant metabolism and their external supply.
14. Propagate (an organism or cell) to make an identical copy of.
15. An electron that is associated with an atom, and that can participate in the formation of a chemical bond.
16. A process in which one substance permeates another; a fluid permeates or is dissolved by a liquid or solid.
17. A fluid or air-filled cavity or sac.
18. The dilatation of blood vessels, which decreases blood pressure.

A. Leukocyte
B. Cloning
C. Vasodilation
D. Element
E. Barr body
F. Bioenergetics
G. Messenger RNA
H. Biophysics
I. Vesicle
J. Plant Nutrition
K. Valence electron
L. Endocytosis
M. Gene
N. Hadron
O. Predation
P. Ectoderm
Q. Amino acid
R. Absorption

17. *Find the hidden words. The words have been placed horizontally, vertically, or diagonally. When you locate a word, draw a circle around it.*

E	N	D	O	S	Y	M	B	I	O	T	I	C	T	H	E	O	R	Y	H
G	T	Y	N	U	C	L	E	O	T	I	D	E	R	J	V	C	X	E	E
P	Q	R	K	G	R	J	P	H	E	N	O	T	Y	P	E	S	C	X	T
C	H	E	R	M	A	P	H	R	O	D	I	T	E	J	P	C	B	O	E
N	E	C	O	L	O	G	I	C	A	L	P	Y	R	A	M	I	D	N	R
T	P	O	P	U	L	A	T	I	O	N	G	E	N	E	T	I	C	S	O
D	F	M	I	C	R	O	E	V	O	L	U	T	I	O	N	D	R	O	S
I	W	P	K	M	O	N	O	M	E	R	V	I	R	U	S	B	A	R	I
G	E	N	E	P	O	O	L	D	J	X	B	O	T	A	N	Y	U	G	S
M	A	R	I	N	E	B	I	O	L	O	G	Y	A	C	T	I	N	A	B
E	P	I	N	E	P	H	R	I	N	E	M	R	A	Z	I	T	L	N	F
M	P	P	O	P	U	L	A	T	I	O	N	E	C	O	L	O	G	Y	P

1. the tendency of a crossbred individual to show qualities superior to those of both parents.
2. A molecule that can be bonded to other identical molecules to form a polymer.
3. The set of observable characteristics of an individual resulting from the interaction of its genotype with the environment.
4. A sub-field of ecology that deals with the dynamics of species populations and how these populations interact with the environment.
5. Any part of a gene that will become a part of the final mature RNA produced by that gene after introns have been removed by RNA splicing.
6. The study of genetic variation within populations, and involves the examination and modeling of changes in the frequencies of genes and alleles.
7. Evolutionary change within a species or small group of organisms, especially over a short period.
8. The stock of different genes in an interbreeding population.
9. a part of an organism that is typically self-contained and has a specific vital function, such as the heart or liver in humans.
10. The study of plants.
11. Organism with both male and female reproductive organs.
12. An evolutionary theory that explains the origin of eukaryotic cells from prokaryotes.
13. Organic molecules that serve as the monomers, or subunits, of nucleic acids like DNA (deoxyribonucleic acid) and RNA (ribonucleic acid).
14. A biological agent that reproduces inside the cells of living hosts.
15. The modern form of the metric system, and is the most widely used system of measurement.
16. Another term for adrenaline.
17. A graphical representation designed to show the biomass or bio productivity at each trophic level in a given ecosystem.
18. One of the proteins into which actomyosin can be split; can exist in either a globular or a fibrous form.
19. The scientific study of organisms in the ocean or other marine bodies of water.
20. The double helix is unwound and each strand acts as a template for the next strand. Bases are matched to synthesize the new partner strands.
21. An application of conservation of mass to the analysis of physical systems.
22. A sequence of three nucleotides forming a unit of genetic code in a transfer RNA molecule, corresponding to a complementary codon in messenger RNA.

A. Epinephrine
B. Gene Pool
C. Heterosis
D. Botany
E. Actin
F. Virus
G. Population Ecology
H. Ecological Pyramid
I. Population Genetics
J. Exon
K. Monomer
L. Endosymbiotic Theory
M. Organ
N. Hermaphrodite
O. International System
P. Anticodon
Q. DNA Replication
R. Nucleotide
S. Phenotype
T. Marine Biology
U. Mass Balance
V. Microevolution

18. *Find the hidden words. The words have been placed horizontally, vertically, or diagonally. When you locate a word, draw a circle around it.*

V	M	C	Z	A	J	V	B	M	J	L	O	C	P	V	D	B	C	A	O
S	O	R	U	T	Y	M	P	B	T	L	S	Y	W	N	H	R	K	I	R
V	L	D	M	O	K	V	W	W	P	F	M	U	D	R	W	J	V	N	N
R	E	T	Y	M	P	O	A	N	A	T	O	M	Y	C	I	C	T	T	I
F	A	M	N	I	O	T	E	S	C	B	S	G	X	W	E	Y	C	E	T
U	E	N	D	O	D	E	R	M	L	S	I	T	R	Q	Q	G	E	R	H
W	O	O	D	V	B	P	D	I	O	Y	S	F	K	Q	H	C	P	L	O
P	O	P	U	L	A	T	I	O	N	E	C	O	L	O	G	Y	R	E	L
D	I	N	E	N	D	O	C	R	I	N	E	S	Y	S	T	E	M	U	O
P	L	A	C	E	B	O	S	N	F	U	Q	Y	T	A	V	A	K	G
M	Y	O	F	I	B	R	I	L	G	W	D	P	D	A	D	R	L	I	Y
S	A	S	Y	P	O	L	Y	P	L	O	I	D	Y	K	H	W	V	N	H

1. Propagate (an organism or cell) to make an identical copy of.
2. The SI unit of measurement used to measure the number of things, usually atoms or molecules.
3. The collection of glands that produce hormones that regulate metabolism, growth and development, tissue function, sexual function, reproduction, sleep, and mood.
4. Organisms that produce an egg composed of shell and membranes that creates a protected environment in which the embryo can develop out of water
5. Containing more than two homologous sets of chromosomes.
6. The smallest component of an element having the chemical properties of the element
7. A branch of zoology that concerns the study of birds.
8. The spontaneous net movement of solvent molecules through a semi-permeable membrane into a region of higher solute concentration.
9. A group of cytokines (secreted proteins and signal molecules) that were first seen to be expressed by white blood cells (leukocytes)
10. The inner layer of the stems of woody plants; composed of xylem.
11. Any of the elongated contractile threads found in striated muscle cells.
12. A chemical reaction in which the standard change in free energy is positive, and energy is absorbed
13. A sub-field of ecology that deals with the dynamics of species populations and how these populations interact with the environment.
14. The branch of biology that studies the development of gametes (sex cells), fertilization, and development of embryos and fetuses.
15. A network of membranous tubules within the cytoplasm of a eukaryotic cell, continuous with the nuclear membrane.
16. A harmless pill, medicine, or procedure prescribed more for the psychological benefit to the patient than for any physiological effect.
17. The first step of gene expression, in which a particular segment of DNA is copied into RNA (mRNA) by the enzyme RNA polymerase.
18. One of the three primary germ layers in the very early human embryo. The other two layers are the ectoderm (outside layer) and mesoderm (middle layer).
19. The genetic contribution of an individual to the next generation's gene pool relative to the average for the population.
20. The branch of morphology that deals with the structure of animals

A. Embryology
E. Myofibril
I. Ornithology
M. Transcription
Q. Endergonic Reaction
B. Cloning
F. Darwinian Fitness
J. Atom
N. Placebo
R. Endoderm
C. Population Ecology
G. Amniotes
K. Wood
O. Endocrine System
S. Interleukin
D. Osmosis
H. Polyploidy
L. Endoplasmic Reticulum
P. Mole
T. Anatomy

19. *Find the hidden words. The words have been placed horizontally, vertically, or diagonally. When you locate a word, draw a circle around it.*

O	C	J	A	U	T	O	I	M	M	U	N	I	T	Y	K	R	K	G	Q
X	L	C	H	O	L	E	S	T	E	R	O	L	J	E	J	U	N	U	M
M	A	C	R	O	N	U	T	R	I	E	N	T	M	E	D	U	L	L	A
L	O	X	I	P	I	H	B	A	D	E	N	I	N	E	B	U	N	H	Z
X	G	G	E	N	E	T	I	C	V	A	R	I	A	T	I	O	N	K	H
U	C	H	M	E	M	B	R	A	N	E	P	O	T	E	N	T	I	A	L
A	R	T	I	F	I	C	I	A	L	S	E	L	E	C	T	I	O	N	X
Y	U	R	E	X	M	Q	V	A	C	U	O	L	E	F	T	J	N	C	R
E	C	O	L	O	G	I	C	A	L	P	Y	R	A	M	I	D	G	W	V
S	N	A	T	U	R	A	L	S	E	L	E	C	T	I	O	N	D	Q	C
F	U	B	U	H	D	O	N	C	O	L	O	G	Y	F	E	T	U	S	L
E	G	H	E	R	M	A	P	H	R	O	D	I	T	E	I	O	N	D	L

1. Also known as selective breeding.
2. Variations of genomes between members of species, or between groups of species thriving in different parts of the world as a result of genetic mutation.
3. A branch of medicine that deals with the prevention, diagnosis and treatment of cancer.
4. The system of immune responses of an organism against its own healthy cells and tissues.
5. A membrane-bound organelle which is present in all plant and fungal cells and some protist, animal and bacterial cells.
6. An atom or molecule with a net electric charge due to the loss or gain of one or more electrons.
7. A process in nature in which organisms possessing certain genotypic characteristics that make them better adjusted to an environment tend to survive.
8. A graphical representation designed to show the biomass or bio productivity at each trophic level in a given ecosystem.
9. One of the two purine nucleobases (the other being guanine) used in forming nucleotides of the nucleic acids.
10. When a nerve or muscle cell is at "rest", its membrane potential is called the resting membrane potential.
11. Organism with both male and female reproductive organs.
12. Nutrients that provide calories or energy. Nutrients are substances needed for growth, metabolism, and for other body functions.
13. The continuation of the spinal cord within the skull, forming the lowest part of the brainstem and containing control centers for the heart and lungs.
14. An organic lipid molecule that is biosynthesized by all animal cells because it is an essential structural component of all animal cell membranes.
15. The independent evolution of similar traits, starting from a similar ancestral condition.
16. The preying of one animal on others.
17. The midsection of the small intestine of many higher vertebrates like mammals, birds, reptiles. It is present between the duodenum and the ileum.
18. The branch of biology dealing with the functions and activities of living organisms and their parts, including all physical and chemical processes.
19. A human embryo after eight weeks of development.
20. Refers to genetically determined structures or attributes that have apparently lost most or all of their ancestral function in a given species.

A. Ecological Pyramid
B. Vestigiality
C. Ion
D. Oncology
E. Jejunum
F. Vacuole
G. Fetus
H. Cholesterol
I. Autoimmunity
J. Genetic Variation
K. Macronutrient
L. Parallel Evolution
M. Predation
N. Hermaphrodite
O. Artificial Selection
P. Membrane Potential
Q. Adenine
R. Natural Selection
S. Medulla
T. Physiology

20. *Find the hidden words. The words have been placed horizontally, vertically, or diagonally. When you locate a word, draw a circle around it.*

R	V	H	A	D	R	O	N	B	I	O	C	A	T	A	L	Y	S	T	S
U	W	A	C	T	I	V	E	T	R	A	N	S	P	O	R	T	G	L	K
W	X	W	S	C	N	T	H	Y	M	I	N	E	T	W	A	E	P	E	B
A	P	Y	V	E	S	T	I	G	I	A	L	I	T	Y	F	V	J	P	I
G	X	E	U	K	A	R	Y	O	T	E	B	I	O	N	I	C	S	T	O
V	E	P	I	G	E	N	E	T	I	C	S	A	M	O	L	E	V	O	P
W	B	P	A	R	A	L	L	E	L	E	V	O	L	U	T	I	O	N	H
D	A	B	V	C	L	O	N	I	N	G	K	K	N	K	F	Q	V	O	Y
T	Y	H	J	Z	H	X	P	A	L	E	O	N	T	O	L	O	G	Y	S
P	A	N	Y	X	X	W	T	E	S	T	O	S	T	E	R	O	N	E	I
M	O	Z	P	O	L	L	I	N	A	T	I	O	N	K	J	A	A	V	C
O	O	N	C	O	L	O	G	Y	B	L	Y	O	L	K	X	M	Q	R	S

1. A steroid hormone from the androgen group and is found in humans and other vertebrates.
2. Any organism whose cells contain a nucleus and other organelles enclosed within membranes.
3. The study, in the field of genetics, of cellular and physiological phenotypic trait variations that are caused by external or environmental factors that switch genes on and off.
4. Transport of a substance (as a protein or drug) across a cell membrane against the concentration gradient; requires an expenditure of energy
5. An interdisciplinary science that applies the approaches and methods of physics to study biological systems.
6. Propagate (an organism or cell) to make an identical copy of.
7. Catalysis in living systems. In biological processes, natural catalysts, such as protein enzymes, perform chemical transformations on organic compounds.
8. One of the four nucleobases in the nucleic acid of DNA that are represented by the letters G–C–A–T.
9. The study of the history of life on Earth as reflected in the fossil record. Fossils are the remains or traces of organisms.
10. The yellow internal part of a bird's egg, which is surrounded by the white, is rich in protein and fat, and nourishes the developing embryo.
11. Refers to genetically determined structures or attributes that have apparently lost most or all of their ancestral function in a given species.
12. The act of transferring pollen grains from the male anther of a flower to the female stigma.
13. The SI unit of measurement used to measure the number of things, usually atoms or molecules.
14. A branch of medicine that deals with the prevention, diagnosis and treatment of cancer.
15. Application of biological methods and systems found in nature to the study and design of engineering systems and modern technology.
16. The independent evolution of similar traits, starting from a similar ancestral condition.
17. Any particle that is made from quarks, anti
18. An elementary, half-integer spin particle that does not undergo strong interactions.

A. Hadron
B. Epigenetics
C. Active Transport
D. Parallel Evolution
E. Paleontology
F. Yolk
G. Mole
H. Vestigiality
I. Bionics
J. Thymine
K. Biocatalysts
L. Oncology
M. Cloning
N. Eukaryote
O. Testosterone
P. Pollination
Q. Lepton
R. Biophysics

1. *Find the hidden words. The words have been placed horizontally, vertically, or diagonally. When you locate a word, draw a circle around it.*

Y	K	W	I	Q	C	A	C	O	E	L	O	M	A	T	E	A	T	N	O
A	B	S	O	L	U	T	E	Z	E	R	O	P	O	L	Y	M	E	R	N
Q	A	B	S	O	R	P	T	I	O	N	S	P	E	C	T	R	U	M	C
B	M	F	B	I	O	I	N	F	O	R	M	A	T	I	C	S	D	Y	O
Q	R	R	Q	G	E	M	E	I	O	S	I	S	M	X	Y	X	E	S	L
Z	K	R	A	U	T	O	I	M	M	U	N	I	T	Y	O	B	C	T	O
O	R	G	A	N	B	C	E	L	L	B	I	P	E	D	A	L	I	E	G
D	M	I	C	R	O	E	V	O	L	U	T	I	O	N	C	A	D	R	Y
A	B	Y	S	S	A	L	Z	O	N	E	J	X	U	S	T	U	U	O	W
A	E	A	W	C	H	O	L	E	S	T	E	R	O	L	M	A	O	I	E
Y	N	E	U	R	O	T	R	A	N	S	M	I	T	T	E	R	U	D	K
E	L	E	C	T	R	I	C	P	O	T	E	N	T	I	A	L	S	E	N

1. The deep sea (2000 meters or more) where there is no light.
2. An organic lipid molecule that is biosynthesized by all animal cells because it is an essential structural component of all animal cell membranes.
3. Means "falling off at maturity" or "tending to fall off", and it is typically used in order to refer to trees or shrubs that lose their leaves seasonally.
4. Animals, like flatworms and jellyfish, that have no body cavity (coelom).
5. A type of cell division that reduces the number of chromosomes in the parent cell by half and produces four gamete cells.
6. The amount of work needed to move a unit charge from a reference point to a specific point against an electric field.
7. An organic compound with four rings arranged in a specific configuration. Examples include the dietary lipid cholesterol and the sex hormones.
8. The lowest theoretically attainable temperature (at which the kinetic energy of atoms and molecules is minimal)
9. A branch of medicine that deals with the prevention, diagnosis and treatment of cancer.
10. A form of terrestrial locomotion where an organism moves by means of its two rear limbs or legs.
11. The spectrum of electromagnetic radiation that has passed through a medium that absorbed radiation of certain wavelengths.
12. The application of computer technology to the management of biological information.
13. Type of lymphocyte in the humeral immunity of the adaptive immune system.
14. Evolutionary change within a species or small group of organisms, especially over a short period.
15. Known as chemical messengers, are endogenous chemicals that enable neurotransmission.
16. A large molecule, or macromolecule, composed of many repeated subunits.
17. The system of immune responses of an organism against its own healthy cells and tissues.
18. Adaptation to a new climate (a new temperature or altitude or environment).
19. a part of an organism that is typically self-contained and has a specific vital function, such as the heart or liver in humans.

A. Cholesterol
E. Acclimatization
I. Microevolution
M. B cell
Q. Polymer

B. Bipedal
F. Bioinformatics
J. Acoelomate
N. Organ
R. Oncology

C. Absolute zero
G. Steroid
K. Abyssal zone
O. Deciduous
S. Neurotransmitter

D. Meiosis
H. Absorption spectrum
L. Electric Potential
P. Autoimmunity

2. *Find the hidden words. The words have been placed horizontally, vertically, or diagonally. When you locate a word, draw a circle around it.*

Z	S	J	E	A	P	M	Y	O	S	I	N	P	L	A	C	E	B	O	I
M	D	E	H	Y	D	R	A	T	I	O	N	R	E	A	C	T	I	O	N
A	N	A	T	O	M	Y	Q	C	E	L	L	M	E	M	B	R	A	N	E
W	G	Q	Y	N	T	A	R	A	C	H	N	O	L	O	G	Y	D	S	U
O	B	W	A	T	E	R	P	O	T	E	N	T	I	A	L	X	B	C	G
C	N	Z	E	K	G	A	M	A	S	S	N	U	M	B	E	R	A	Y	N
W	K	L	D	E	S	T	R	O	G	E	N	E	N	D	E	M	I	S	M
E	L	G	R	O	A	O	S	D	C	E	L	L	T	H	E	O	R	Y	I
D	E	O	X	Y	R	I	B	O	N	U	C	L	E	I	C	A	C	I	D
E	P	I	D	E	M	I	O	L	O	G	Y	Y	B	I	O	M	E	X	W
Z	T	N	S	Y	H	Y	D	R	O	C	A	R	B	O	N	Q	C	C	M
P	D	B	K	W	H	I	T	E	B	L	O	O	D	C	E	L	L	V	F

1. Large superfamily of motor proteins that move along actin filaments, while hydrolyzing ATP.
2. The total number of protons and neutrons (together known as nucleons) in an atomic nucleus
3. Usually defined as a chemical reaction that involves the loss of a water molecule from the reacting molecule.
4. In organic chemistry, a hydrocarbon is an organic compound consisting entirely of hydrogen and carbon.
5. The primary female sex hormone. It is responsible for the development and regulation of the female reproductive system and secondary sex characteristics.
6. A harmless pill, medicine, or procedure prescribed more for the psychological benefit to the patient than for any physiological effect.
7. The study and analysis of the patterns, causes, and effects of health and disease conditions in defined populations.
8. A measure of the potential energy in water as well as the difference between the potential in a given water sample and pure water.
9. Scientific study of spiders, scorpions, pseudo-scorpions, and harvestmen, collectively called arachnids.
10. Very large ecological areas on the earth's surface, with fauna and flora (animals and plants) adapting to their environment.
11. The semipermeable membrane surrounding the cytoplasm of a cell.
12. Component of the blood that functions in the immune system. Also known as a leukocyte.
13. The four bases found in DNA are adenine, cytosine, guanine and thymine. These four bases are attached to the sugar
14. The theory that all living things are made up of cells.
15. The branch of morphology that deals with the structure of animals
16. The ecological state of a species being unique to a defined geographic location, such as an island, nation, country or other defined zone, or habitat type.
17. Refers to the provision of essential nutrients necessary to support human life and health.
18. How your body recognizes and defends itself against bacteria, viruses, and substances that appear foreign and harmful.
19. a nerve cell (neuron) whose cell body is located in the spinal cord and whose fiber (axon) projects outside the spinal cord to directly or indirectly control effector organs.

A. Hydrocarbon
E. Arachnology
I. Human Nutrition
M. Dehydration Reaction
Q. Water Potential
B. Biome
F. Anatomy
J. Deoxyribonucleic Acid
N. Mass Number
R. Epidemiology
C. Myosin
G. Motor Neuron
K. Cell membrane
O. Cell theory
S. Estrogen
D. Endemism
H. Immune Response
L. White Blood Cell
P. Placebo

3. *Find the hidden words. The words have been placed horizontally, vertically, or diagonally. When you locate a word, draw a circle around it.*

P	U	J	J	D	N	A	R	E	P	L	I	C	A	T	I	O	N	B	W
A	E	C	G	U	L	A	R	P	O	L	Y	P	L	O	I	D	Y	R	C
R	F	K	C	H	L	O	R	O	P	L	A	S	T	D	A	L	T	O	N
A	F	E	X	O	N	L	Z	V	X	A	N	T	H	O	P	H	Y	L	L
S	E	Z	H	H	D	E	N	A	T	U	R	A	T	I	O	N	Y	B	G
I	C	Y	Q	G	G	K	M	C	E	N	D	O	D	E	R	M	I	S	F
T	T	G	K	K	N	O	E	U	E	X	O	C	Y	T	O	S	I	S	M
O	O	O	X	P	O	A	R	O	M	I	I	I	P	M	J	M	V	Y	D
L	R	T	X	X	U	F	I	L	E	A	N	T	I	C	O	D	O	N	C
O	W	E	S	O	I	O	Z	E	A	B	Y	S	S	A	L	Z	O	N	E
G	Y	L	I	P	O	P	R	O	T	E	I	N	O	H	Y	F	E	U	W
Y	Y	B	I	O	M	E	D	I	C	A	L	R	E	S	E	A	R	C	H

1. A biochemical assembly that contains both proteins and lipids, bound to the proteins, which allow fats to move through the water inside and outside cells.
2. Containing more than two homologous sets of chromosomes.
3. Work to convert light energy of the Sun into sugars that can be used by cells.
4. A membrane-bound organelle which is present in all plant and fungal cells and some protist, animal and bacterial cells.
5. Of or pertaining to the throat.
6. An inner layer of cells in the cortex of a root and of some stems, surrounding a vascular bundle.
7. The pursuit of answers to medical questions. These investigations lead to discoveries, which in turn lead to the development of new preventions, therapies and cures.
8. A process by which the contents of a cell vacuole are released to the exterior through fusion of the vacuole membrane with the cell membrane.
9. A process in which proteins or nucleic acids lose the quaternary structure, tertiary structure and secondary structure which is present in their native state.
10. The double helix is unwound and each strand acts as a template for the next strand. Bases are matched to synthesize the new partner strands.
11. A diploid cell resulting from the fusion of two haploid gametes; a fertilized ovum.
12. The study of parasites, their hosts, and the relationship between them.
13. A unit of mass (also known as an atomic mass unit, amu), equal to the mass of a hydrogen atom (1.67 x 1024 g).
14. The deep sea (2000 meters or more) where there is no light.
15. Component of the blood that functions in the immune system. Also known as a leukocyte.
16. An organ or cell that acts in response to a stimulus.
17. Any part of a gene that will become a part of the final mature RNA produced by that gene after introns have been removed by RNA splicing.
18. The yellow colored photosynthetic pigments.
19. An electron that is associated with an atom, and that can participate in the formation of a chemical bond.
20. A sequence of three nucleotides forming a unit of genetic code in a transfer RNA molecule, corresponding to a complementary codon in messenger RNA.

A. White Blood Cell
E. Parasitology
I. Gular
M. Exon
Q. DNA Replication

B. Anticodon
F. Abyssal zone
J. Lipoprotein
N. Polyploidy
R. Chloroplast

C. Xanthophyll
G. Biomedical research
K. Effector
O. Zygote
S. Vacuole

D. Exocytosis
H. Endodermis
L. Valence electron
P. Denaturation
T. Dalton

4. *Find the hidden words. The words have been placed horizontally, vertically, or diagonally. When you locate a word, draw a circle around it.*

D	N	A	C	P	H	E	R	O	M	O	N	E	J	L	Y	S	J	M	L
F	M	E	M	B	R	A	N	E	P	O	T	E	N	T	I	A	L	L	I
G	E	P	X	M	A	J	J	Q	Q	E	P	L	D	A	L	T	O	N	G
C	N	R	C	O	Z	T	K	I	Z	P	R	E	D	A	T	I	O	N	A
U	A	O	M	A	R	I	N	E	B	I	O	L	O	G	Y	B	Z	P	M
I	N	K	J	A	P	E	L	E	C	T	R	O	N	S	H	E	L	L	E
J	T	A	E	N	Z	S	O	N	U	C	L	E	O	B	A	S	E	A	N
R	I	R	J	Z	C	R	Y	O	B	I	O	L	O	G	Y	E	U	C	T
Y	O	Y	U	C	W	L	I	P	I	D	S	C	Q	F	S	U	R	E	T
D	M	O	N	A	L	A	R	V	A	U	L	F	H	A	N	L	J	B	H
P	E	T	U	L	K	A	E	N	D	O	C	Y	T	O	S	I	S	O	W
Q	R	E	M	M	Y	C	O	L	O	G	Y	X	P	Y	L	Y	I	Q	X

1. The scientific study of organisms in the ocean or other marine bodies of water.
2. The midsection of the small intestine of many higher vertebrates like mammals, birds, reptiles. It is present between the duodenum and the ileum.
3. The fibrous connective tissue that connects bones to other bones.
4. A chemically defined as a substance that is insoluble in water and soluble in alcohol, ether, and chloroform. The basis for fats and oils.
5. An electron shell is the outside part of an atom around the atomic nucleus. It is a group of atomic orbitals with the same value of the principal quantum number n.
6. When a nerve or muscle cell is at "rest", its membrane potential is called the resting membrane potential.
7. Stereoisomers that are non-superimposable mirror images. A molecule with 1 chiral carbon atom exists as 2 stereoisomers termed enantiomers.
8. A distinct juvenile form many animals undergo before metamorphosis into adults. Animals with indirect development such as insects, amphibians, or cnidarians.
9. A chemical substance produced and released into the environment by an animal, especially a mammal or an insect, affecting the behavior or physiology of others of its species.
10. A unit of mass (also known as an atomic mass unit, amu), equal to the mass of a hydrogen atom (1.67 x 1024 g).
11. A microscopic single
12. A harmless pill, medicine, or procedure prescribed more for the psychological benefit to the patient than for any physiological effect.
13. The branch of biology concerned with the study of fungi, including their genetic and biochemical properties, their taxonomy and their use to humans.
14. The branch of biology that studies the effects of low temperatures on living things within Earth's cryosphere or in science.
15. The preying of one animal on others.
16. A form of active transport in which a cell transports molecules (such as proteins) into the cell (endo
17. Cytosine, Guanine, Adenine (which can be found in DNA and RNA), Thymine (found only in DNA), and Uracil (found only in RNA).
18. Also known as antibodies, They act as a critical part of the immune response by specifically recognizing and binding to particular antigens, and aiding in their destruction.
19. The hereditary material in humans and almost all other organisms.

A. Mycology	B. Dalton	C. Ligament	D. Jejunum	E. DNA
F. Pheromone	G. Lipid	H. Electron Shell	I. Endocytosis	J. Membrane Potential
K. Placebo	L. Cryobiology	M. Nucleobase	N. Predation	O. Enantiomer
P. Larva	Q. Prokaryote	R. Marine Biology	S. Immunogloblin	

5. *Find the hidden words. The words have been placed horizontally, vertically, or diagonally. When you locate a word, draw a circle around it.*

U	T	E	R	U	S	C	E	L	L	T	H	E	O	R	Y	L	O	N	D
U	K	N	E	U	R	O	N	E	U	M	Y	O	F	I	B	R	I	L	E
D	R	D	H	P	M	A	C	R	O	N	U	T	R	I	E	N	T	U	S
D	E	N	I	T	R	I	F	I	C	A	T	I	O	N	D	X	U	L	M
R	D	G	C	C	L	I	P	O	P	R	O	T	E	I	N	D	W	C	O
C	A	G	R	I	C	U	L	T	U	R	E	A	E	R	O	B	I	C	S
O	C	H	E	M	I	S	T	R	Y	M	O	S	M	O	S	I	S	G	O
O	N	A	T	U	R	A	L	S	E	L	E	C	T	I	O	N	D	B	M
T	P	E	P	H	E	R	M	A	P	H	R	O	D	I	T	E	H	D	E
S	T	E	R	O	I	D	C	H	R	O	M	O	S	O	M	E	T	D	M
L	I	P	I	D	B	I	O	G	E	O	G	R	A	P	H	Y	U	B	Z
E	S	O	W	V	G	E	N	E	T	I	C	C	O	D	E	D	S	A	R

1. Organism with both male and female reproductive organs.
2. Nutrients that provide calories or energy. Nutrients are substances needed for growth, metabolism, and for other body functions.
3. A threadlike strand of DNA in the cell nucleus that carries the genes in a linear order.
4. An electrically excitable cell that processes and transmits information through electrical and chemical signals.
5. The theory that all living things are made up of cells.
6. The practice of cultivating land, growing food, and raising stock.
7. Any of the elongated contractile threads found in striated muscle cells.
8. A branch of physical science that studies the composition, structure, properties and change of matter.
9. The nucleotide triplets of DNA and RNA molecules that carry genetic information in living cells.
10. Depending on free oxygen or air.
11. The study of the distribution of species and ecosystems in geographic space and through time.
12. A biochemical assembly that contains both proteins and lipids, bound to the proteins, which allow fats to move through the water inside and outside cells.
13. A microbially facilitated process of nitrate reduction that may ultimately produce molecular nitrogen.
14. Also known as a macula adhaerens, is a cell structure specialized for cell to cell adhesion.
15. A chemically defined as a substance that is insoluble in water and soluble in alcohol, ether, and chloroform. The basis for fats and oils.
16. An organic compound with four rings arranged in a specific configuration. Examples include the dietary lipid cholesterol and the sex hormones.
17. A process in nature in which organisms possessing certain genotypic characteristics that make them better adjusted to an environment tend to survive.
18. The spontaneous net movement of solvent molecules through a semi-permeable membrane into a region of higher solute concentration.
19. The organ in the lower body of a woman or female mammal where offspring are conceived and in which they gestate before birth; the womb.

A. Denitrification
B. Desmosome
C. Hermaphrodite
D. Genetic Code
E. Cell theory
F. Chromosome
G. Steroid
H. Aerobic
I. Biogeography
J. Neuron
K. Macronutrient
L. Osmosis
M. Chemistry
N. Agriculture
O. Uterus
P. Lipid
Q. Myofibril
R. Natural Selection
S. Lipoprotein

6. *Find the hidden words. The words have been placed horizontally, vertically, or diagonally. When you locate a word, draw a circle around it.*

```
M  P  B  I  O  I  N  F  O  R  M  A  T  I  C  S  J  C  D  T
M  F  O  U  D  M  M  N  A  B  S  O  R  P  T  I  O  N  Z  S
H  T  R  O  X  O  R  C  E  L  L  T  H  E  O  R  Y  B  Q  P
M  D  G  T  C  L  C  E  D  D  U  Q  U  A  R  K  K  T  K  Q
E  G  A  X  F  E  C  E  E  W  A  O  D  O  I  S  X  E  G  G
D  L  N  L  N  F  F  X  S  C  E  L  L  N  U  C  L  E  U  S
W  B  I  O  N  I  C  S  M  X  R  C  G  I  B  R  I  C  A  S
T  C  S  J  O  B  W  J  O  V  O  N  E  C  M  Y  U  A  E  Z
S  R  M  H  E  N  N  U  S  G  B  D  Q  Z  Y  G  O  T  E  W
H  A  B  I  T  A  T  B  O  L  I  P  O  P  R  O  T  E  I  N
E  N  D  O  P  L  A  S  M  I  C  R  E  T  I  C  U  L  U  M
N  M  E  M  B  R  A  N  E  P  O  T  E  N  T  I  A  L  N  M
```

1. Also known as a macula adhaerens, is a cell structure specialized for cell to cell adhesion.
2. Application of biological methods and systems found in nature to the study and design of engineering systems and modern technology.
3. The "control room" for the cell. The nucleus gives out all the orders.
4. The application of computer technology to the management of biological information.
5. The female reproductive cell (gamete) in oogamous organisms.
6. Depending on free oxygen or air.
7. A process in which one substance permeates another; a fluid permeates or is dissolved by a liquid or solid.
8. The scientific study of nature and of Earth's biodiversity with the aim of protecting species, their habitats, and ecosystems from excessive rates of extinction.
9. An individual animal, plant, or single-celled life form.
10. When a nerve or muscle cell is at "rest", its membrane potential is called the resting membrane potential.
11. A network of membranous tubules within the cytoplasm of a eukaryotic cell, continuous with the nuclear membrane.
12. The SI unit of measurement used to measure the number of things, usually atoms or molecules.
13. An elementary particle and a fundamental constituent of matter; combine to form composite particles called hadrons, the most stable of which are protons and neutrons.
14. The theory that all living things are made up of cells.
15. A group of cytokines (secreted proteins and signal molecules) that were first seen to be expressed by white blood cells (leukocytes)
16. A biochemical assembly that contains both proteins and lipids, bound to the proteins, which allow fats to move through the water inside and outside cells.
17. A diploid cell resulting from the fusion of two haploid gametes; a fertilized ovum.
18. A place for animals, people and plants and non-living things

A. Endoplasmic Reticulum
B. Desmosome
C. Lipoprotein
D. Absorption
E. Habitat
F. Interleukin
G. Bionics
H. Bioinformatics
I. Egg
J. Cell theory
K. Aerobic
L. Conservation Biology
M. Organism
N. Mole
O. Cell nucleus
P. Membrane Potential
Q. Zygote
R. Quark

7. *Find the hidden words. The words have been placed horizontally, vertically, or diagonally. When you locate a word, draw a circle around it.*

H	U	P	H	Y	S	I	O	L	O	G	Y	H	A	D	E	N	I	N	E
Z	X	Y	P	O	J	P	B	F	K	D	E	S	M	O	S	O	M	E	M
Q	R	Q	E	N	R	F	E	T	U	S	E	L	E	M	E	N	T	H	N
I	I	O	N	I	C	B	O	N	D	E	N	T	O	M	O	L	O	G	Y
E	N	D	O	P	L	A	S	M	I	C	R	E	T	I	C	U	L	U	M
V	N	P	K	C	T	R	O	P	H	I	C	L	E	V	E	L	T	R	P
Y	F	E	S	T	R	O	G	E	N	J	V	V	C	E	S	Q	W	M	E
W	U	B	I	O	E	N	G	I	N	E	E	R	I	N	G	E	Z	F	N
K	C	P	Y	S	X	C	E	L	L	T	H	E	O	R	Y	M	C	U	Z
M	B	I	O	M	E	D	I	C	A	L	R	E	S	E	A	R	C	H	Y
D	A	R	W	I	N	I	A	N	F	I	T	N	E	S	S	M	M	H	M
O	N	V	S	L	I	N	K	E	D	G	E	N	E	S	A	C	Z	A	E

1. The complete transfer of valence electron(s) between atoms. It is a type of chemical bond that generates two oppositely charged ions.
2. The genetic contribution of an individual to the next generation's gene pool relative to the average for the population.
3. A network of membranous tubules within the cytoplasm of a eukaryotic cell, continuous with the nuclear membrane.
4. The branch of biology dealing with the functions and activities of living organisms and their parts, including all physical and chemical processes.
5. A human embryo after eight weeks of development.
6. Each of several hierarchical levels in an ecosystem, comprising organisms that share the same function in the food chain and the same nutritional relationship.
7. Also known as a macula adhaerens, is a cell structure specialized for cell to cell adhesion.
8. The theory that all living things are made up of cells.
9. Biological molecules (proteins) that act as catalysts and help complex reactions occur everywhere in life.
10. The pursuit of answers to medical questions. These investigations lead to discoveries, which in turn lead to the development of new preventions, therapies and cures.
11. When two genes are close together on the same chromosome, they do not assort independently.
12. The primary female sex hormone. It is responsible for the development and regulation of the female reproductive system and secondary sex characteristics.
13. The application of concepts and methods of biology to solve real world problems.
14. The study of insects.
15. A species of atoms having the same number of protons in their atomic nuclei (i.e. the same atomic number, Z).
16. One of the two purine nucleobases (the other being guanine) used in forming nucleotides of the nucleic acids.
17. The application of computer technology to the management of biological information.
18. A type of microscope that uses a beam of electrons to create an image of the specimen. It is capable of much higher magnifications.

A. Estrogen
E. Biomedical research
I. Entomology
M. Electron Microscope
Q. Desmosome

B. Bioinformatics
F. Cell theory
J. Fetus
N. Adenine
R. Physiology

C. Element
G. Darwinian Fitness
K. Linked Genes
O. Trophic level

D. Endoplasmic Reticulum
H. Ionic Bond
L. Enzyme
P. Bioengineering

8. *Find the hidden words. The words have been placed horizontally, vertically, or diagonally. When you locate a word, draw a circle around it.*

T	B	D	C	P	L	A	S	M	O	L	Y	S	I	S	R	E	G	E	F
C	R	E	E	D	G	P	M	S	H	U	O	T	K	A	F	S	S	P	C
E	C	O	L	N	G	R	R	F	I	B	I	O	N	I	C	S	C	I	M
O	T	X	L	T	S	O	C	S	P	E	C	I	E	S	A	B	G	S	O
O	N	Y	M	C	U	K	E	M	B	R	Y	O	L	O	G	Y	E	T	L
W	Y	R	Y	E	G	A	H	A	B	S	O	R	P	T	I	O	N	A	A
O	G	I	O	L	V	R	D	E	S	M	O	S	O	M	E	G	O	S	R
B	K	B	S	L	K	Y	G	A	O	T	L	Q	W	P	R	Z	M	I	I
N	W	O	I	J	P	O	L	L	I	N	A	T	I	O	N	B	E	S	T
S	S	S	N	Z	E	T	T	M	E	N	E	U	T	R	I	N	O	X	Y
F	J	E	U	M	V	E	Q	V	S	Z	Q	M	O	N	O	M	E	R	V
X	A	R	T	I	F	I	C	I	A	L	S	E	L	E	C	T	I	O	N

1. Often defined as the largest group of organisms in which two individuals are capable of reproducing fertile offspring, typically using sexual reproduction.
2. Contraction of the protoplast of a plant cell as a result of loss of water from the cell.
3. A lymphocyte of a type produced or processed by the thymus gland and actively participating in the immune response.
4. A process in which one substance permeates another; a fluid permeates or is dissolved by a liquid or solid.
5. Also known as selective breeding.
6. A microscopic single
7. The haploid set of chromosomes in a gamete or microorganism, or in each cell of a multicellular organism.
8. An elementary particle with half-integer spin, that interacts only via the weak subatomic force and gravity. Its mass is tiny compared to other subatomic particles.
9. A molecule that can be bonded to other identical molecules to form a polymer.
10. A monosaccharide. Its name indicates that it is a deoxy sugar, meaning that it is derived from the sugar ribose by loss of an oxygen atom.
11. The interaction of genes that are not alleles, in particular the suppression of the effect of one such gene by another.
12. Large superfamily of motor proteins that move along actin filaments, while hydrolyzing ATP.
13. Also known as a macula adhaerens, is a cell structure specialized for cell to cell adhesion.
14. The collection of glands that produce hormones that regulate metabolism, growth and development, tissue function, sexual function, reproduction, sleep, and mood.
15. Application of biological methods and systems found in nature to the study and design of engineering systems and modern technology.
16. The act of transferring pollen grains from the male anther of a flower to the female stigma.
17. The branch of biology that studies the development of gametes (sex cells), fertilization, and development of embryos and fetuses.
18. The structural and functional unit of all organisms; an autonomous self
19. Rain containing acids that form in the atmosphere when industrial gas emissions (especially sulfur dioxide and nitrogen oxides) combine with water.
20. A unit of concentration measuring the number of moles of a solute per liter of solution.

A. Deoxyribose
F. Myosin
K. Monomer
P. Neutrino

B. Pollination
G. Absorption
L. Genome
Q. Species

C. Embryology
H. Epistasis
M. Prokaryote
R. T Cell

D. Acid precipitation
I. Desmosome
N. Bionics
S. Endocrine System

E. Plasmolysis
J. Cell
O. Molarity
T. Artificial Selection

9. *Find the hidden words. The words have been placed horizontally, vertically, or diagonally. When you locate a word, draw a circle around it.*

A	G	M	B	D	B	I	O	I	N	F	O	R	M	A	T	I	C	S	U
P	P	E	N	G	B	I	O	E	N	G	I	N	E	E	R	I	N	G	S
K	E	S	U	A	S	E	N	A	N	T	I	O	M	E	R	D	T	D	N
C	U	O	C	E	F	F	E	C	T	O	R	C	E	L	L	H	M	P	X
P	T	N	L	N	E	H	I	S	T	O	L	O	G	Y	I	X	T	R	M
L	C	F	E	Z	A	G	R	O	B	I	O	L	O	G	Y	V	W	H	P
A	E	K	O	Y	A	E	R	O	B	I	C	B	O	I	S	O	M	E	R
C	L	B	I	M	O	F	O	R	G	A	N	C	B	O	U	R	E	A	B
E	L	P	D	E	U	O	R	G	A	N	I	S	M	A	S	F	M	U	D
B	Q	D	E	N	I	T	R	I	F	I	C	A	T	I	O	N	M	G	K
O	C	H	E	M	I	C	A	L	R	E	A	C	T	I	O	N	J	X	U
W	L	E	P	T	O	N	I	M	M	U	N	O	G	L	O	B	L	I	N

1. A microbially facilitated process of nitrate reduction that may ultimately produce molecular nitrogen.
2. An irregularly shaped region within the cell of a prokaryote that contains all or most of the genetic material, called gonophore.
3. A lymphocyte of a type produced or processed by the thymus gland and actively participating in the immune response.
4. The study of the microscopic anatomy of cells and tissues of plants and animals.
5. Stereoisomers that are non-superimposable mirror images. A molecule with 1 chiral carbon atom exists as 2 stereoisomers termed enantiomers.
6. An elementary, half-integer spin particle that does not undergo strong interactions.
7. Plasma cells, also called plasma B cells, plasmocytes, plasmacytes, or effector B cells, are white blood cells that secrete large volumes of antibodies.
8. Serves an important role in the metabolism of nitrogen-containing compounds by animals, and is the main nitrogen-containing substance in the urine of mammals.
9. Also known as antibodies, They act as a critical part of the immune response by specifically recognizing and binding to particular antigens, and aiding in their destruction.
10. The study of plant nutrition and growth especially as a way to increase crop yield
11. a part of an organism that is typically self-contained and has a specific vital function, such as the heart or liver in humans.
12. Depending on free oxygen or air.
13. Hadronic subatomic particles composed of one quark and one antiquark, bound together by the strong interaction.
14. The application of concepts and methods of biology to solve real world problems.
15. Usually characterized by a chemical change, and they yield one or more products, which usually have properties different from the reactants
16. Biological molecules (proteins) that act as catalysts and help complex reactions occur everywhere in life.
17. A molecule with the same chemical formula as another molecule, but with a different chemical structure.
18. The application of computer technology to the management of biological information.
19. A harmless pill, medicine, or procedure prescribed more for the psychological benefit to the patient than for any physiological effect.
20. An individual animal, plant, or single-celled life form.

A. Meson	B. Enantiomer	C. Denitrification	D. Agrobiology	E. Enzyme
F. T Cell	G. Immunogloblin	H. Lepton	I. Organ	J. Organism
K. Isomer	L. Aerobic	M. Nucleoid	N. Bioengineering	O. Urea
P. Bioinformatics	Q. Effector Cell	R. Chemical reaction	S. Placebo	T. Histology

10. *Find the hidden words. The words have been placed horizontally, vertically, or diagonally. When you locate a word, draw a circle around it.*

U	T	Z	Y	F	B	I	O	M	A	S	S	W	G	A	E	A	J	H	V
M	A	A	P	H	Y	T	O	P	A	T	H	O	L	O	G	Y	A	X	A
E	L	E	C	T	R	O	N	M	I	C	R	O	S	C	O	P	E	E	S
D	C	D	B	I	O	P	H	Y	S	I	C	S	D	F	N	N	R	C	O
E	A	U	T	O	I	M	M	U	N	I	T	Y	Q	D	J	A	O	T	D
N	S	W	H	I	T	E	B	L	O	O	D	C	E	L	L	O	B	O	I
D	R	N	Z	Q	G	E	F	O	O	D	C	H	A	I	N	B	I	T	L
R	H	O	C	H	E	M	I	C	A	L	B	O	N	D	Z	C	O	H	A
I	S	U	H	Q	I	E	F	F	E	C	T	O	R	C	E	L	L	E	T
T	P	A	T	H	O	B	I	O	L	O	G	Y	F	A	U	Z	O	R	I
E	U	M	E	T	A	P	H	A	S	E	P	R	X	S	V	J	G	M	O
C	H	R	O	M	O	S	O	M	E	V	A	L	E	N	C	E	Y	H	N

1. A hierarchical series of organisms each dependent on the next as a source of food.
2. The study or practice of pathology with greater emphasis on the biological than on the medical aspects.
3. A lasting attraction between atoms that enables the formation of chemical compounds.
4. The study of organic particles, such as bacteria, fungal spores, very small insects, pollen grains and viruses, which are passively transported by the air.
5. An interdisciplinary science that applies the approaches and methods of physics to study biological systems.
6. The science of diagnosing and managing plant diseases.
7. A type of microscope that uses a beam of electrons to create an image of the specimen. It is capable of much higher magnifications.
8. A short branched extension of a nerve cell, along which impulses received from other cells at synapses are transmitted to the cell body
9. Refers to the number of elements to which it can connect.
10. Plasma cells, also called plasma B cells, plasmocytes, plasmacytes, or effector B cells, are white blood cells that secrete large volumes of antibodies.
11. The dilatation of blood vessels, which decreases blood pressure.
12. A threadlike strand of DNA in the cell nucleus that carries the genes in a linear order.
13. A organism in which internal physiological sources of heat are of relatively small or quite negligible importance in controlling body temperature. "Cold blooded".
14. The third phase of mitosis, the process that separates duplicated genetic material carried in the nucleus of a parent cell into two identical daughter cells.
15. The system of immune responses of an organism against its own healthy cells and tissues.
16. Organic matter derived from living, or recently living organisms.
17. Component of the blood that functions in the immune system. Also known as a leukocyte.
18. Giving birth to one of its kind, sexually or asexually.
19. A kind of swallowing cell, which means it functions by literally swallowing up other particles or smaller cells.

A. Electron Microscope
E. Chemical bond
I. Autoimmunity
M. Dendrite
Q. Phytopathology
B. Pathobiology
F. Chromosome
J. Macrophage
N. Vasodilation
R. Aerobiology
C. Biophysics
G. Valence
K. White Blood Cell
O. Effector Cell
S. Reproduction
D. Food Chain
H. Biomass
L. Metaphase
P. Ectotherm

11. *Find the hidden words. The words have been placed horizontally, vertically, or diagonally. When you locate a word, draw a circle around it.*

N	E	D	A	R	W	I	N	I	A	N	F	I	T	N	E	S	S	O	P
S	E	G	L	M	O	L	E	C	U	L	A	R	P	H	Y	S	I	C	S
X	H	E	I	I	Y	E	U	K	A	R	Y	O	T	E	A	M	J	S	S
S	V	N	P	H	F	M	E	Q	A	W	Q	J	J	V	G	W	A	C	F
S	D	O	O	I	R	B	N	L	Y	O	W	M	Q	V	S	J	T	D	N
V	M	M	P	J	M	R	D	U	K	O	V	H	S	F	J	N	O	T	E
D	O	E	R	E	I	Y	O	W	U	D	F	U	M	I	V	C	M	P	U
U	R	U	O	J	T	O	S	Y	U	W	F	E	L	L	I	P	I	D	R
M	H	W	T	U	O	L	P	K	R	E	B	S	C	Y	C	L	E	V	O
X	O	L	E	N	S	O	E	B	A	R	R	B	O	D	Y	K	O	J	N
Z	J	Q	I	U	I	G	R	B	I	O	C	H	E	M	I	S	T	R	Y
P	N	W	N	M	S	Y	M	N	U	C	L	E	I	C	A	C	I	D	B

1. A tissue produced inside the seeds of most of the flowering plants around the time of fertilization.
2. A chemically defined as a substance that is insoluble in water and soluble in alcohol, ether, and chloroform. The basis for fats and oils.
3. A series of chemical reactions used by all aerobic organisms to generate energy through the oxidation of acetyl
4. The branch of biology that studies the development of gametes (sex cells), fertilization, and development of embryos and fetuses.
5. The genetic contribution of an individual to the next generation's gene pool relative to the average for the population.
6. The inactive X chromosome in a female somatic cell, rendered inactive in a process called lionization
7. The study of the physical properties of molecules, the chemical bonds between atoms as well as the molecular dynamics.
8. The midsection of the small intestine of many higher vertebrates like mammals, birds, reptiles. It is present between the duodenum and the ileum.
9. Rain containing acids that form in the atmosphere when industrial gas emissions (especially sulfur dioxide and nitrogen oxides) combine with water.
10. The inner layer of the stems of woody plants; composed of xylem.
11. A biochemical assembly that contains both proteins and lipids, bound to the proteins, which allow fats to move through the water inside and outside cells.
12. The haploid set of chromosomes in a gamete or microorganism, or in each cell of a multicellular organism.
13. A succession of letters that indicate the order of nucleotides within a DNA (using GACT) or RNA (GACU) molecule.
14. A complex organic substance present in living cells, especially DNA or RNA, whose molecules consist of many nucleotides linked in a long chain.
15. The smallest component of an element having the chemical properties of the element
16. The branch of science that explores the chemical processes within and related to living organisms.
17. The branch of biology concerned with the relations between organisms and their environment.
18. The process in which a eukaryotic cell nucleus splits in two, followed by division of the parent cell into two daughter cells.
19. Any organism whose cells contain a nucleus and other organelles enclosed within membranes.
20. An electrically excitable cell that processes and transmits information through electrical and chemical signals.

A. Nucleic Acid Sequence
E. Jejunum
I. Eukaryote
M. Lipid
Q. Embryology

B. Genome
F. Atom
J. Nucleic Acid
N. Endosperm
R. Neuron

C. Darwinian Fitness
G. Krebs Cycle
K. Molecular physics
O. Mitosis
S. Lipoprotein

D. Acid precipitation
H. Biochemistry
L. Environmental Biology
P. Barr body
T. Wood

12. *Find the hidden words. The words have been placed horizontally, vertically, or diagonally. When you locate a word, draw a circle around it.*

C	H	B	E	N	T	H	I	C	Z	O	N	E	W	J	J	N	B	A	G
S	D	P	X	N	W	Z	O	N	C	O	L	O	G	Y	E	A	B	M	G
W	V	A	L	E	N	C	E	B	A	N	D	S	B	W	Q	M	I	I	C
C	B	I	O	T	E	C	H	N	O	L	O	G	Y	U	M	N	C	N	E
G	E	E	L	E	C	T	R	O	N	D	O	N	O	R	C	I	H	O	N
S	E	X	U	A	L	R	E	P	R	O	D	U	C	T	I	O	N	A	T
C	S	U	Y	I	C	D	T	U	D	A	L	T	O	N	P	T	F	C	R
L	V	B	I	O	E	N	E	R	G	E	T	I	C	S	M	E	B	I	O
M	A	E	O	B	I	O	D	I	V	E	R	S	I	T	Y	S	I	D	S
R	C	E	L	L	T	H	E	O	R	Y	D	A	F	R	N	H	P	B	O
E	P	I	D	E	M	I	O	L	O	G	Y	B	I	P	E	D	A	L	M
T	R	A	N	S	C	R	I	P	T	I	O	N	Z	L	A	R	V	A	E

1. A unit of mass (also known as an atomic mass unit, amu), equal to the mass of a hydrogen atom (1.67 x 1024 g).
2. The first step of gene expression, in which a particular segment of DNA is copied into RNA (mRNA) by the enzyme RNA polymerase.
3. The variety of life in the world or in a particular habitat or ecosystem.
4. A branch of medicine that deals with the prevention, diagnosis and treatment of cancer.
5. Type of reproduction in which cells from two parents unite to form the first cell of a new organism.
6. A class of organic compounds containing an amino group and a carboxylic acid group
7. The study of the transformation of energy in living organisms.
8. In cell biology, an organelle that is the main place where cell microtubules get organized. They occur only in plant and animal cells.
9. The theory that all living things are made up of cells.
10. The highest range of electron energies in which electrons are normally present at absolute zero temperature.
11. A form of terrestrial locomotion where an organism moves by means of its two rear limbs or legs.
12. An electron donor is a chemical entity that donates electrons to another compound.
13. The ecological region at the lowest level of a body of water such as an ocean or a lake, including the sediment surface and some sub
14. A distinct juvenile form many animals undergo before metamorphosis into adults. Animals with indirect development such as insects, amphibians, or cnidarians.
15. The use of living systems and organisms to develop or make products, or "any technological application that uses biological systems, living organisms or derivatives thereof.
16. The modern form of the metric system, and is the most widely used system of measurement.
17. Also known as antibodies, They act as a critical part of the immune response by specifically recognizing and binding to particular antigens, and aiding in their destruction.
18. The study and analysis of the patterns, causes, and effects of health and disease conditions in defined populations.
19. A microbially facilitated process of nitrate reduction that may ultimately produce molecular nitrogen.
20. Organisms that produce an egg composed of shell and membranes that creates a protected environment in which the embryo can develop out of water

A. Bioenergetics
E. Electron Donor
I. Benthic zone
M. Biotechnology
Q. Larva

B. Denitrification
F. International System
J. Valence band
N. Biodiversity
R. Centrosome

C. Bipedal
G. Sexual Reproduction
K. Transcription
O. Epidemiology
S. Amino acid

D. Amniotes
H. Cell theory
L. Oncology
P. Dalton
T. Immunogloblin

13. *Find the hidden words. The words have been placed horizontally, vertically, or diagonally. When you locate a word, draw a circle around it.*

Z	N	B	B	I	V	A	G	V	C	S	A	P	E	W	Z	M	D	M	C
X	L	I	R	L	E	G	E	N	P	T	S	A	X	Z	B	E	C	A	P
T	Q	L	Y	A	R	R	N	O	E	E	H	R	P	U	U	S	O	S	R
V	C	E	P	C	R	I	E	J	F	R	N	A	R	Q	A	S	G	S	K
Z	A	M	H	T	P	C	P	E	F	O	O	S	E	F	M	E	P	D	N
M	R	Y	A	E	S	U	O	W	E	I	C	I	S	X	N	N	X	E	Y
H	B	C	S	A	X	L	O	D	C	D	N	T	S	T	I	G	B	N	E
P	O	O	L	U	C	T	U	V	T	A	V	O	I	Z	O	E	Z	S	M
P	N	L	C	U	Z	U	P	B	O	S	B	L	V	B	T	R	V	I	U
C	A	O	R	P	X	R	R	S	R	B	V	O	I	T	E	R	C	T	W
G	T	G	F	K	V	E	S	I	C	L	E	G	T	P	S	N	D	Y	D
U	E	Y	B	A	R	R	B	O	D	Y	N	Y	Y	R	A	A	S	K	N

1. The branch of biology concerned with the study of fungi, including their genetic and biochemical properties, their taxonomy and their use to humans.
2. Variations in a phenotype among individuals carrying a particular genotype.
3. Density is mass per volume.
4. The practice of cultivating land, growing food, and raising stock.
5. The stock of different genes in an interbreeding population.
6. Organisms that produce an egg composed of shell and membranes that creates a protected environment in which the embryo can develop out of water
7. The study of parasites, their hosts, and the relationship between them.
8. Any of various molecules that are capable of accepting one or two electrons from one molecule and donating them to another in the process of electron transport.
9. An organic compound with four rings arranged in a specific configuration. Examples include the dietary lipid cholesterol and the sex hormones.
10. The inactive X chromosome in a female somatic cell, rendered inactive in a process called lionization
11. A lymphatic capillary that absorbs dietary fats in the villi of the small intestine.
12. Any member of two classes of chemical compounds derived from carbonic acid or carbon dioxide.
13. Glands that secrete their products, hormones, directly into the blood rather than through a duct.
14. A fluid or air-filled cavity or sac.
15. A very large molecule, such as protein, commonly created by polymerization of smaller subunits (monomers).
16. An organ or cell that acts in response to a stimulus.
17. Also known as antibodies, They act as a critical part of the immune response by specifically recognizing and binding to particular antigens, and aiding in their destruction.
18. The form of RNA in which genetic information transcribed from DNA as a sequence of bases is transferred to a ribosome.
19. A dark green to yellowish brown fluid, produced by the liver of most vertebrates, that aids the digestion of lipids in the small intestine.
20. Organism which is capable of producing energy through aerobic respiration and then switching to anaerobic respiration depending on the amounts of oxygen.

A. Gene Pool
E. Endocrine Gland
I. Amniotes
M. Lacteal
Q. Bile

B. Effector
F. Parasitology
J. Carbonate
N. Macromolecule
R. Mycology

C. Agriculture
G. Barr body
K. Steroid
O. Facultative Anaerobe
S. Expressivity

D. Mass Density
H. Immunogloblin
L. Electron Carrier
P. Vesicle
T. Messenger RNA

14. *Find the hidden words. The words have been placed horizontally, vertically, or diagonally. When you locate a word, draw a circle around it.*

E	N	D	O	C	Y	T	O	S	I	S	V	X	D	Z	S	Q	E	B	N
P	H	E	N	O	T	Y	P	E	M	Y	B	A	R	R	B	O	D	Y	U
D	A	R	W	I	N	I	A	N	F	I	T	N	E	S	S	H	C	X	C
M	W	P	L	A	N	T	N	U	T	R	I	T	I	O	N	F	D	H	L
A	B	I	O	P	H	Y	S	I	C	S	T	H	E	G	J	S	B	W	E
M	P	O	Z	Y	P	H	E	R	P	E	T	O	L	O	G	Y	O	H	O
M	N	E	T	B	A	C	T	E	R	I	O	P	H	A	G	E	T	J	T
A	H	B	C	E	N	T	R	O	I	D	B	H	A	O	T	J	A	E	I
L	O	C	E	L	L	B	I	O	L	O	G	Y	C	A	K	H	N	E	D
O	X	I	S	G	M	Y	O	S	I	N	X	L	T	R	F	X	Y	X	E
G	A	C	T	I	V	E	S	I	T	E	V	L	I	M	A	V	Z	O	O
Y	M	O	L	A	R	I	T	Y	K	T	R	P	N	U	Y	U	N	N	S

1. The yellow colored photosynthetic pigments.
2. A unit of concentration measuring the number of moles of a solute per liter of solution.
3. The study of plants.
4. The study of the chemical elements and compounds necessary for plant growth, plant metabolism and their external supply.
5. The set of observable characteristics of an individual resulting from the interaction of its genotype with the environment.
6. The part of an enzyme or antibody where the chemical reaction occurs
7. A chemical reaction in which the standard change in free energy is positive, and energy is absorbed
8. Any part of a gene that will become a part of the final mature RNA produced by that gene after introns have been removed by RNA splicing.
9. The inactive X chromosome in a female somatic cell, rendered inactive in a process called lionization
10. A measure of the tendency of an atom to attract a bonding pair of electrons. The Pauling scale is the most commonly used.
11. The genetic contribution of an individual to the next generation's gene pool relative to the average for the population.
12. Large superfamily of motor proteins that move along actin filaments, while hydrolyzing ATP.
13. Organic molecules that serve as the monomers, or subunits, of nucleic acids like DNA (deoxyribonucleic acid) and RNA (ribonucleic acid).
14. The intersection of the three medians of the triangle (each median connecting a vertex with the midpoint of the opposite side).
15. The branch of zoology concerned with reptiles and amphibians.
16. One of the proteins into which actomyosin can be split; can exist in either a globular or a fibrous form.
17. An interdisciplinary science that applies the approaches and methods of physics to study biological systems.
18. Virus that infects and multiplies within bacteria.
19. A form of active transport in which a cell transports molecules (such as proteins) into the cell (endo
20. The study of mammals. A class of vertebrates with characteristics such as homeothermic metabolism, fur, four
21. Explains the structure, organization of the organelles they contain, their physiological properties, metabolic processes, signaling pathways, life cycle, and interactions.

A. Xanthophyll
E. Cell biology
I. Myosin
M. Electronegativity
Q. Phenotype
U. Bacteriophage

B. Herpetology
F. Barr body
J. Darwinian Fitness
N. Centroid
R. Mammalogy

C. Active site
G. Exon
K. Endocytosis
O. Nucleotide
S. Endergonic Reaction

D. Plant Nutrition
H. Botany
L. Biophysics
P. Molarity
T. Actin

15. *Find the hidden words. The words have been placed horizontally, vertically, or diagonally. When you locate a word, draw a circle around it.*

O	T	Q	D	E	P	H	A	R	M	A	C	O	L	O	G	Y	D	N	A
P	H	Y	T	O	P	A	T	H	O	L	O	G	Y	C	W	Z	U	N	P
O	R	G	A	N	I	S	M	E	N	D	O	S	P	E	R	M	U	E	O
A	D	E	N	Y	L	A	T	E	C	Y	C	L	A	S	E	R	X	U	L
Z	O	O	L	O	G	Y	L	I	P	O	P	R	O	T	E	I	N	T	Y
Q	O	A	B	S	C	I	S	I	C	A	C	I	D	M	T	J	B	R	P
P	H	E	T	E	R	O	S	I	S	R	K	P	O	G	U	A	Q	I	L
Z	V	N	T	V	U	N	U	C	L	E	O	L	U	S	M	K	B	N	O
Q	Z	T	A	Z	B	M	P	H	A	S	E	N	V	N	H	G	Z	O	I
D	E	C	T	O	T	H	E	R	M	Z	T	C	L	O	N	I	N	G	D
B	B	E	H	A	V	I	O	R	A	L	E	C	O	L	O	G	Y	Y	Y
P	O	P	U	L	A	T	I	O	N	G	E	N	E	T	I	C	S	C	F

1. A organism in which internal physiological sources of heat are of relatively small or quite negligible importance in controlling body temperature. "Cold blooded".
2. A biochemical assembly that contains both proteins and lipids, bound to the proteins, which allow fats to move through the water inside and outside cells.
3. The study of the evolutionary basis for animal behavior due to ecological pressures.
4. a plant hormone.
5. A small dense spherical structure in the nucleus of a cell during interphase.
6. The study of genetic variation within populations, and involves the examination and modeling of changes in the frequencies of genes and alleles.
7. Containing more than two homologous sets of chromosomes.
8. The science of drug action on biological systems.
9. Propagate (an organism or cell) to make an identical copy of.
10. An individual animal, plant, or single-celled life form.
11. An enzyme that catalyzes the formation of cyclic AMP from ATP.
12. An elementary particle with half-integer spin, that interacts only via the weak subatomic force and gravity. Its mass is tiny compared to other subatomic particles.
13. the tendency of a crossbred individual to show qualities superior to those of both parents.
14. The science of diagnosing and managing plant diseases.
15. A tissue produced inside the seeds of most of the flowering plants around the time of fertilization.
16. Mitosis and cytokinesis together define this phase of an animal cell cycle-the division of the mother cell into two daughter cells, genetically identical to each other and the parent.
17. The study of the history of life on Earth as reflected in the fossil record. Fossils are the remains or traces of organisms.
18. The branch of biology that relates to the animal kingdom, including the structure, embryology, evolution, classification, habits, and distribution of all animals.
19. An inner layer of cells in the cortex of a root and of some stems, surrounding a vascular bundle.
20. Nutrients that provide calories or energy. Nutrients are substances needed for growth, metabolism, and for other body functions.

A. Ectotherm
B. Zoology
C. Neutrino
D. Heterosis
E. Abscisic acid
F. Polyploidy
G. Lipoprotein
H. Endosperm
I. Macronutrient
J. Nucleolus
K. Organism
L. Population Genetics
M. Adenylate cyclase
N. Paleontology
O. Behavioral ecology
P. Phytopathology
Q. Pharmacology
R. Cloning
S. Endodermis
T. M phase

16. *Find the hidden words. The words have been placed horizontally, vertically, or diagonally. When you locate a word, draw a circle around it.*

V	A	N	H	J	H	C	L	O	N	I	N	G	G	E	N	E	C	S	F
E	M	L	X	U	E	C	T	O	D	E	R	M	Q	M	E	A	W	G	C
S	I	Q	B	D	B	I	O	E	N	E	R	G	E	T	I	C	S	T	P
I	N	R	K	W	E	N	D	O	C	Y	T	O	S	I	S	G	G	B	M
C	O	E	L	E	M	E	N	T	B	I	O	P	H	Y	S	I	C	S	O
L	A	N	P	L	A	N	T	N	U	T	R	I	T	I	O	N	M	R	K
E	C	A	Q	N	A	B	S	O	R	P	T	I	O	N	E	Z	S	H	Q
R	I	C	T	F	W	Z	J	M	E	S	S	E	N	G	E	R	R	N	A
D	D	V	L	V	A	L	E	N	C	E	E	L	E	C	T	R	O	N	K
P	R	E	D	A	T	I	O	N	B	A	R	R	B	O	D	Y	I	U	X
P	Z	H	A	D	R	O	N	V	A	S	O	D	I	L	A	T	I	O	N
L	V	M	L	E	U	K	O	C	Y	T	E	D	Y	I	G	D	V	U	Z

1. Any particle that is made from quarks, anti
2. The inactive X chromosome in a female somatic cell, rendered inactive in a process called lionization
3. The study of the transformation of energy in living organisms.
4. The form of RNA in which genetic information transcribed from DNA as a sequence of bases is transferred to a ribosome.
5. The outermost layer of cells or tissue of an embryo in early development, or the parts derived from this, which include the epidermis, nerve tissue, and nephridia.
6. A colorless cell which circulates in the blood and body fluids and is involved in counteracting foreign substances and disease; a white (blood) cell.
7. A form of active transport in which a cell transports molecules (such as proteins) into the cell (endo
8. An interdisciplinary science that applies the approaches and methods of physics to study biological systems.
9. A gene is a locus (or region) of DNA that encodes a functional RNA or protein product, and is the molecular unit of heredity.
10. A species of atoms having the same number of protons in their atomic nuclei (i.e. the same atomic number, Z).
11. The preying of one animal on others.
12. A class of organic compounds containing an amino group and a carboxylic acid group
13. The study of the chemical elements and compounds necessary for plant growth, plant metabolism and their external supply.
14. Propagate (an organism or cell) to make an identical copy of.
15. An electron that is associated with an atom, and that can participate in the formation of a chemical bond.
16. A process in which one substance permeates another; a fluid permeates or is dissolved by a liquid or solid.
17. A fluid or air-filled cavity or sac.
18. The dilatation of blood vessels, which decreases blood pressure.

A. Leukocyte
B. Cloning
C. Vasodilation
D. Element
E. Barr body
F. Bioenergetics
G. Messenger RNA
H. Biophysics
I. Vesicle
J. Plant Nutrition
K. Valence electron
L. Endocytosis
M. Gene
N. Hadron
O. Predation
P. Ectoderm
Q. Amino acid
R. Absorption

17. *Find the hidden words. The words have been placed horizontally, vertically, or diagonally. When you locate a word, draw a circle around it.*

E	N	D	O	S	Y	M	B	I	O	T	I	C	T	H	E	O	R	Y	H
G	T	Y	N	U	C	L	E	O	T	I	D	E	R	J	V	C	X	E	E
P	Q	R	K	G	R	J	P	H	E	N	O	T	Y	P	E	S	C	X	T
C	H	E	R	M	A	P	H	R	O	D	I	T	E	J	P	C	B	O	E
N	E	C	O	L	O	G	I	C	A	L	P	Y	R	A	M	I	D	N	R
T	P	O	P	U	L	A	T	I	O	N	G	E	N	E	T	I	C	S	O
D	F	M	I	C	R	O	E	V	O	L	U	T	I	O	N	D	R	O	S
I	W	P	K	M	O	N	O	M	E	R	V	I	R	U	S	B	A	R	I
G	E	N	E	P	O	O	L	D	J	X	B	O	T	A	N	Y	U	G	S
M	A	R	I	N	E	B	I	O	L	O	G	Y	A	C	T	I	N	A	B
E	P	I	N	E	P	H	R	I	N	E	M	R	A	Z	I	T	L	N	F
M	P	P	O	P	U	L	A	T	I	O	N	E	C	O	L	O	G	Y	P

1. the tendency of a crossbred individual to show qualities superior to those of both parents.
2. A molecule that can be bonded to other identical molecules to form a polymer.
3. The set of observable characteristics of an individual resulting from the interaction of its genotype with the environment.
4. A sub-field of ecology that deals with the dynamics of species populations and how these populations interact with the environment.
5. Any part of a gene that will become a part of the final mature RNA produced by that gene after introns have been removed by RNA splicing.
6. The study of genetic variation within populations, and involves the examination and modeling of changes in the frequencies of genes and alleles.
7. Evolutionary change within a species or small group of organisms, especially over a short period.
8. The stock of different genes in an interbreeding population.
9. a part of an organism that is typically self-contained and has a specific vital function, such as the heart or liver in humans.
10. The study of plants.
11. Organism with both male and female reproductive organs.
12. An evolutionary theory that explains the origin of eukaryotic cells from prokaryotes.
13. Organic molecules that serve as the monomers, or subunits, of nucleic acids like DNA (deoxyribonucleic acid) and RNA (ribonucleic acid).
14. A biological agent that reproduces inside the cells of living hosts.
15. The modern form of the metric system, and is the most widely used system of measurement.
16. Another term for adrenaline.
17. A graphical representation designed to show the biomass or bio productivity at each trophic level in a given ecosystem.
18. One of the proteins into which actomyosin can be split; can exist in either a globular or a fibrous form.
19. The scientific study of organisms in the ocean or other marine bodies of water.
20. The double helix is unwound and each strand acts as a template for the next strand. Bases are matched to synthesize the new partner strands.
21. An application of conservation of mass to the analysis of physical systems.
22. A sequence of three nucleotides forming a unit of genetic code in a transfer RNA molecule, corresponding to a complementary codon in messenger RNA.

A. Epinephrine
E. Actin
I. Population Genetics
M. Organ
Q. DNA Replication
U. Mass Balance

B. Gene Pool
F. Virus
J. Exon
N. Hermaphrodite
R. Nucleotide
V. Microevolution

C. Heterosis
G. Population Ecology
K. Monomer
O. International System
S. Phenotype

D. Botany
H. Ecological Pyramid
L. Endosymbiotic Theory
P. Anticodon
T. Marine Biology

18. *Find the hidden words. The words have been placed horizontally, vertically, or diagonally. When you locate a word, draw a circle around it.*

V	M	C	Z	A	J	V	B	M	J	L	O	C	P	V	D	B	C	A	O
S	O	R	U	T	Y	M	P	B	T	L	S	Y	W	N	H	R	K	I	R
V	L	D	M	O	K	V	W	W	P	F	M	U	D	R	W	J	V	N	N
R	E	T	Y	M	P	O	A	N	A	T	O	M	Y	C	I	C	T	T	I
F	A	M	N	I	O	T	E	S	C	B	S	G	X	W	E	Y	C	E	T
U	E	N	D	O	D	E	R	M	L	S	I	T	R	Q	Q	G	E	R	H
W	O	O	D	V	B	P	D	I	O	Y	S	F	K	Q	H	C	P	L	O
P	O	P	U	L	A	T	I	O	N	E	C	O	L	O	G	Y	R	E	L
D	I	N	E	N	D	O	C	R	I	N	E	S	Y	S	T	E	M	U	O
P	L	A	C	E	B	O	B	S	N	F	U	Q	Y	T	A	V	A	K	G
M	Y	O	F	I	B	R	I	L	G	W	D	P	D	A	D	R	L	I	Y
S	A	S	Y	P	O	L	Y	P	L	O	I	D	Y	K	H	W	V	N	H

1. Propagate (an organism or cell) to make an identical copy of.
2. The SI unit of measurement used to measure the number of things, usually atoms or molecules.
3. The collection of glands that produce hormones that regulate metabolism, growth and development, tissue function, sexual function, reproduction, sleep, and mood.
4. Organisms that produce an egg composed of shell and membranes that creates a protected environment in which the embryo can develop out of water
5. Containing more than two homologous sets of chromosomes.
6. The smallest component of an element having the chemical properties of the element
7. A branch of zoology that concerns the study of birds.
8. The spontaneous net movement of solvent molecules through a semi-permeable membrane into a region of higher solute concentration.
9. A group of cytokines (secreted proteins and signal molecules) that were first seen to be expressed by white blood cells (leukocytes)
10. The inner layer of the stems of woody plants; composed of xylem.
11. Any of the elongated contractile threads found in striated muscle cells.
12. A chemical reaction in which the standard change in free energy is positive, and energy is absorbed
13. A sub-field of ecology that deals with the dynamics of species populations and how these populations interact with the environment.
14. The branch of biology that studies the development of gametes (sex cells), fertilization, and development of embryos and fetuses.
15. A network of membranous tubules within the cytoplasm of a eukaryotic cell, continuous with the nuclear membrane.
16. A harmless pill, medicine, or procedure prescribed more for the psychological benefit to the patient than for any physiological effect.
17. The first step of gene expression, in which a particular segment of DNA is copied into RNA (mRNA) by the enzyme RNA polymerase.
18. One of the three primary germ layers in the very early human embryo. The other two layers are the ectoderm (outside layer) and mesoderm (middle layer).
19. The genetic contribution of an individual to the next generation's gene pool relative to the average for the population.
20. The branch of morphology that deals with the structure of animals

A. Embryology
E. Myofibril
I. Ornithology
M. Transcription
Q. Endergonic Reaction

B. Cloning
F. Darwinian Fitness
J. Atom
N. Placebo
R. Endoderm

C. Population Ecology
G. Amniotes
K. Wood
O. Endocrine System
S. Interleukin

D. Osmosis
H. Polyploidy
L. Endoplasmic Reticulum
P. Mole
T. Anatomy

19. *Find the hidden words. The words have been placed horizontally, vertically, or diagonally. When you locate a word, draw a circle around it.*

O	C	J	A	U	T	O	I	M	M	U	N	I	T	Y	K	R	K	G	Q
X	L	C	H	O	L	E	S	T	E	R	O	L	J	E	J	U	N	U	M
M	A	C	R	O	N	U	T	R	I	E	N	T	M	E	D	U	L	L	A
L	O	X	I	P	I	H	B	A	D	E	N	I	N	E	B	U	N	H	Z
X	G	G	E	N	E	T	I	C	V	A	R	I	A	T	I	O	N	K	H
U	C	H	M	E	M	B	R	A	N	E	P	O	T	E	N	T	I	A	L
A	R	T	I	F	I	C	I	A	L	S	E	L	E	C	T	I	O	N	X
Y	U	R	E	X	M	Q	V	A	C	U	O	L	E	F	T	J	N	C	R
E	C	O	L	O	G	I	C	A	L	P	Y	R	A	M	I	D	G	W	V
S	N	A	T	U	R	A	L	S	E	L	E	C	T	I	O	N	D	Q	C
F	U	B	U	H	D	O	N	C	O	L	O	G	Y	F	E	T	U	S	L
E	G	H	E	R	M	A	P	H	R	O	D	I	T	E	I	O	N	D	L

1. Also known as selective breeding.
2. Variations of genomes between members of species, or between groups of species thriving in different parts of the world as a result of genetic mutation.
3. A branch of medicine that deals with the prevention, diagnosis and treatment of cancer.
4. The system of immune responses of an organism against its own healthy cells and tissues.
5. A membrane-bound organelle which is present in all plant and fungal cells and some protist, animal and bacterial cells.
6. An atom or molecule with a net electric charge due to the loss or gain of one or more electrons.
7. A process in nature in which organisms possessing certain genotypic characteristics that make them better adjusted to an environment tend to survive.
8. A graphical representation designed to show the biomass or bio productivity at each trophic level in a given ecosystem.
9. One of the two purine nucleobases (the other being guanine) used in forming nucleotides of the nucleic acids.
10. When a nerve or muscle cell is at "rest", its membrane potential is called the resting membrane potential.
11. Organism with both male and female reproductive organs.
12. Nutrients that provide calories or energy. Nutrients are substances needed for growth, metabolism, and for other body functions.
13. The continuation of the spinal cord within the skull, forming the lowest part of the brainstem and containing control centers for the heart and lungs.
14. An organic lipid molecule that is biosynthesized by all animal cells because it is an essential structural component of all animal cell membranes.
15. The independent evolution of similar traits, starting from a similar ancestral condition.
16. The preying of one animal on others.
17. The midsection of the small intestine of many higher vertebrates like mammals, birds, reptiles. It is present between the duodenum and the ileum.
18. The branch of biology dealing with the functions and activities of living organisms and their parts, including all physical and chemical processes.
19. A human embryo after eight weeks of development.
20. Refers to genetically determined structures or attributes that have apparently lost most or all of their ancestral function in a given species.

A. Ecological Pyramid   B. Vestigiality   C. Ion   D. Oncology   E. Jejunum
F. Vacuole   G. Fetus   H. Cholesterol   I. Autoimmunity   J. Genetic Variation
K. Macronutrient   L. Parallel Evolution   M. Predation   N. Hermaphrodite   O. Artificial Selection
P. Membrane Potential   Q. Adenine   R. Natural Selection   S. Medulla   T. Physiology

20. *Find the hidden words. The words have been placed horizontally, vertically, or diagonally. When you locate a word, draw a circle around it.*

R	V	H	A	D	R	O	N	B	I	O	C	A	T	A	L	Y	S	T	S
U	W	A	C	T	I	V	E	T	R	A	N	S	P	O	R	T	G	L	K
W	X	W	S	C	N	T	H	Y	M	I	N	E	T	W	A	E	P	E	B
A	P	Y	V	E	S	T	I	G	I	A	L	I	T	Y	F	V	J	P	I
G	X	E	U	K	A	R	Y	O	T	E	B	I	O	N	I	C	S	T	O
V	E	P	I	G	E	N	E	T	I	C	S	A	M	O	L	E	V	O	P
W	B	P	A	R	A	L	L	E	L	E	V	O	L	U	T	I	O	N	H
D	A	B	V	C	L	O	N	I	N	G	K	K	N	K	F	Q	V	O	Y
T	Y	H	J	Z	H	X	P	A	L	E	O	N	T	O	L	O	G	Y	S
P	A	N	Y	X	X	W	T	E	S	T	O	S	T	E	R	O	N	E	I
M	O	Z	P	O	L	L	I	N	A	T	I	O	N	K	J	A	A	V	C
O	O	N	C	O	L	O	G	Y	B	L	Y	O	L	K	X	M	Q	R	S

1. A steroid hormone from the androgen group and is found in humans and other vertebrates.
2. Any organism whose cells contain a nucleus and other organelles enclosed within membranes.
3. The study, in the field of genetics, of cellular and physiological phenotypic trait variations that are caused by external or environmental factors that switch genes on and off.
4. Transport of a substance (as a protein or drug) across a cell membrane against the concentration gradient; requires an expenditure of energy
5. An interdisciplinary science that applies the approaches and methods of physics to study biological systems.
6. Propagate (an organism or cell) to make an identical copy of.
7. Catalysis in living systems. In biological processes, natural catalysts, such as protein enzymes, perform chemical transformations on organic compounds.
8. One of the four nucleobases in the nucleic acid of DNA that are represented by the letters G–C–A–T.
9. The study of the history of life on Earth as reflected in the fossil record. Fossils are the remains or traces of organisms.
10. The yellow internal part of a bird's egg, which is surrounded by the white, is rich in protein and fat, and nourishes the developing embryo.
11. Refers to genetically determined structures or attributes that have apparently lost most or all of their ancestral function in a given species.
12. The act of transferring pollen grains from the male anther of a flower to the female stigma.
13. The SI unit of measurement used to measure the number of things, usually atoms or molecules.
14. A branch of medicine that deals with the prevention, diagnosis and treatment of cancer.
15. Application of biological methods and systems found in nature to the study and design of engineering systems and modern technology.
16. The independent evolution of similar traits, starting from a similar ancestral condition.
17. Any particle that is made from quarks, anti
18. An elementary, half-integer spin particle that does not undergo strong interactions.

A. Hadron
F. Yolk
K. Biocatalysts
P. Pollination

B. Epigenetics
G. Mole
L. Oncology
Q. Lepton

C. Active Transport
H. Vestigiality
M. Cloning
R. Biophysics

D. Parallel Evolution
I. Bionics
N. Eukaryote

E. Paleontology
J. Thymine
O. Testosterone

Glossary

Abscisic acid: a plant hormone.

Abscission: Shedding of flowers and leaves and fruit following formation of scar tissue in a plant.

Absolute zero: The lowest theoretically attainable temperature (at which the kinetic energy of atoms and molecules is minimal)

Absorption: A process in which one substance permeates another; a fluid permeates or is dissolved by a liquid or solid.

Absorption spectrum: The spectrum of electromagnetic radiation that has passed through a medium that absorbed radiation of certain wavelengths.

Abyssal zone: The deep sea (2000 meters or more) where there is no light.

Acclimatization: Adaptation to a new climate (a new temperature or altitude or environment).

Acid precipitation: Rain containing acids that form in the atmosphere when industrial gas emissions (especially sulfur dioxide and nitrogen oxides) combine with water.

Acoelomate: Animals, like flatworms and jellyfish, that have no body cavity (coelom). Semi-solid mesodermal tissues between the gut and body wall hold their organs in place.

Actin: One of the proteins into which actomyosin can be split; can exist in either a globular or a fibrous form.

Action potential: The local voltage change across the cell wall as a nerve impulse is transmitted.

Activation energy: The energy that an atomic system must acquire before a process (such as an emission or reaction) can occur.

Active site: The part of an enzyme or antibody where the chemical reaction occurs

Active Transport: Transport of a substance (as a protein or drug) across a cell membrane against the concentration gradient; requires an expenditure of energy

Adenine: One of the two purine nucleobases (the other being guanine) used in forming nucleotides of the nucleic acids.

Adenosine Triphosphate: A nucleotide derived from adenosine that occurs in muscle tissue; the major source of energy for cellular reactions.

Adenylate cyclase: An enzyme that catalyzes the formation of cyclic AMP from ATP.

Aerobic: Depending on free oxygen or air.

Aerobiology: The study of organic particles, such as bacteria, fungal spores, very small insects, pollen grains and viruses, which are passively transported by the air.

Agriculture: The practice of cultivating land, growing food, and raising stock.

Agrobiology: The study of plant nutrition and growth especially as a way to increase crop yield

Amino acid: A class of organic compounds containing an amino group and a carboxylic acid group

Amniotes: Organisms that produce an egg composed of shell and membranes that creates a protected environment in which the embryo can develop out of water

Anatomy: The branch of morphology that deals with the structure of animals

Antibiotic: A class of drug used to kill bacteria.

Anticodon: A sequence of three nucleotides forming a unit of genetic code in a transfer RNA molecule, corresponding to a complementary codon in messenger RNA.

Arachnology: Scientific study of spiders, scorpions, pseudo-scorpions, and harvestmen, collectively called arachnids.

Artificial Selection: Also known as selective breeding.

Asexual Reproduction: Process of reproduction involving a single parent that results in offspring that are genetically identical to the parent.

Astrobiology: The branch of biology concerned with the effects of outer space on living organisms and the search for extraterrestrial life

Atom: The smallest component of an element having the chemical properties of the element

Autoimmunity: The system of immune responses of an organism against its own healthy cells and tissues.

B cell: Type of lymphocyte in the humeral immunity of the adaptive immune system.

Bacteria: Single-cell microscopic organisms which lack a true nucleus. They represent one of the three domains.

Bacteriophage: Virus that infects and multiplies within bacteria.

Barr body: The inactive X chromosome in a female somatic cell, rendered inactive in a process called lionization

Basal body: An organelle formed from a centriole, and a short cylindrical array of microtubules.

Behavioral Ecology: The study of the evolutionary basis for animal behavior due to ecological pressures.

Benthic zone: The ecological region at the lowest level of a body of water such as an ocean or a lake, including the sediment surface and some sub-surface layers.

Bile: A dark green to yellowish brown fluid, produced by the liver of most vertebrates, that aids the digestion of lipids in the small intestine.

Binary fission: One cell dividing into two identical daughter cells.

Biocatalysts: Catalysis in living systems. In bio catalytic processes, natural catalysts, such as protein enzymes, perform chemical transformations on organic compounds.

Biochemistry: The branch of science that explores the chemical processes within and related to living organisms. It is a laboratory based science that brings together biology and chemistry.

Biodiversity: The variety of life in the world or in a particular habitat or ecosystem.

Bioengineering: The application of concepts and methods of biology to solve real-world problems.

Bioenergetics: The study of the transformation of energy in living organisms.

Biogeography: The study of the distribution of species and ecosystems in geographic space and through time.

Bioinformatics: The application of computer technology to the management of biological information.

Biology: Study of living organisms.

Biomass: Organic matter derived from living, or recently living organisms.

Biomathematics: The field is also called mathematical.

Biome: Very large ecological areas on the earth's surface, with fauna and flora (animals and plants) adapting to their environment.

Biomechanics: The study of the structure and function of biological systems by means of the methods of "mechanics."

Biomedical engineering: The application of engineering principles and design concepts to medicine and biology for healthcare purposes (e.g. diagnostic or therapeutic).

Biomedical research: The pursuit of answers to medical questions. These investigations lead to discoveries, which in turn lead to the development of new preventions, therapies and cures.

Bionics: Application of biological methods and systems found in nature to the study and design of engineering systems and modern technology.

Biophysics: An interdisciplinary science that applies the approaches and methods of physics to study biological systems.

Biotechnology: The use of living systems and organisms to develop or make products, or "any technological application that uses biological systems, living organisms or derivatives thereof.

Bipedal: A form of terrestrial locomotion where an organism moves by means of its two rear limbs or legs.

Blastocyst: A mammalian blastula in which some differentiation of cells has occurred.

Blood: The red liquid that circulates in the arteries and veins of humans and other vertebrate animals, carrying oxygen to and carbon dioxide from the tissues of the body.

Botany: The study of plants.

Bowman's capsule: A cup-like sac at the beginning of the tubular component of a nephron in the mammalian kidney that performs the first step in the filtration of blood to form urine.

Cell: The structural and functional unit of all organisms; an autonomous self-replicating unit that may exist as functional independent unit of life.

Carbonate: Any member of two classes of chemical compounds derived from carbonic acid or carbon dioxide.

Cell biology: Explains the structure, organization of the organelles they contain, their physiological properties, metabolic processes, signaling pathways, life cycle, and interactions.

Cell membrane: The semipermeable membrane surrounding the cytoplasm of a cell.

Cell nucleus: The "control room" for the cell. The nucleus gives out all the orders.

Cell theory: The theory that all living things are made up of cells.

Centroid: The centroid of a triangle is the intersection of the three medians of the triangle (each median connecting a vertex with the midpoint of the opposite side).

Centrosome: In cell biology, the centrosome is an organelle that is the main place where cell microtubules get organized. They occur only in plant and animal cells.

Chemical bond: A lasting attraction between atoms that enables the formation of chemical compounds.

Chemical compound: A chemical substance consisting of two or more different chemically bonded chemical elements, with a fixed ratio determining the composition.

Chemical equilibrium: The state in which both reactants and products are present in concentrations which have no further tendency to change with time.

Chemical kinetics: The study and discussion of chemical reactions with respect to reaction rates, effect of various variables, re-arrangement of atoms, formation of intermediates etc.

Chemical reaction: Usually characterized by a chemical change, and they yield one or more products, which usually have properties different from the reactants

Chemistry: A branch of physical science that studies the composition, structure, properties and change of matter.

Chloride: A compound of chlorine with another element or group, especially a salt of the anion or an organic compound with chlorine bonded to an alkyl group.

Chloroplast: Work to convert light energy of the Sun into sugars that can be used by cells.

Cholesterol: An organic lipid molecule that is biosynthesized by all animal cells because it is an essential structural component of all animal cell membranes.

Chromosome: A threadlike strand of DNA in the cell nucleus that carries the genes in a linear order.

Cloning: Propagate (an organism or cell) as a clone, to make an identical copy of.

Conservation Biology: The scientific study of nature and of Earth's biodiversity with the aim of protecting species, their habitats, and ecosystems from excessive rates of extinction.

Cryobiology: The branch of biology that studies the effects of low temperatures on living things within Earth's cryosphere or in science.

Dalton: A unit of mass (also known as an atomic mass unit, amu), equal to the mass of a hydrogen atom (1.67×1024 g).

Darwinian Fitness: The genetic contribution of an individual to the next generation's gene pool relative to the average for the population.

Deciduous: Means "falling off at maturity" or "tending to fall off", and it is typically used in order to refer to trees or shrubs that lose their leaves seasonally (most commonly during autumn).

Dehydration Reaction: Usually defined as a chemical reaction that involves the loss of a water molecule from the reacting molecule.

Denaturation: A process in which proteins or nucleic acids lose the quaternary structure, tertiary structure and secondary structure which is present in their native state.

Dendrite: A short branched extension of a nerve cell, along which impulses received from other cells at synapses are transmitted to the cell body

Denitrification: A microbially facilitated process of nitrate reduction (performed by a large group of heterotrophic facultative anaerobic bacteria) that may ultimately produce molecular nitrogen.

Deoxyribonucleic Acid:The four bases found in DNA are adenine (abbreviated A), cytosine (C), guanine (G) and thymine (T). These four bases are attached to the sugar-phosphate.

Deoxyribose: A monosaccharide. Its name indicates that it is a deoxy sugar, meaning that it is derived from the sugar ribose by loss of an oxygen atom.

Depolarization: The process of reversing the charge across a cell membrane (usually a NEURON), so causing an ACTION POTENTIAL.

Desmosome: Also known as a macula adhaerens, is a cell structure specialized for cell-to-cell adhesion

DNA: The hereditary material in humans and almost all other organisms.

DNA Replication: The double helix is unwound and each strand acts as a template for the next strand. Bases are matched to synthesize the new partner strands.

DNA Sequencing: The process of determining the precise order of nucleotides within a DNA molecule.

Dynein: A motor protein (also called molecular motor or motor molecule) in cells which converts the chemical energy contained in ATP into the mechanical energy of movement

Ecdysone: A steroidal prohormone of the major insect molting hormone is secreted from the prothoracic glands. Insect molting hormones are generally called ecdysteroids

Ecological Efficiency: Describes the efficiency with which energy is transferred from one trophic level to the next.

Ecological Niche: An ecological niche is the role and position a species has in its environment; how it meets its needs for food and shelter, how it survives, and how it reproduces.

Ecological Pyramid: A graphical representation designed to show the biomass or bio productivity at each trophic level in a given ecosystem.

Ecological Succession: The term used to describe what happens to an ecological community over time.

Ecology: The scientific analysis and study of interactions among organisms and their environment. It is an interdisciplinary field that includes biology, geography and Earth science.

Ecosystem: An interaction of living things and non-living things in a physical environment.

Ecotype: Describes a genetically distinct geographic variety, population or race within a species, which is adapted to specific environmental conditions.

Ectoderm: The outermost layer of cells or tissue of an embryo in early development, or the parts derived from this, which include the epidermis, nerve tissue, and nephridia.

Ectotherm: A organism in which internal physiological sources of heat are of relatively small or quite negligible importance in controlling body temperature. "Cold blooded".

Effector: An organ or cell that acts in response to a stimulus.

Effector Cell: Plasma cells, also called plasma B cells, plasmocytes, plasmacytes, or effector B cells, are white blood cells that secrete large volumes of antibodies.

Efferent: Conducted or conducting outwards or away from something (for nerves, the central nervous system; for blood vessels, the organ supplied).

Egg: The female reproductive cell (gamete) in oogamous organisms.

Electric Potential: The amount of work needed to move a unit charge from a reference point to a specific point against an electric field.

Electrochemical Gradient: A gradient of electrochemical potential, usually for an ion that can move across a membrane.

Electromagnetic Spectrum: The collective term for all possible frequencies of electromagnetic radiation.

Electron: A subatomic particle with a negative elementary electric charge.

Electron Acceptor: A chemical entity that accepts electrons transferred to it from another compound. It is an oxidizing agent that, by virtue of its accepting electrons, is itself reduced in the process.

Electron Carrier: Any of various molecules that are capable of accepting one or two electrons from one molecule and donating them to another in the process of electron transport.

Electron Donor: An electron donor is a chemical entity that donates electrons to another compound.

Electron Microscope: A type of microscope that uses a beam of electrons to create an image of the specimen. It is capable of much higher magnifications and has a greater resolving power than a light microscope, allowing it to see much smaller objects in finer detail.

Electron Shell: An electron shell is the outside part of an atom around the atomic nucleus. It is a group of atomic orbitals with the same value of the principal quantum number n.

Electron Transport Chain: The site of oxidative phosphorylation in eukaryotes.

Electronegativity: A measure of the tendency of an atom to attract a bonding pair of electrons. The Pauling scale is the most commonly used.

Element: A species of atoms having the same number of protons in their atomic nuclei (i.e. the same atomic number, Z). There are 118 elements that have been identified.

Embryo: Developing stage of a multicellular organism

Embryo Sac: The female gametophyte of a seed plant, within which the embryo develops. ... (in flowering plants) a large cell of the rudimentary seed, within which the embryo develops.

Embryology: The branch of biology that studies the development of gametes (sex cells), fertilization, and development of embryos and fetuses.

Enantiomer: Stereoisomers that are non-superimposable mirror images. A molecule with 1 chiral carbon atom exists as 2 stereoisomers termed enantiomers.

Endangered Species: Threatened by factors such as habitat loss, hunting, disease and climate change, and usually have declining populations or a very limited range.

Endemism: The ecological state of a species being unique to a defined geographic location, such as an island, nation, country or other defined zone, or habitat type.

Endemic Species: The ecological state of a species being unique to a defined geographic location, such as an island, nation, country or other defined zone, or habitat type.

Endergonic Reaction: A chemical reaction in which the standard change in free energy is positive, and energy is absorbed

Endocrine Gland: Glands of the endocrine system that secrete their products, hormones, directly into the blood rather than through a duct.

Endocrine System: The collection of glands that produce hormones that regulate metabolism, growth and development, tissue function, sexual function, reproduction, sleep, and mood.

Endocytosis: A form of active transport in which a cell transports molecules (such as proteins) into the cell (endo: + cytosis) by engulfing them in an energy-using process.

Endoderm: One of the three primary germ layers in the very early human embryo. The other two layers are the ectoderm (outside layer) and mesoderm (middle layer).

Endodermis: An inner layer of cells in the cortex of a root and of some stems, surrounding a vascular bundle.

Endoplasmic Reticulum: A network of membranous tubules within the cytoplasm of a eukaryotic cell, continuous with the nuclear membrane.

Endosperm: A tissue produced inside the seeds of most of the flowering plants around the time of fertilization. It surrounds the embryo and provides nutrition in the form of starch.

Endosymbiotic Theory: An evolutionary theory that explains the origin of eukaryotic cells from prokaryotes.

Endotherm: An animal that is dependent on or capable of the internal generation of heat; a warm-blooded animal.

Entomology: The study of insects, but etymology is the study of words

Environmental Biology: The branch of biology concerned with the relations between organisms and their environment. bionomics, ecology.

Enzyme: Biological molecules (proteins) that act as catalysts and help complex reactions occur everywhere in life.

Epicotyl: The region of an embryo or seedling stem above the cotyledon.

Epidemiology: The study and analysis of the patterns, causes, and effects of health and disease conditions in defined populations.

Epigenetics: The study, in the field of genetics, of cellular and physiological phenotypic trait variations that are caused by external or environmental factors that switch genes on and off.

Epinephrine: Another term for adrenaline.

Epiphyte: A plant that grows harmlessly upon another plant and derives its moisture and nutrients from the air, rain, and sometimes from debris accumulating around it.

Epistasis: The interaction of genes that are not alleles, in particular the suppression of the effect of one such gene by another.

Estrogen: The primary female sex hormone. It is responsible for the development and regulation of the female reproductive system and secondary sex characteristics.

Ethology: The scientific and objective study of non-human animal behavior rather than human behavior and usually with a focus on behavior under natural conditions.

Eukaryote: Any organism whose cells contain a nucleus and other organelles enclosed within membranes.

Evolution: The change in genetic composition of a population over successive generations, which may be caused by natural selection, inbreeding, hybridization, or mutation.

Evolutionary Biology: The subfield of biology that studies the evolutionary processes that produced the diversity of life on Earth starting from a single origin of life.

Exocytosis: A process by which the contents of a cell vacuole are released to the exterior through fusion of the vacuole membrane with the cell membrane.

Exon: Any part of a gene that will become a part of the final mature RNA produced by that gene after introns have been removed by RNA splicing.

Expressivity: Variations in a phenotype among individuals carrying a particular genotype.

External Fertilization: Sperm units with egg in the open, rather than inside the body of the parents

Facultative Anaerobe: Organism which is capable of producing energy through aerobic respiration and then switching to anaerobic respiration depending on the amounts of oxygen.

Fetus: A human embryo after eight weeks of development.

FIRST: For Inspiration and Recognition of Science and Technology. An organization founded to develop ways to inspire students in engineering and technology fields.

Food Chain: A hierarchical series of organisms each dependent on the next as a source of food.

Founder Effect: The reduced genetic diversity that results when a population is descended from a small number of colonizing ancestors.

Ganglion: A cluster (functional group) of nerve cell bodies in a centralized nervous system.

Gene: A gene is a locus (or region) of DNA that encodes a functional RNA or protein product, and is the molecular unit of heredity.

Gene Pool: The stock of different genes in an interbreeding population.

Genetic Code: The nucleotide triplets of DNA and RNA molecules that carry genetic information in living cells.

Genetic Drift: Variation in the relative frequency of different genotypes in a small population, owing to the chance disappearance of particular genes as individuals die or do not reproduce.

Genetics: The study of heredity

Genetic Variation: Variations of genomes between members of species, or between groups of species thriving in different parts of the world as a result of genetic mutation.

Genome: The haploid set of chromosomes in a gamete or microorganism, or in each cell of a multicellular organism.

Guanine: One of the four main nucleobases found in the nucleic acids DNA and RNA, the others being adenine, cytosine, and thymine. In DNA, guanine is paired with cytosine.

Gular: Of or pertaining to the throat.

Habitat: A place for animals, people and plants and non-living things

Hadron: A hadron is any particle that is made from quarks, anti-quarks and gluons. (If you want to learn more about quarks and gluons.

Hermaphrodite: Organism with both male and female reproductive organs.

Herpetology: The branch of zoology concerned with reptiles and amphibians.

Heterosis: the tendency of a crossbred individual to show qualities superior to those of both parents.

Histology: The study of the microscopic anatomy of cells and tissues of plants and animals.

Hormone: A chemical substance produced in the body that controls and regulates the activity of certain cells or organs.

Human Nutrition: Refers to the provision of essential nutrients necessary to support human life and health.

Hydrocarbon: In organic chemistry, a hydrocarbon is an organic compound consisting entirely of hydrogen and carbon.

Ichthyology: Known as Fish Science, is the branch of biology devoted to the study of fish.

Immune Response: The immune response is how your body recognizes and defends itself against bacteria, viruses, and substances that appear foreign and harmful.

Immunogloblin: Also known as antibodies, they act as a critical part of the immune response by specifically recognizing and binding to particular antigens, and aiding in their destruction.

Incomplete Dominance: A form of intermediate inheritance in which one allele for a specific trait is not completely expressed over its paired allele.

Insulin: Helps keeps your blood sugar level from getting too high (hyperglycemia) or too low (hypoglycemia).

Interferon: A group of signaling proteins made and released by host cells in response to the presence of several pathogens, such as viruses, bacteria, parasites, and also tumor cells.

Integrative Biology: A label frequently used to describe various forms of cross-disciplinary and multitaxon research.

Interleukin: A group of cytokines (secreted proteins and signal molecules) that were first seen to be expressed by white blood cells (leukocytes)

Internal Fertilization: Fertilization that takes place inside the egg-producing individual.

International System: The modern form of the metric system, and is the most widely used system of measurement.

Invertebrate: A group of animals that have no backbone, unlike animals such as reptiles, amphibians, fish, birds and mammals who all have a backbone.

Ion: An atom or molecule with a net electric charge due to the loss or gain of one or more electrons.

Ionic Bond: The complete transfer of valence electron(s) between atoms. It is a type of chemical bond that generates two oppositely charged ions.

Isomer: A molecule with the same chemical formula as another molecule, but with a different chemical structure.

Isotonic Solution: An isotonic solution refers to two solutions having the same osmotic pressure across a semipermeable membrane.

Jejunum: The midsection of the small intestine of many higher vertebrates like mammals, birds, reptiles is called as jejunum. It is present between the duodenum and the ileum.

Krebs Cycle: A series of chemical reactions used by all aerobic organisms to generate energy through the oxidation of acetyl-CoA derived from carbohydrates, fats and proteins.

Lacteal: A lymphatic capillary that absorbs dietary fats in the villi of the small intestine.

Larva: A distinct juvenile form many animals undergo before metamorphosis into adults. Animals with indirect development such as insects, amphibians, or cnidarians.

Law of Independent Assortment: The principle, originated by Gregor Mendel, stating that when two or more characteristics are inherited, individual hereditary factors assort independently.

Lepton: An elementary, half-integer spin particle that does not undergo strong interactions.

Leukocyte: A colorless cell which circulates in the blood and body fluids and is involved in counteracting foreign substances and disease; a white (blood) cell.

Ligament: The fibrous connective tissue that connects bones to other bones and is also known as articular ligament, articular larua, fibrous ligament, or true ligament.

Linked Genes: When two genes are close together on the same chromosome, they do not assort independently and are said to be linked.

Lipid: A chemically defined as a substance that is insoluble in water and soluble in alcohol, ether, and chloroform. Together with carbohydrates and proteins, lipids are the main constituents of plant and animal cells. Cholesterol and triglycerides are lipids.

Lipoprotein: A biochemical assembly that contains both proteins and lipids, bound to the proteins, which allow fats to move through the water inside and outside cells.

M phase: Mitosis and cytokinesis together define this phase of an animal cell cycle- the division of the mother cell into two daughter cells, genetically identical to each other and the parent.

Macroevolution: Evolution on a scale of separated gene pools. Studies focus on change that occurs at or above the level of species, in contrast with microevolution.

Macromolecule: A very large molecule, such as protein, commonly created by polymerization of smaller subunits (monomers). They are typically composed of thousands or more atoms.

Macronutrient: Nutrients that provide calories or energy. Nutrients are substances needed for growth, metabolism, and for other body functions.

Macrophage: A kind of swallowing cell, which means it functions by literally swallowing up other particles or smaller cells. Macrophages engulf and digest debris (like dead cells).

Mammalogy: The study of mammals – a class of vertebrates with characteristics such as homeothermic metabolism, fur, four-chambered hearts, and complex nervous systems.

Marine Biology: The scientific study of organisms in the ocean or other marine bodies of water.

Mass Balance: An application of conservation of mass to the analysis of physical systems.

Mass Density: Density is mass per volume.

Mass Number: The mass number (A), also called atomic mass number or nucleon number, is the total number of protons and neutrons (together known as nucleons) in an atomic nucleus

Mast Cell: A cell filled with basophil granules, found in numbers in connective tissue and releasing histamine and other substances during inflammatory and allergic reactions.

Medulla: The continuation of the spinal cord within the skull, forming the lowest part of the brainstem and containing control centers for the heart and lungs.

Meiosis: A type of cell division that reduces the number of chromosomes in the parent cell by half and produces four gamete cells.

Membrane Potential: When a nerve or muscle cell is at "rest", its membrane potential is called the resting membrane potential.

Meson: Hadronic subatomic particles composed of one quark and one antiquark, bound together by the strong interaction.

Messenger RNA: The form of RNA in which genetic information transcribed from DNA as a sequence of bases is transferred to a ribosome.

Metaphase: The third phase of mitosis, the process that separates duplicated genetic material carried in the nucleus of a parent cell into two identical daughter cells.

Microbiology: The study of microscopic organisms, such as bacteria, viruses, archaea, fungi and protozoa.

Microevolution: evolutionary change within a species or small group of organisms, especially over a short period.

Mitosis: The process in which a eukaryotic cell nucleus splits in two, followed by division of the parent cell into two daughter cells.

Molarity: A unit of concentration measuring the number of moles of a solute per liter of solution.

Mole: The SI unit of measurement used to measure the number of things, usually atoms or molecules. One mole of something is equal to Avogadro's number.

Molecule: A molecule is the smallest particle in a chemical element or compound that has the chemical properties of that element or compound.

Molecular biology: A branch of science concerning biological activity at the molecular level.

Molecular physics: The study of the physical properties of molecules, the chemical bonds between atoms as well as the molecular dynamics.

Monomer: A molecule that can be bonded to other identical molecules to form a polymer.

Motor Neuron: a nerve cell (neuron) whose cell body is located in the spinal cord and whose fiber (axon) projects outside the spinal cord to directly or indirectly control effector organs.

Mucous Membrane: An epithelial tissue that secretes mucus and that lines many body cavities and tubular organs including the gut and respiratory passages.

Muon: An unstable subatomic particle. Among all known unstable subatomic particles, only the neutron (lasting around 15 minutes) and some atomic nuclei have a longer decay lifetime.

Mycology: The branch of biology concerned with the study of fungi, including their genetic and biochemical properties, their taxonomy and their use to humans.

Myofibril: Any of the elongated contractile threads found in striated muscle cells.

Myosin: Large superfamily of motor proteins that move along actin filaments, while hydrolyzing ATP.

Natural Selection: A process in nature in which organisms possessing certain genotypic characteristics that make them better adjusted to an environment tend to survive.

Neurobiology: The study of cells of the nervous system and the organization of these cells into functional circuits that process information and mediate behavior.

Neuromuscular Junction: A chemical synapse formed by the contact between a motor neuron and a muscle fiber.

Neuron: An electrically excitable cell that processes and transmits information through electrical and chemical signals.

Neurotransmitter: Known as chemical messengers, are endogenous chemicals that enable neurotransmission.

Neutrino: An elementary particle with half-integer spin, that interacts only via the weak subatomic force and gravity. Its mass is tiny compared to other subatomic particles.

Nucleic Acid: A complex organic substance present in living cells, especially DNA or RNA, whose molecules consist of many nucleotides linked in a long chain.

Nucleic Acid Sequence: A succession of letters that indicate the order of nucleotides within a DNA (using GACT) or RNA (GACU) molecule.

Nucleobase: Cytosine, Guanine, Adenine (which can be found in DNA and RNA), Thymine (found only in DNA), and Uracil (found only in RNA).

Nucleoid: An irregularly shaped region within the cell of a prokaryote that contains all or most of the genetic material, called gonophore.

Nucleolus: A small dense spherical structure in the nucleus of a cell during interphase.

Nucleotide: Organic molecules that serve as the monomers, or subunits, of nucleic acids like DNA (deoxyribonucleic acid) and RNA (ribonucleic acid).

Organ: a part of an organism that is typically self-contained and has a specific vital function, such as the heart or liver in humans.

Organism: An individual animal, plant, or single-celled life form.

Oncology: Oncology is a branch of medicine that deals with the prevention, diagnosis and treatment of cancer.

Ornithology: Ornithology is a branch of zoology that concerns the study of birds.

Osmosis: The spontaneous net movement of solvent molecules through a semi-permeable membrane into a region of higher solute concentration.

Paleontology: The study of the history of life on Earth as reflected in the fossil record. Fossils are the remains or traces of organisms.

Parallel Evolution: The independent evolution of similar traits, starting from a similar ancestral condition.

Parasitology: The study of parasites, their hosts, and the relationship between them.

Pathobiology: The study or practice of pathology with greater emphasis on the biological than on the medical aspects.

Pathology: A medical specialty that is concerned with the diagnosis of disease based on the laboratory analysis of bodily fluids such as blood and urine.

pH: A numeric scale used to specify the acidity or basicity (alkalinity) of an aqueous solution. It is roughly the negative of the logarithm to base 10 of the concentration.

Pharmacology: The science of drug action on biological systems. In its entirety, it embraces knowledge of the sources, chemical properties, biological effects and therapeutic uses of drugs.

Phenotype: The set of observable characteristics of an individual resulting from the interaction of its genotype with the environment.

Pheromone: A chemical substance produced and released into the environment by an animal, especially a mammal or an insect, affecting the behavior or physiology of others of its species.

Phloem: The vascular tissue in plants that conducts sugars and other metabolic products downward from the leaves.

Physiology: The branch of biology dealing with the functions and activities of living organisms and their parts, including all physical and chemical processes.

Phytopathology: Plant pathology is the science of diagnosing and managing plant diseases.

Placebo: A harmless pill, medicine, or procedure prescribed more for the psychological benefit to the patient than for any physiological effect.

Plant Nutrition: The study of the chemical elements and compounds necessary for plant growth, plant metabolism and their external supply.

Plasmolysis: Contraction of the protoplast of a plant cell as a result of loss of water from the cell.

Pollination: The act of transferring pollen grains from the male anther of a flower to the female stigma.

Polygene: A gene whose individual effect on a phenotype is too small to be observed, but which can act together with others to produce observable variation.

Polymer: A large molecule, or macromolecule, composed of many repeated subunits.

Polymerase Chain Reaction: A technique used in molecular biology to amplify a single copy or a few copies of a piece of DNA across several orders of magnitude.

Polyploidy: Containing more than two homologous sets of chromosomes.

Population Biology: The study of populations of organisms, especially the regulation of population size, life history traits such as clutch size, and extinction.

Population Ecology: A sub-field of ecology that deals with the dynamics of species populations and how these populations interact with the environment.

Population Genetics: The study of genetic variation within populations, and involves the examination and modeling of changes in the frequencies of genes and alleles.

Predation: The preying of one animal on others.

Primase: An enzyme that synthesizes short RNA sequences called primers.

Prokaryote: A microscopic single-celled organism that has neither a distinct nucleus with a membrane nor other specialized organelles. Prokaryotes include the bacteria and cyanobacteria.

Protein: Large biomolecules, or macromolecules, consisting of one or more long chains of amino acid residues.

Psychobiology: The application of the principles of biology to the study of physiological, genetic, and developmental mechanisms of behavior in humans and other animals.

Quark: An elementary particle and a fundamental constituent of matter. Quarks combine to form composite particles called hadrons, the most stable of which are protons and neutrons.

Reproduction: Giving birth to one of its kind, sexually or asexually.

RNA: Stands for ribonucleic acid. It is an important molecule with long chains of nucleotides. A nucleotide contains a nitrogenous base, a ribose sugar, and a phosphate.

Sexual Reproduction: Type of reproduction in which cells from two parents unite to form the first cell of a new organism.

SI units: A system of physical units-based on the meter, kilogram, second, ampere, kelvin, candela, and mole, together with a set of prefixes.

Sociobiology: A field of scientific study that is based on the hypothesis that social behavior has resulted from evolution and attempts to explain and examine social behavior within that context.

Species: Often defined as the largest group of organisms in which two individuals are capable of reproducing fertile offspring, typically using sexual reproduction.

Stem cell: An undifferentiated cell of a multicellular organism that is capable of giving rise to indefinitely more cells of the same type.

Steroid: An organic compound with four rings arranged in a specific configuration. Examples include the dietary lipid cholesterol and the sex hormones.

Structural Biology: A branch of molecular biology, biochemistry, and biophysics concerned with the molecular structure of biological macromolecules, especially proteins and nucleic acids.

Symbiogenesis: An evolutionary theory that explains the origin of eukaryotic cells from prokaryotes.

Synthetic Biology: An interdisciplinary branch of biology and engineering.

Systematics: The branch of biology that deals with classification and nomenclature; taxonomy.

T Cell: A lymphocyte of a type produced or processed by the thymus gland and actively participating in the immune response.

Testosterone: A steroid hormone from the androgen group and is found in humans and other vertebrates. Testosterone is secreted primarily by the testicles of males.

Thymine: One of the four nucleobases in the nucleic acid of DNA that are represented by the letters G–C–A–T.

Transcription: The first step of gene expression, in which a particular segment of DNA is copied into RNA (mRNA) by the enzyme RNA polymerase.

Transfer RNA: RNA consisting of folded molecules that transport amino acids from the cytoplasm of a cell to a ribosome.

Translation: The decoding of genetic instructions for making proteins.

Trophic level: Each of several hierarchical levels in an ecosystem, comprising organisms that share the same function in the food chain and the same nutritional relationship.

Uracil: One of the four nucleobases in the nucleic acid of RNA that are represented by the letters A, G, C and U.

Urea: Serves an important role in the metabolism of nitrogen- containing compounds by animals, and is the main nitrogen-containing substance in the urine of mammals.

Uric acid: A heterocyclic compound of carbon, nitrogen, oxygen, and hydrogen. It forms ions and salts known as urates and acid urates, such as ammonium acid urate.

Urine: A liquid by- product of the body secreted by the kidneys through a process called urination (or micturition) and excreted through the urethra.

Uterus: The organ in the lower body of a woman or female mammal where offspring are conceived and in which they gestate before birth; the womb.

Vacuole: A membrane-bound organelle which is present in all plant and fungal cells and some protist, animal and bacterial cells.

Valence: In several fields the valence of an element refers to the number of elements to which it can connect: Valence (chemistry), the valence of an atom.

Valence band: The valence band is the highest range of electron energies in which electrons are normally present at absolute zero temperature.

Valence bond theory: A straightforward extension of Lewis structures. Valence bond theory says that electrons in a covalent bond reside in a region that is the overlap of individual atomic orbitals.

Valence electron: An electron that is associated with an atom, and that can participate in the formation of a chemical bond.

Valence shell: The electrons in the outermost occupied shell (or shells) determine the chemical properties of the atom; it is called the valence shell.

Vasodilation: The dilatation of blood vessels, which decreases blood pressure.

Vegetative reproduction: A form of asexual reproduction of a plant. Only one plant is involved and the offspring is the result of one parent. The new plant is genetically identical to the parent.

Vesicle: A fluid or air-filled cavity or sac.

Vestigiality: Refers to genetically determined structures or attributes that have apparently lost most or all of their ancestral function in a given species.

Virology: The study of viruses- submicroscopic, parasitic particles of genetic material contained in a protein coat and virus-like agents.

Virus: A biological agent that reproduces inside the cells of living hosts.

Water Potential: A measure of the potential energy in water as well as the difference between the potential in a given water sample and pure water.

White Blood Cell: Component of the blood that functions in the immune system. Also known as a leukocyte.

Whole Genome Sequencing: A laboratory process that determines the complete DNA sequence of an organism's genome at a single time.

Wobble Base Pair: A pairing between two nucleotides in RNA molecules that does not follow Watson-Crick base pair rules.

Wood: The inner layer of the stems of woody plants; composed of xylem.

Xanthophyll: The yellow colored photosynthetic pigments.

Xylem: The vascular tissue in plants that conducts water and dissolved nutrients upward from the root and also helps to form the woody element in the stem.

Yolk: The yellow internal part of a bird's egg, which is surrounded by the white, is rich in protein and fat, and nourishes the developing embryo.

Zoology: The branch of biology that relates to the animal kingdom, including the structure, embryology, evolution, classification, habits, and distribution of all animals.

Zygote: A diploid cell resulting from the fusion of two haploid gametes; a fertilized ovum.